Graham Seal is Emeritus Professor of Folklore at Curtin University. He is a leading expert on Australian cultural history and the bestselling author of *Great Australian Stories, Larrikins, Bush Tales and Other Great Australian Stories, Great Bush Stories, Great Convict Stories, Australia's Funniest Yarns* and *Great Australian Mysteries*.

Great Australian Stories

'A fair dinkum insight into the richness of Australian story telling.' —*The Weekly Times*

'A treasure trove of material from our nation's historical past' —*Courier Mail*

The Savage Shore

'Colourful stories about the spirit of navigation and exploration, and of courageous and miserable adventures at sea.' —*National Geographic*

Larrikins, Bush Tales and Other Great Australian Stories

'Another collection of yarns, tall tales, bush legends and colourful characters ... from one of our master storytellers.' —*Queensland Times*

Great Anzac Stories

'They are pithy short pieces . . . stories you will remember for much longer than you would expect.'—*Ballarat Courier*

Great Australian Journeys

'Readers familiar with Graham Seal's work will know he finds and writes ripper, fair-dinkum, true blue Aussie yarns. His books are great reads and do a lot for ensuring cultural stories are not lost.' —*The Weekly Times*

Great Convict Stories

'More than just a retelling of some of the most fascinating yarns, Seal is interested in how folklore around the convicts grew from the colourful tales of transportation and what impact that had on how we see our convict heritage.' —*Daily Telegraph*

Great Bush Stories

'Takes us back to a time when "the bush" was central to popular notions of Australian identity, with the likes of Henry Lawson and "Banjo" Paterson serving to both celebrate and mythologise it.' —*Writing WA*

Australia's Funniest Yarns

'*Australia's Funniest Yarns* is full of songs, stories, poems, rules and quizzes. It is a lovely book for those who want to catch a glimpse of the old characters who used their stories and language to make the Australia of the past much more colourful than it is today.' —*Glam Adelaide*

Great Australian Mysteries

'Seal brings to life the enigmas and puzzles behind unsolved crimes, lost treasures and strange phenomena . . . a fascinating read.' —*Canberra Weekly*

'Succeeded in making me laugh out loud and bamboozling me at the same time.' —*Goodreads*

Also by Graham Seal

Great Australian Stories
Great Anzac Stories
Larrikins, Bush Tales and Other Great Australian Stories
The Savage Shore
Great Australian Journeys
Great Convict Stories
Great Bush Stories
Australia's Funniest Yarns
Great Australian Mysteries
Condemned

GREAT AUSTRALIAN PLACES

GRAHAM SEAL

ALLEN&UNWIN
SYDNEY·MELBOURNE·AUCKLAND·LONDON

First published in 2022

Copyright © Graham Seal 2022

All rights reserved. No part of this book may be reproduced or transmitted in any form or by any means, electronic or mechanical, including photocopying, recording or by any information storage and retrieval system, without prior permission in writing from the publisher. The Australian *Copyright Act 1968* (the Act) allows a maximum of one chapter or 10 per cent of this book, whichever is the greater, to be photocopied by any educational institution for its educational purposes provided that the educational institution (or body that administers it) has given a remuneration notice to the Copyright Agency (Australia) under the Act.

p. 129: Grateful acknowledgement is given to Bruce Watson for permission to quote the last stanzas of the song 'The Man and the Woman and the Edison Phonograph' from the album *Balance* © 2009 by Bruce Watson. The late Ronnie Summers wrote the last stanza.

p. 291–292: Grateful acknowledgement is given to Phyl Lobl for permission to quote 'The Derby' lyrics from the album *Alcyone* © 2003 by Phyl Lobl.

Every effort has been made to trace the holders of copyright material. If you have any information concerning copyright material in this book please contact the publishers at the address below.

Allen & Unwin
Cammeraygal Country
83 Alexander Street
Crows Nest NSW 2065
Australia
Phone: (61 2) 8425 0100
Email: info@allenandunwin.com
Web: www.allenandunwin.com

Allen & Unwin acknowledges the Traditional Owners of the Country on which we live and work. We pay our respects to all Aboriginal and Torres Strait Islander Elders, past and present.

 A catalogue record for this book is available from the National Library of Australia

ISBN 978 1 76106 713 6

Cover photographs: ALAMY (lifesaver Joseph N. Callahan, Uluru, old car and caravan, Mr Whippy van, lifesaver cap); SHUTTERSTOCK (ice cream, stamp, gold 'foil', cockatoo, texture, road)
Set in 11.5/17 pt Stempel Schneidler by Bookhouse, Sydney
Printed in Australia by McPherson's Printing Group

10 9 8 7 6 5 4 3 2 1

 The paper in this book is FSC® certified. FSC® promotes environmentally responsible, socially beneficial and economically viable management of the world's forests.

CONTENTS

Introduction What a Place! 1

1   Pioneering Places 7

    Turn Again 7
    Possession Island 9
    The Futile Fort 12
    The Bloody Bridge 15
    Long Harry's Legacy 17
    Mrs Penfold's 19
    Old Ireland at Baker's Flat 23
    The Land We Live Inn 25
    Glorious News for the Diggers! 29
    The Singing Wire 33
    Sea Lines 37
    The Wire Frontier 40
    The Sheds 43
    A Golden Pipeline 47

2 Dangerous Places — 51

- The Eye of the Needle — 51
- B LXV — 54
- Stringybark Creek — 58
- The Street of Evil — 62
- Windy Gully Candles — 66
- The Fatal Railway Station — 69
- Razorhurst — 73
- Escaping the Island — 77
- Greased Lightning Let Loose — 81
- The Woman Who Ran the Radio — 83
- Two Up, One Down — 87
- Saving Silver Town — 89
- The Field of Thunder — 93

3 Sacred Places — 97

- The Rock — 97
- The Wurrwurrwuy Stones — 100
- The Devil's Marbles — 102
- Hallowed Grounds — 105
- The Tree of Knowledge — 108
- Mer — 111
- Sad Waterlilies — 113
- Places in the Heart — 116
- 'Here is their spirit' — 121
- Misery Hill — 124
- 'I am the last of the Tasmanians' — 127
- The Star of Taroom — 129
- A Plait of Hair — 132

4	**Unsettling Places**	**137**
	Hell's Gate	137
	The Massacre Hill	141
	Cullin-La-Ringo	145
	A Troubled Light	149
	Ironstone Mountain	152
	Visions Splendid	155
	The Country Knows the Rest	158
	A Troubled Triangle	163
	Unexplained Ipswich Phenomena	166
	'Populate or Perish!'	170
	The Spirit Stones	173
	Mysteries within Mysteries	176
	Toxic Town	178
5	**Wild Places**	**183**
	Ghost Gum Dreaming	183
	The Great Divide	185
	'A Small, Woody Island'	189
	Dark Emu in the Stars	193
	The Burning Mountain	195
	The Coral Kingdom	196
	Sea Country	199
	Not So Sunny	201
	Red Palms in the Desert	204
	The Pelican Spree	206
	High Country	210
	Paroo Legends	214
	A Home in the Blizzard	218

6	**Imagined Places**	225
	Where the Pelican Builds Its Nest	225
	The Outside Track	228
	Matilda Country	232
	The Prince of Ballyhoo	235
	Cuppacumalonga Hill	238
	The Pub with No Beer	240
	The Land where the Crow Flies Backwards	242
	The Roaring Days	246
	'Where they rise the sun with a golden bar'	250
	The Everywhere Man	255
	Capricornia	258
	The Borders	261
7	**Our Place**	267
	Big Australia	267
	The Old Tin Shed	271
	What Did the King Say to the Duke?	274
	The Bridge	276
	'She's a Beauty!'	279
	The Bushranger of Research	282
	The Show	285
	The Country Hall	288
	The Milk Bar	292
	Sun, Sand and Surf	295
	The Centre of Australia	298

Acknowledgements	303
Image Credits	305
Notes	307

Introduction
WHAT A PLACE!

In a country the size of Australia there are many places and a lot of things have happened in them. Wherever you go—around, across or over this continent—you will stumble into ancient legends, tales of exploration and discovery, yarns of the roaring days of gold and bushranging, war exploits, unexplained events, crimes and a seemingly never-ending cast of sometimes quirky characters. Every tongue has a tale to tell, every pen a story to write and everyone has an ear to listen.

This ongoing conversation tells us a lot about the land, those who have lived here and those who still do. From the most local to the most nationally significant, places are a fundamental part of our lives and understanding of the world. Where we come from. Where we go to. Where important events happened. Even the most familiar places can have intriguing histories—accounts of discovery, violence, survival, mystery, danger and of the many things that people do in them, good and bad. Australia's long history of human occupation is etched into the country through stories like those in this book.

Finding places, settling them and developing them are deep-rooted themes of our history. Sixty-five thousand or more years ago people reached this place and settled it, spreading from the north down through the continent to its southern extremity, now severed from the mainland and known as Tasmania. From the earliest European arrivals by sea, through the rigours of inland exploration, pioneering, goldrushes and bold nation-building projects that have aimed to tie the country together, modern Australia has always been in in the process of becoming. It still is.

Fire, flood and drought have always been regular dangers for Australians, now worse with the impact of climate change. Other hazards include fraught sea passages, unsafe mines and the consequences of nuclear weapons testing. Even railway stations, suburban streets and island backwaters can be risky. There has been no shortage of dangerous places and hair-raising stories about what happened in them.

Australians have traditionally been reluctant to pay much attention to formal faiths. Religious observation has often been nominal—births, deaths, marriages—and more than a third of the population declared in the 2021 Census that they follow no religious belief. But there is a spiritual dimension to our past and present.

The powerful connection of First Australians to Country is only now beginning to be more broadly understood. The extreme duration of First Nations peoples' occupation means that there are a vast number of sacred sites. They include mountains, rivers, rocks and caves as well as the traditional ways that connect them through song, story and belief.

More recent events have also created sacred places; some religious, some secular. Some are a bit of both, a characteristically Australian response to a need to commemorate, celebrate and remember struggle, war, tragedy and even those sports many follow with almost religious devotion.

Modern Australia has achieved a great deal since what most observers considered to be, at the very least, an unpromising start in 1788. Sadly, many of these successes were built on the violent dispossession of the original inhabitants. Sites of frontier confrontation and massacre are being unearthed and, slowly, acknowledged. Other places with unsettling resonances include penal settlements, killing grounds of rebellions and industrial conflict, tragic lighthouses, institutions for the supposed care of children, deadly roads and even entire towns.

With one of the largest landmasses on the planet, a great many islands and a slice of Antarctica, Australia is blessed with natural wonder of many kinds. Many unique plant species are found here, together with a great variety of unusual, often confronting, animals and insects. These may be found in the bush, the deserts, in mountain ranges and in the surrounding seas. All these wild locations seem to possess outstanding beauty, from the massive jumble of the Great Dividing Range or the glowing corals wreathing our coasts, to the sombre magnificence of arid landscapes and the quiet beauty of the outback night skies.

As well as places that have a physical presence, there are others that live in the heart and mind. Poets, writers and artists have created places that may not exist yet reflect something of the history and traditions of a country that is, in its entirety, endlessly fascinating. In our shared idea of the country we inhabit we can still surprise ourselves. The COVID-19 pandemic that began in 2020 revealed a country whose seemingly settled borders and governance were anything but, as states and territories looked to the interests of their people with limited reference to the Commonwealth government. It has been the colonial era all over again.

The everyday places and pleasures of Australian life have often been borrowed from elsewhere. The milk bar came from America, the agricultural show from Britain. We have remade these in our own unique fashion. The scattered patterns of settlement have produced distinctive places like the halls that the people of even the smallest hamlet erected for meetings and for music and dance. The 'pub' or 'hotel' is a central institution everywhere. As well as playing hard, we have worked hard in factories, shops, offices, shearing sheds and even laboratories. These important locations all have their own stories to tell.

Other places have become heavy with local, state or national symbolism—Sydney's Harbour Bridge, Old Parliament House in Canberra and of course the beach, the bush and the outback. And we like to celebrate the vastness of the country in quirkier ways. Where exactly is the centre of Australia? Trickier to work out than you might think. Then there are all those BIG things that seem to spring up wherever you go around the map, testament to our delight in sending ourselves up—and pretty much everything else as well.

Although we tend not to think much about it, the meanings we give to places are made up of the stories and traditions that we cannot escape. Australia's human history is very long, stretching from ancient First Nations occupation through maritime discovery by Europeans, colonial settlement, the convict era, inland exploration, pioneering, gold and mineral rushes, economic depression and industrial conflict in the 1890s, World War I, another deep depression, World War II, mass immigration, social change from the 1960s and into the technological revolutions and global financial crises of the twenty-first century, followed by the looming consequences of climate change and the COVID-19 pandemic from 2020.

What we have made of these momentous experiences, good and bad, is something else again. Despite the realities of urban living for most, we still romanticise the pioneering past and the values we identify with bush life and legend. We cling to ideals like the 'fair go', anti-authoritarianism and a rugged independence. Sometimes, we live up to these. Often we do not, because such ideals are hard to maintain, either by individuals or groups, far less by an entire nation.

Yet we cling to our aspirations. Why? Because every group of people—tribes, clans, states, to nations—needs sustaining beliefs that express their ideals and collective identity. These ways of seeing the world and where we stand in it are what make us tick. They are expressed not in official history and government policies but in stories, songs, art, literature, dance and other creative forms. They are part of our accumulated social and historical experience, forming a shared idea of ourselves that gives meaning to the big place—and the smaller places—where we live.

A school celebration in 1924 of the centenary of the establishment of Fort Dundas on Melville Island in 1824.

1
PIONEERING PLACES

Turn Again

In February 1606, Willem Jansz (also known as Janszoon) and his few men aboard the *Duyfken*—'Little Dove'—were completely lost. In their small ship they had sailed from the Dutch East India Company (VOC) base in Java with the usual orders to look out for trading opportunities along the coast of what is now Papua New Guinea. The voyage did not go well.

All VOC skippers were under firm instructions to establish trade links with the people of whatever new region they reached on their travels. It was also desirable to kidnap one or two to gain intelligence about any resources that might lie in newfound lands. This was standard practice wherever the VOC went and, indeed, for any of the other European mercantile adventurers braving the unknown seas of the south.

Not surprisingly, spiriting folk away often led to conflict rather than cooperation between explorers and Indigenous peoples. Jansz and his men did not have much luck in convincing the New Guineans to sign up to the one-sided VOC trade agenda, so they kept sailing. Travelling further and further south, it was difficult for the mariners to tell what was an island and what was a larger landmass. The maps and charts of the time were not very reliable and no one had ever been this far off them before.

Eventually, the *Duyfken* made landfall on what we now call Cape York Peninsula. Jansz's logbook is lost but we do have some account of what happened next from the hearsay report of a Tamil sailor. According to the man, the 'Flemming's Pinnasse', as he called the small *Duyfken*, had landed in search of natives 'to intreate of Trade' but had been violently repulsed and nine of the intruders were 'killed by the Heathens' who were also, it was claimed, 'man-eaters'. Having seen no tradeable commodities or exploitable resources while ashore, the *Duyfken* men decided to return to the safety of their ship 'finding no good to be done there'. It is thought that this encounter took place on the Pennefather River, making this spot 'one of the most significant historical sites in Australia'.

The visit of the *Duyfken* is still remembered in the oral traditions of the Wik-Mungkan, traditional owners of the western Cape York area. According to some of these accounts the Dutch were first sighted north of the Kirke River. They describe the wooden windship—which they believed to be *Duyfken*—as 'a big mob of logs' and their sailors as 'devils'. The Dutch, now seriously depleted in numbers, came ashore for fresh water and convinced the local inhabitants to help them dig a well. Relations were cordial at first, though the behaviour of the sailors towards them eventually convinced the Wik-Mungkan that they were *onya*, malevolent nuisances.

One day, when the Dutch climbed back into one of the numerous wells they were digging with the help of the now reluctant local people, the warriors waited until last, then jumped in on top of the luckless sailors and killed them. This sparked a battle during which a number of Wik-Mungan men were shot and some of the incomers speared. The remaining Dutch retreated to their ship and sailed away. Jansz named the point from which he left *keer weer*. In Dutch this means to 'turn again' or to 'turn back'. That place is now known as Cape Keerweer, the first part of the country to be impacted by the transformational magic of naming.

As far as anyone knows, this was the first time Europeans walked on Australian soil. These first encounters with Indigenous Australians were not promising for future relations. Brief and often bloody confrontations like this would be repeated in one form or another as other navigators and later settlers came to what had once been an unknown south land.

Possession Island

As navigator James Cook charted his way along the east coast of New Holland, later to be 'Australia', he and those aboard HMB *Endeavour* made continual observations of the new land. They saw many fires ashore and assumed these were lit by people, perhaps for cooking, perhaps as signals. What Cook and his companions did not know was that they, too, were being observed. From the shore, many eyes closely watched the progress of the ship and began to form some ideas about it.

The Yuin people of what is now Victoria thought the sailing ship looked like Gurung-gubba, the pelican. In Yuin tradition, the pelican is a mischievous thief, likely to steal your fish, so it was a good idea to watch the newcomers closely. Signal fires were lit to warn groups further north that possible trouble was on the way. An early omen was Cook's unwitting naming of Mount Dromedary on the south coast of what is New South Wales. He thought the imposing mountain resembled a camel. However, the mountain is sacred and known as Gulaga, the originary mother of the Yuin people, so the European name is an unintended insult to that belief.

On 29 April 1770 Cook eventually set foot on the continent at the place that would come to be known as Botany Bay (Kamay). Here, insult became injury when he encountered two Gweagal men with wide stripes of white daubed across their bodies. Not knowing the custom of seeking consent to enter Country, the sailors of the *Endeavour* barged in. One Gweagal man threw a rock at the newcomers, a clear warning to depart from their spiritual and physical home, possibly because the newcomers' white skin made him think they were ghosts. In response, Cook's sailors fired, wounding one of the men, who ran back to nearby dwellings and returned with others who threw spears. More shots were fired, though it seems that there were no further injuries.

When Cook and his men inspected the huts, they found only a few children; everyone else had fled. Cook left some trinkets as gifts of peace. The newcomers helped themselves to spears and other items they found, some of which now reside at Cambridge University. A bark shield held by the British Museum was long thought to have been that collected at Botany Bay, though recent research suggests otherwise. The hole in the shield was often said to have been caused by a ball from a musket, though it is now thought that it may have been made through earlier damage, possibly another spear or other weapon.

As they made their way further north, Cook and his men had further interactions with Indigenous Australians; some friendly, some not. After the *Endeavour* was nearly lost near what is now Cooktown, the Europeans established mostly positive relations with the Guugu Yimithirr people during the four months they were stranded repairing their ship. *Endeavour* then zig-zagged on through the maze of reefs, shoals and sandbanks to Possession Island, where Cook did exactly that—comprehensively. On 22 August 1770 he wrote in his journal:

> Notwithstand[ing] I had in the Name of his Majesty taken posession of several places upon this coast I now once more hoisted English Coulers and in the Name of His Majesty King George the Third took posession of the whole Eastern Coast from ... Latitude [38° South] down to this place by the Name of New South Wales together with all the Bays, Harbours Rivers and Islands situate upon the said coast ...

Three volleys were fired onshore and echoed by another three from the *Endeavour*. Cook finally cleared the reef five days later and made for home. Many of his crew were sick, succumbing to fever and dysentery on the return voyage to England. Cook's report on the country he had claimed was generally negative as far as trade and settlement were concerned.

But when the British government was desperately seeking a place to send its convicts, James Cook's acquisition of an almost completely unknown land at the southern end of the planet was remembered. The rest is history.

The Futile Fort

There's not much of it left. The crumbling ruins of the first European outpost in Australia's north have almost returned to the Tiwi Islands jungle from which they were hacked out in 1824. Melville Island's Fort Dundas, as the settlement was called, existed for barely five years. The fierce Tiwi people were such capable warriors that they managed to keep the British garrison effectively bottled up in their wooden stockade. Eventually, after three commandants and deaths on both sides, the British gave up. Ratuati Irara, named Bathurst and Melville islands by the British, was left to decay and forgetting.

Eighty kilometres offshore from what is now Darwin and around 700 kilometres from Timor-Leste, the Tiwi Islands have long been home to one of Australia's most tenacious First Peoples. In their tradition, the Tiwi have lived on their homeland since the beginning of time. They say that in the Palaneri, or Creation era, an old blind woman named Mudungkala appeared from the ground with three children and journeyed north. As she went, she made the straits between the islands and the mainland. She covered the islands in plants and animals to feed her children, then disappeared.

Cut off from the mainland by rising sea levels around 15,000 years ago, the islands had already been inhabited for at least 25,000 years. The Tiwi continued to live in almost complete isolation until Dutch navigators arrived in the seventeenth century. They were followed by Macassan trepangers from islands to the north of Australia, possibly Portuguese slave-traders, as well as French and British navigators in the nineteenth century. All these outsiders were effectively beaten off by the Tiwi.

Despite these unpromising precedents, the British Colonial Office decided to establish a military outpost on Melville Island to bolster Britain's territorial claims. Poorly planned and equipped, the first European settlement in the north of the continent struggled to maintain a tentative toehold on the islands. Around 120 marines, soldiers, convicts and a few free settlers came into mostly violent contact with the bewildered and defensive Tiwi, establishing a relationship of mutual distrust that doomed the occupation to a short and troubled history.

There were a few more positive interactions. The Tiwi were especially interested in the metal axes of the newcomers, not only as useful weapons but for more efficiently crafting their spears and the traditional Pukumani funeral poles. Axes and other goods were gifted to the Tiwi. No trade took place as, apart from their basic but deadly spears and throwing sticks, the British did not value the small stock of Tiwi possessions. None of the British knew the island language and the mostly hostile nature of their dealings meant that no pidgin speech could develop to lubricate intercultural relations. The Tiwi and the British remained enigmas to each other as the newcomers succumbed to disease or were picked off by the original inhabitants.

By March 1829, Fort Dundas had been abandoned. As well as the effective guerrilla attacks of the inhabitants, the place had proven unpromising for agriculture and too isolated for the planned trade with the islands to the north. The British left behind thirty-four dead and a memory of attempted invasion reflected in some local oral traditions and lore. Their legacy also included a population of Timorese water buffalo intended for food and labour. And they left the ruins of their fort, where the first European wedding and birth in the country's north took place.

The Tiwi would not be troubled by newcomers again until the late nineteenth and early twentieth centuries when buffalo-shooting and timber-milling industries were established. In 1909 missionaries began arriving to convert the Tiwi to Christianity and suppress their traditions. They were followed by the Royal Australian Air Force in 1929, as concern grew about Japanese activity in the area and then by Japanese pearlers in the 1930s.

During World War II, the Tiwi played important roles as coastwatchers, rescuers of Allied airmen, and forward scouts for commando raiders in enemy-occupied islands. A Tiwi man, Matthias Ulungura, made the first capture of a Japanese prisoner of war on Australian territory. Several Japanese troops were also killed by Tiwi soldiers. These and other efforts in defence of the country went unpaid and unrewarded for twenty years. When they were remunerated, it was at a reduced rate.

The remains of Fort Dundas can barely be seen today, but they are still there, mouldering under the foliage. At the time of writing they are in the process of being heritage listed, as they should be, a reminder of colonial calamity and the determination of the Tiwi to hold their ancestral home, as they still do. Today, the Tiwi are known for their art, some serious footballing skills and a fierce resolve to continue occupying, owning and caring for Country.

The Bloody Bridge

Legend has it that the convicts building the bridge were suffering under an especially cruel overseer. Eventually they could stand the flogging and beating no more and dispatched the tyrant with a pick in his head. To hide their crime, they interred the body in the stones of the bridge and mortared it up. Of course, there were questions about the sudden disappearance of the overseer, but the bridge-building gang seemed to be getting away with it—until the new overseer saw blood seeping through the damp mortar joints. This being Norfolk Island, retribution would have been swift, brutal and terminal.

Norfolk Islanders tell this tale about the picturesque Bloody Bridge at the eastern end of Quality Row, the remaining administrative precinct of the convict era. The bridge spans one of the many beautiful spots on the subtropical island, its gory folklore at odds with the surrounding grassy hills and stunning sea views. It is a typically Norfolk Island contrast, a place of outstanding natural beauty with a dark history.

'N'fk', as the islanders call it, is an extremely isolated place around 1600 kilometres from Sydney, 1100 kilometres from Auckland and just over 700 kilometres south-east of Noumea. It was first settled by Polynesians during the fifteenth or sixteenth centuries. They left a few generations later and the island lay undisturbed until James Cook 'discovered' it in 1774 during his second global voyage. He gave it a good report, being impressed with the pines he thought would be useful as masts for naval ships, and the abundance of flax, much used at that time for sailcloth.

Cook sailed away to further navigational glories and it was not until shortly after the First Fleet arrived at far-away Botany Bay that humans again walked the island. Based on Cook's report, Governor Phillip's orders included an instruction to settle the island as soon as possible, as a source of food and lumber. Six weeks after the arrival of the First Fleet, HMS *Supply* was dispatched to the island under the command of Lieutenant Philip Gidley King.

The first settlement lasted only a few decades. The otherwise magnificent pines turned out to be useless for masts and the flax unsuitable for sail-making. The colony was closed down in 1814 and it was another eleven years before the next was founded, in 1825. This time, the intention was to build a serious penal establishment that would not only develop and exploit the island's natural resources but house those convicts considered the worst of the worst: these unfortunates would suffer 'the extremist punishment short of death'. Norfolk's confronting history relates mainly to this period.

The second settlement was a period of sadistic commandants, brutal floggings and other punishments, convict mutinies and mass hangings. It was said that men made murder pacts in which one agreed to be killed by the other who would gratefully go to his execution, death a better fate than the misery of life on Norfolk. While the grislier aspects of these times have been much mythologised, even a benign reading of what went on here leaves no doubt that Norfolk Island's grim reputation was well—or badly—deserved.

By 1855, the penal colony was closed. A few old lags and settlers stayed behind in the impressive stone structures of Kingston, living off the island's natural bounty and whatever they could grow. The British thought Norfolk was strategically important and were keen to maintain a colony there. It was at this time that the Pitcairners arrived.

After the mutiny led by Fletcher Christian against Captain Bligh of HMS *Bounty* in 1789, the mutineers settled on Pitcairn Island far across the Pacific off the coast of South America. After a few generations their tiny island became too small for them and most were moved to Norfolk in 1856. Today, the Pitcairners, with their distinctive language and customs, are a major part of a unique community with strong links to the South Pacific and New Zealand, as well as to Australia. A few remained on Pitcairn and there are still strong links between their descendants and modern-day Norfolk Islanders.

The islanders are proudly independent and not all are happy with the political and administrative External Territory relationship to the Commonwealth of Australia. This ongoing cause of tension is politely but firmly explained to the tourists who come to see the extensive ruins of the convict era and the many beauty spots, and to meet the friendly people of one of Australia's most amazing places.

Long Harry's Legacy

Towns are not usually named after bushrangers. Codrington on Victoria's Portland Bay seems to be the one exception. The story is an unusual one.

Henry Rouse was born in Leicestershire in 1818. His family circumstances were difficult, and he had only a limited education. The tall, thin youth was remembered by a former employer as having 'a rather unprepossessing countenance'. He became a cooper, or wooden barrel maker, but began his criminal career in the 1840s. A theft of cloth sent him to Australia for ten years, firstly to Norfolk Island, then to Hobart. After his release he followed his trade around Geelong.

In 1850, using the improbable alias 'Codrington Revingstone', Rouse bailed up the Portland to Port Fairy Mail coach, not once but three times. His favoured location for these attacks became known as 'Codrington's Forest'.

Living in Ballarat under the name Garrett, 'Long Harry' as he was now also known, and three others robbed the local branch of the Bank of Victoria in 1854. They stole several fortunes and Long Harry escaped to England with a very large amount of gold dust, which he presented to a London bank. Unknown to him, one of his accomplices had confessed to police and Long Harry was arrested and brought back to Melbourne to face trial. Ten years hard labour served on the very unpleasant prison hulks was the result. He was given a ticket of leave in 1861 and went to New Zealand.

Here, Harry wasted no time in robbing a gunsmith and subsequently holding up fifteen gold diggers. He and his accomplices escaped with a good deal of loot, but Rouse was again betrayed and captured in Sydney where he had fled. He was deported and given eight years gaol in Dunedin. After a failed escape attempt, Rouse found God with the Plymouth Brethren and was released in 1868, returning to Victoria. They didn't want him there and sent him straight back to Dunedin.

It was not long before he was again arrested after robbing a chemist's shop of goods and poison. Possession of lethal substances and his extensive criminal record meant that the trial did not go well: Long Harry received another ten years. Released in 1882, he was arrested a few months later for stealing wine and given a seven-year term with hard labour. Old and ailing, he was eventually sent to hospital where he died of 'chronic bronchitis' in September 1885.

Although Henry Rouse was a habitual criminal who spent around fifty of his sixty-seven years of life inside prisons in England, Norfolk Island, Van Diemen's Land, Victoria and New Zealand, he displayed some dash and style in his crimes. When Governor La Trobe offered a £30 reward for the bushranger, Rouse published a newspaper notice pledging £100 'to any man or old woman who will deliver into my hands Charles Joseph La Trobe, and my word if I get hold of him I'll work the shine out of his carcass!'

Rouse also made several notable escape attempts and seems not to have killed anyone. Normally, these would be prime traits for outlaw hero status, but this mantle eluded Rouse and we hear nothing of him in folklore. Instead, his pseudonymous legacy was the naming of a projected township on Portland Bay after him when it was surveyed in 1870. Although a post office was established there, no town developed and few live there today. A forgotten bushranger and a forgotten town.

Mrs Penfold's

They came with grapevine cuttings in their luggage. It was 1844 and Mary, Christopher and four-year-old Georgina sailed from

England to make new lives in South Australia. They would also plant the vines that became the famous Penfold's wines.

They were solid middle-class folk, exactly the kind of immigrants the free colony of South Australia wanted. Christopher was a doctor; Mary came from a well-off family and had received a good education. With them came Mary's companion, Ellen Kimbrell. The family bought a 500-acre (200-hectare) block and home, called The Grange, near Magill in the Mount Lofty Ranges. Christopher worked as the busy local doctor and Mary, with the help of Ellen and other employees, looked after the property. They planted their French grenache vines in the good soil of the farm, later adding to the stock with other varieties.

The first fruits of their labour became wine in the 1850s. It was a time when wine growing, and drinking, was in vogue. People drank it for pleasure, of course, but it was also widely used in medicine. Christopher was a staunch advocate for the medicinal qualities of wine, as were many medicos of the era, and much of the early production was used in this way. But the Penfold vintages also garnered a growing reputation in the colony and beyond. By the end of the 1860s they had 59 acres (24 hectares) under vines. A variety of reds and whites were being produced for consumption in Australia and export to India. They also began to win international awards.

Mary, assisted by Ellen, was the main operator and developer of the business. Her sharp business sense and a self-taught ability to grow grapes and blend increasingly palatable wines was complemented by a forward-looking approach. She was an early adopter of new technology, including steam-driven crushing devices, concrete vats and other labour-saving machinery, including a pioneering gadget for corking and labelling bottles.

Christopher Penfold died in 1870 and was much missed by a grateful local community. Ellen Kimbrell was already dead, leaving Mary to manage the business in partnership with another local vigneron and her family. Georgina had married civil servant Thomas Hyland, and their eight-year-old daughter, Inez, came to the vineyard to live with her grandmother in 1872. Mary effectively became the girl's mother and guardian, supervising her education, encouraging her literary gifts and caring for her poor health.

In 1884, Mary retired from the business. She was sixty-eight and much of her life had been productively spent in raising a family and pioneering a business and an industry. Her retirement was spent mainly in her garden with Inez as a much-loved companion. Sadly, this relationship was fated to last only another eight years: Inez died at the age of twenty-nine in 1892.

Mary arranged a posthumous publication of Inez's work in a book titled *In Sunshine and in Shadow*. Inez's intense nature verse was praised by reviewers, who lamented the too-early passing of a very promising literary talent. Mary lived the rest of her life with her daughter's family in Melbourne and died aged seventy-nine. Her body was brought back to the place the locals knew as 'Mrs Penfold's' and laid to rest with Christopher and Inez at St George's Church in nearby Woodforde.

The enterprise that Mary and her helper Ellen established lived on. Penfolds Wines went from strength to strength and became a household name throughout Australia. In the 1950s, European winemaker Max Schubert was responsible for creating Penfolds'—and Australia's—most famous wine, Grange Hermitage. A bottle of the first vintage, from 1951, will set you back over $160,000. While Schubert perfected his legendary drop long after the pioneering Penfolds, it would never have happened without what was basically a hopeful gamble on a few vine cuttings wrapped in canvas and transported carefully from one side of the planet to the other.

Wine may or may not have medicinal qualities but it is certainly one of the world's most popular tipples. If there is any more to the ancient fluid, then perhaps Inez came close to catching the magic in her 'Bread and Wine':

> A cup of opal
> Through which there glows
> The cream of the pearl,
> The heart of the rose;
> And the blue of the sea
> Where Australia lies,
> And the amber flush
> Of her sunset skies,
> And the emerald tints
> Of the dragon fly
> Shall stain my cup
> With their brilliant dye.
> And into this cup
> I would pour the wine
> Of youth and health
> And the gifts divine
> Of music and song,

And the sweet content
Which must ever belong
To a life well spent.
And what bread would I break
With my wine, think you?
The bread of a love
That is pure and true.

Old Ireland at Baker's Flat

By the end of the nineteenth century, the census recorded well over 200,000 Irish-born citizens, almost certainly an underestimation. The Irish immigration to Australia, voluntary or otherwise, has been one of the defining features of the nation and remains a powerful element of cultural background, history and folklore. Among the many Irish influences in religion, politics and culture was an ancient arrangement of living and working together.

Until well into the nineteenth century, it was not unusual for people in rural Ireland to live in communities known as *clachans*. A *clachan* was a small gathering of thirty to forty cottages erected on land of varying quality. The people who lived there, often related, farmed scattered allotments surrounding their houses under some form of communal ownership that allowed them to—just—survive. This system began to fall apart under the linked effects of privatisation of the land and the disruption of immigration.

During the 1850s, a group of Irish immigrants came to the Kapunda area of South Australia. They set up the only *clachan* yet to be found outside Ireland, Scotland or the Isle of Man, where a similar system operated. It is certainly the only example of this way of living to be found in Australia. We only know about this unusual place through the work of archaeologists who have revealed the remains of the *clachan* at Baker's Flat using ground-penetrating radar—and a little bit of Irish luck.

Copper was the reason for the settlement of Kapunda in the early 1840s. Many arrived to dig it out of the earth; others came to farm, including a group of Irish settlers who squatted on around 148 acres (60 hectares) and proceeded to set up a *clachan*. They ran stock and grew crops just as they had back home. It is thought that possibly 500 people may have lived there at any one time. Despite repeated attempts by the legal owners to evict them from the land, the Irish endured for a century or so until the 1950s, when the buildings and infrastructure were gradually demolished. Only the determined research of archaeologist Susan Arthure and her colleagues has unearthed the lost *clachan* of Baker's Flat.

Dr Arthure had heard vague stories about a lost Irish town that set her searching for evidence. After some hunting in archives and court records, she found an old map that gave her the location of the settlement. At first, excavations revealed fragments of domestic items. When the geophysical radar technology was used, it showed the outlines of a significant settlement beneath the ground, complete with fence lines and tracks. The archaeologists were able to excavate one of the clay and stone cottages and also found a well-used dance floor. It seems the people of Baker's Flat kept up their traditions with dancing to the tunes of pipes or fiddle long into the night, lighted by fires and no doubt lubricated by alcohol, possibly the fiery Irish home-brewed spirit known as poitín or poteen and also called 'mountain dew' or 'devil's spittle'.

As well as farming in the traditional *clachan* manner, the Irish of Baker's Flat also worked as local labourers. Otherwise, they seem to have kept mostly to themselves, gaining a reputation as a 'lawless little community', deserved or not. Their lives were undoubtedly hard compared with those of our own time, but they were probably better, even much better, than they might have been in Ireland. The archaeologists found pottery and other artefacts that suggest a reasonable level of comfort and lifestyle, much like that of most nineteenth-century settlers.

Who the Irish of Baker's flat were and from what part of Ireland they came, we do not know. Did they immigrate as a group, as sometimes happened, or did they somehow come together after they had reached South Australia? How did they manage to settle on the considerable block of someone else's land on which they made their lives? And are there any other *clachans* in Australia? Further research might one day answer these questions. Until then, Baker's Flat remains a unique outpost of old Ireland in Australia's vast history.

The Land We Live Inn

People called it 'Calico Town'. Goldrush Sofala, New South Wales, was a sea of canvas tents in the early 1850s. The only building of consequence was the weatherboard pub imaginatively named The Land We Live Inn. This establishment had a long and not always illustrious history and was the location for many a yarn.

One of the earliest was said to have taken place in 1858 when one of the hard-bitten local diggers stopped by for a few rums, the favoured spirit of the day. His name was Bill Simpson, a hard worker and, like most of the miners, a hard drinker. Conditions were pretty primitive on the goldfields, even by the standards of the era, and Bill was not exactly well groomed. His hair hung down in locks 'like a surf ripple', overly lubricated with the then-popular pomade, castor oil. Bathing was not something diggers did a lot and Bill was well on the nose. As he approached the bar the other drinkers slid away from him, but soon got used to the smell when Bill began shouting drinks all round. Bill got stuck into the numerous nobblers he would put away that afternoon but eventually called it quits and decided to have a snooze. This provided a golden opportunity for a bit of vengeful fun at the malodorous digger's expense.

'Freddy the Fossicker' tipped Susie Slapp the barmaid with a small piece of gold and suggested that she might get a pair of scissors. Susie knew just what he meant. She found some shears and took to Bill's oily locks with a will, leaving most of his hair on the bar-room floor before he finally woke up. As the teller of this tale recounted it eighty years later:

> When Bill awoke and missed his locks he raved like a madman, rushing round swearing to do for the publican and the rest of the company. He shot stones, collected in the road, at the bottles, liberating much good spirit, some at least of which was sucked up hog fashion, by several diggers sprawled upon their knees on the floor. It took five men to tie his hands behind him and get him away to his

hut, minus his oily old hat which Susie Slapp bore away on the end of a poker and hung on a post in the yard to bleach.

Tales of big finds are always an important part of goldfields pub lore and the World We Live Inn was no different. The biggest was the lump of pure gold that caused great excitement in January 1858. Publican Bill Rogers had employed a few men to prospect on his behalf at Nuggetty Creek. The men fossicked for a few hours without much luck and knocked off for a smoko around eleven. To pass the time, they began throwing clods of earth at each other. As the game proceeded the clods got bigger, until one man grabbed an especially large lump of clay. As he made to hurl it towards his mates, it crumbled, revealing a pure gold nugget said to be the largest ever found on the Turon goldfield.

After debating whether to tell their employer about the find, the men decided the right thing to do was to let him know and carried the shining lump up to the pub in a red bandana, hallooing as they went. Rogers was cutting lunch for the men at the time but soon forgot that mundane task when he saw what the commotion was about and 'seeing the glitter of the nugget picked it up, jumped up on to the table, waved it round and hurrahed till he was hoarse, his family dancing round the room'.

The nugget had to be assayed for official weight and value at Bathurst, a difficult and potentially dangerous journey once news of the find got out, which it quickly did. Undaunted, the publican's seventeen-year-old daughter, Mary Ann, slipped the nugget into a pillowcase and rode with it side-saddle on her horse along the bush short cut. The gold was assayed at 132 ounces (3.75 kg) and fetched the then-enormous sum of £528, which Mary Ann had to carry back the way she had come, eluding several attempts to waylay her. Rogers paid the three honest diggers the rather measly bonus of £5 each but at least they were able to celebrate, or perhaps commiserate, with as many drinks as they liked when the now-enriched publican declared a free house day at the Land We Live Inn.

Plucky Mary Ann later married Cobb & Co driver James Lowe and became a noted horsewoman in the district. She died aged ninety in 1927, a celebrated pioneer 'after a life crowded with adventure', as her obituary put it.

As well as running the pub and looking for gold, Bill Rogers had another sideline as an undertaker. One morning a digger came into the Land We Live Inn and morosely downed a couple of rums. Then he told Bill his wife had just died. Never one to let a business opportunity pass by, Bill asked who was going to bury her.

'Oh, you'd better do that, Bill,' replied the digger. 'You knowed her, and she knowed you, and you was always a friend to us both.'

Bill began preparations as the tipsy widower made his unsteady way to the establishment of Bill's rival, a man named Davis who also ran a funeral business. Forgetting he had arranged with Rogers to bury his wife, the befuddled digger hired Davis for the same job. Next day, Rogers arrived at the bereaved man's hut with a well-made coffin at the same time as Davis turned up with a rough-and-ready pine casket. Equally enraged, the two publicans went for each other in proper goldrush manner, forcing the digger to adjudicate: 'Rogers has made a decent coffin; yours ain't fit to bury a dorg in, Davis, you can take it back home again.'

The digger's wife was soon laid to rest at Sofala in Bill Rogers' coffin. He was there to pay his respects as well as to receive his pay. As he left the cemetery, he ran straight into the waiting Davis who promptly punched him on the nose. As a later newspaper account put it: 'A brief and bloody fistic skirmish followed, and when the next court day came round, the rival undertakers were each fined for disorderly conduct.'

The legendary The Land We Live Inn carried on well into the twentieth century, a nostalgic memory of the glory days of gold, wild yarns and quirky characters. Still standing, it is now a private residence.

Glorious News for the Diggers!

The city now known as Forbes, New South Wales, has seen a thing or two in the nearly 200 years it has been growing. Founded in the 1830s, the next big excitement to hit Forbes was the goldrushes of the 1860s. This was shortly followed by some epic outbreaks of bushranging starring Frank Gardiner, Ben Hall, John Gilbert and a colourful cast of other villains celebrated in folk ballads and yarns, all trying to relieve the diggers of their earnings.

On the wild and woolly goldfields of the Lachlan rush, diggers hoped to strike it rich but mostly struggled to make a living. After a tough week they at least had the delights of Forbes nightlife to look forward to, as one Saturday night reveller described them in 1862:

We are at that portion of Rankin or Main street where it is intersected by Brown street, and looking towards the Caledonia and Victoria leads. Underfoot it seems as if some immense soap-boiling establishment has been emptied of its contents, making locomotion pretty easy from the tops of the numerous little mounds in the directions of the nearest mud puddles, and you can scarcely imagine the difficulty of keeping your feet from going from under you, thereby bringing your posteriors to an anchor in a very unenviable position.

The writer went on to describe how, after avoiding the mud, you could quickly lose a lot of money at 'pitch and toss' or 'two-up', as it now known:

A group is collected at one corner; a man standing in the midst throws his hand upwards, and instantly all the faces are turned upwards. In a second they are down again, and a slight rattle of silver amidst an avalanche of curses tell us that it is 'pitch and toss'.
'A note I heads 'em.'
'A——note you don't.'
'Done.'
Up go the half-crowns.
'Two to one. I does it again.'
This blackguard game is continued all day, until the knowing ones have nothing more to win.

While all this, and more, was going on, hungry diggers got a chance to buy their meat direct from the cart of a butcher who had immigrated from London's Whitechapel area. His meat was the cheapest and best, he bellowed in a hoarse voice to a crowd of several hundred potential customers in the light of a slush lamp:

> Who says the Vitechapel butcher ain't the poa man's friend? Yere's your rosy meat. 'Buy, buy will yon buy, honly freehapence a pound. The butchers tries to keep hup the price of meat. They'd sooner ha' see hit a 'angin in their shops than hin a poor digger's belly, but I'll bring 'em down, I'll sell meat on Monday night for a penny a pound, hand hif they sells it for a penny, vy, I sells it for a 'apenny'.

Still expertly working the crowd, the butcher elicits a cheer from his delighted audience as he proceeds to another competing meat stall and confronts the luckless owner 'who accordingly vents his displeasure in a host of a disgusting appellations'. The rivals continue their slanging match 'which generally turns to the advantage of the Whitechapel butcher, who has the crowd cheering him all the time'.

Further along the street is another merchant selling food, according to some of dubious quality, but he is still 'taking money as fast as he can pocket it'. His large shop is 'covered with posters, announcing "Glorious news for the diggers! Skillicorn the renowned has opened! Bread down to sixteenpence, meat one penny, and potatoes twelve pounds for a 'tanner'!"

Over at the Exchange Hotel the dance floor is, typically, full of men. When the partiers go inside 'we find the floor occupied by fifteen men and one woman going through the different movements of a set of quadrilles, a piano and violin forming the "quadrille band" mentioned in the advertisement. On either side of the dancers are a number of men of all shades of color, and so closely wedged together, that we can scarcely pass.'

Dancing and drinking are not the only attractions of the Exchange. It was also possible to enjoy the latest medical technology, for a price:

> At a little distance a large lump upon a table arrests our progress, the man in charge of which is unburdening his mind to several half-scared individuals in the following manner—'take a shock from the galvanic battery, gents, you can have hit has heasy has you likes, hor, has ard as you likes, it circulates the blood, cures the rheumatism, removes the 'eadache, softens the muscles palevates pains hin the back, will make the old feel young, hand the charge his only sixpence. Try a shock gents, try a shock.'

Then the lamplit Cobb & Co coach arrives, carrying some dubious characters, flashing rolls of banknotes, or 'sugar', and calling for wagers. The streets are crowded with diggers seeking some Saturday night diversion. Vigilant for pickpockets, the revellers move on to some further entertainment in the very smoky premises of the grandly named Exhibition Concert Room: basically a pub. Entrance to the crowded room is one shilling and there are:

> stools on each side; every stool provided with a little shelf to hold the glass or pint-pot of its occupant (for every person is expected to drink; at least I think so from the waiters constantly calling out 'give your orders, gentlemen', and

watching dart upon any glass that may be empty). The performance consisted of a sort of miscellaneous entertainment. Every person drank or smoked as much as he or *she* liked. The smoking seemed to annoy the performer much; it was almost impossible for the ladies to keep upon their countenances that stereotyped smile so necessary upon the stage, it was painful to witness the twitching of the lips and the nose, generally resulting in something between a sneeze and a cough, as every cloud of smoke rolled over the stage . . .

Between acts, the patrons engaged in 'a great deal of colonial wit'. The show finished with a light show of some sort, though the author couldn't see the colours through the clouds of smoke.

Then it was time to return to the diggings, so 'we made our way to our tents, on the banks of a filthy lagoon about half a mile from the main street' to sleep despite the croaking of the bullfrogs.

It seems that a night out on the diggings might have been as exhausting as mining for gold.

The Singing Wire

The single strand of galvanised iron wire linking Port Augusta in South Australia to Darwin in the Northern Territory had many names. One was the prosaic but accurate Overland Telegraph, rapidly abbreviated to the 'OT'. More romantic was 'the singing wire', a poetic take on the sound of wind resonating through the posts and wire as the line marched across more than 1864 miles (3000 kilometres) of some of the hardest country in the world. Those who worked on surveying and building the Overland Telegraph had other, unprintable, names for their creation. Probably the greatest engineering accomplishment of nineteenth-century Australian nation-building, the OT was an epic struggle against desert, flood and time.

When the explorer John McDouall Stuart and his party achieved the first successful European south–north crossing of the continent in 1862, the idea of linking the north and south of Australia by telegraph went from wishful thinking to a definite possibility. The determined Scotsman recommended the suitability of the route as 'nearly a straight line for telegraphic purposes'. Like the current National Broadband Network (NBN) it would be enormously expensive and difficult. But Stuart, mostly following a traditional First Nations trade route, had shown that it was possible to travel overland from one end of the continent to the other and back again—although the hardships he suffered contributed to his early death, in 1866.

There was the usual squabbling between colonies as the honour of mounting the visionary project was discussed. In the end, South Australia won because it controlled the Northern Territory, providing the only north–south corridor free of borders. Work on the line began in 1870. Following Stuart's maps, Charles Todd, the Superintendent of Telegraphs for South Australia, began surveying and preparing the route.

The plan was to break the project into three geographical sections: the southern section beginning in Port Augusta and the northern section in Darwin. These would both be constructed by the British Australian Telegraph Company, which was also laying the first undersea cable from Darwin to Java. The plan was for the Overland Telegraph and the cable to be completed at nearly the same time, not only connecting the Australia colonies to each other but also to Britain and so to the rest of the world. The lengthy and most isolated central section would be built by the South Australian government.

As well as the massive logistics challenge involved in providing iron and native timber poles, insulators, batteries and wire, and feeding and sheltering three large armies of workers and animals across almost uncharted distances, there was a deadline. If the line was late being completed, the South Australian government would have to pay the British Australian Telegraph Company a very large amount of compensation. No pressure.

It began well. Then 'the wet' set in. Work on the northern section was bogged down. There were disagreements between the government and contractors as well as strikes, eventually resulting in the cancellation of the contract. Todd now had to take responsibility for building another 435 miles (700 kilometres) of line.

To add further drama to the situation, the British Australian Telegraph Company finished laying the Darwin–Java cable ahead of schedule, well before the telegraph line was completed. Messages could now be sent and received through the cable but there was a gap of more than 186 miles (300 kilometres) in the line. This was overcome by pony express riders taking messages by hand until 22 August 1872, when the wires of the Overland Telegraph were finally joined at Frew Ponds, Birdum, in the Northern Territory. Todd had the honour of sending the first official message:

> We have this day, within two years, completed a line of communications two thousand miles long through the very

centre of Australia, until a few years ago a Terra Incognita believed to be a desert . . .

The OT was up: an enormous engineering, technical and logistical feat involving intense hardship for those who built it. Six workers died and many others were injured or suffered sickness. But the OT fulfilled its backers' dreams, and more. Alice Springs was established around the telegraph repeater station built there. Gold was discovered and exploration of the interior was encouraged through the existence of a physical structure and repeater stations along its route providing landmarks and occasional shelter for travellers. And most of the country got to communicate quickly with the world and between colonies for the first time.

Upkeep and maintenance of the line was a continual source of trouble but also of employment and development. Floods regularly washed the posts away and white ants destroyed many timber poles. Aboriginal groups quickly discovered how useful the glass insulators were for making sharp tools and weapons. There were also attacks on repeater stations leading to reprisals, most fatally at Barrow Creek in 1874, where many Kaititja (Kaytetye) people were killed.

In 1877, Western Australia was connected to the Overland Telegraph through a line built across the Nullarbor Plain, another epic encounter between harsh terrain and hard work. The OT continued to provide vital communication within the nation and with other nations across the world for many years until superseded by wireless and telephone technologies. Nowadays, the OT is part of Australia's national development story, its remnants a draw for tourists and those with a passion for technological and communication history.

Sea Lines

From the middle of the nineteenth century there was a rapid boom in the making and laying of undersea cables from country to country. France and England were connected, shakily, from the early 1850s, followed by England and Germany and then an increasing number of longer and longer undersea cables were laid between more and more countries. The growing system of transcontinental cables was not quite the nineteenth-century equivalent of today's internet, but it brought about an international communications revolution.

The first undersea cable in the southern hemisphere was laid under Bass Strait in 1859, connecting Tasmania at Low Head on the Tamar River and the mainland at Cape Otway. At the time, it was said to have been the longest such cable in the world. But the first international connection with Australia was between Darwin and Java in 1871.

As it got light on the morning of 7 November that year, hundreds of men began the difficult task of bringing one end of the heavy cable that would be dropped beneath the waves all the way to Java onto the shore at Port Darwin. Large loops of cable were brought ashore from the *Hibernia*, one of the three cable-laying ships anchored half a mile (800 metres) out to sea. On the beach, workers attached the cable to a shackle and began to haul: 'The scene was a most animated one, the men singing at their work, the officers waving flags, and the inhabitants of the settlement looking on'. Over the next few hours, the thick cable was guided up a shallow trench to an iron hut, where it was attached to an 'electrical apparatus'.

The ships, now connected to the land, were signalled along the cable and steamed away for Java. As they went, rolling the great wire down onto the seabed, telegraphic messages kept those in Darwin informed of progress. A week or so later, the ships were within 6 miles of the Java coast. All they needed to do now was cut the cable, seal it and get it to shore where it would be connected to another electrical apparatus. Four days later, a telegraphic message reached the Darwin station saying that the link had been made. Australia was connected to Java and, through other cables on the island, to Britain and other parts of the world for the first time.

The speed and efficiency of this British Australian Telegraph Company operation was astonishing, considering that the technology allowing it had only been developed over the previous twenty years or so. The challenges involved in making a wire able to carry an electric current across vast distances and to lay it at the bottom of the sea were enormous for the manufacturing and shipping facilities of the day. And yet, by the 1870s, such underwater cables were commonplace around the world.

Not everything went according to plan, of course. Cables frequently broke during laying or were rubbed against rocks beneath the sea, quickly parting and losing the connection. These outages were usually repaired quickly, or troublesome cables were replaced with more advanced and stronger models. The Darwin–Java cable failed in its first year of operation. It took four months to restore it. A second cable was laid between

Darwin and Java in 1880 but after only a few years a volcanic disturbance in the Bali Straits ruptured the cables, reinforcing the need for another link from Australia.

By 1889, Broome on the western coast was also connected to Java, providing a backup facility. The original cable station was converted into the Broome Court House after the cable link was discontinued in 1914, replaced by the cheaper and more flexible technology of wireless telegraphy. Today, tourists enjoy camel rides and impressive sunsets on Broome's Cable Beach. Unless they read the plaque commemorating this slice of communication history, they will probably be unaware of the significance of the place they are enjoying.

In the next few years other Australian undersea cables were connected from Bundaberg to New Caledonia and through Norfolk Island and Fiji to Canada. The era of international cable telegraphy was a boost for all connected countries. For Australia, it was especially important. The cable connections, together with the Overland Telegraph, freed the country from the twin tyrannies of distance and time The telegraph, using both land lines and undersea cables, 'girdled the earth'. It was now possible to quickly send and receive news and other information between the colonies, as well as to and from the world. Business, government and the press of the day were the greatest users of these services, but individuals and families could also rapidly send and receive messages of events, both joyous and sad. Although telegraphy has long been obsolete, it is the modern international network of submarine cables, mostly using fibre-optic technology, that make the internet possible.

The Wire Frontier

Visible from space and said to be one of the world's largest structures, the dingo fence snakes more than 5000 kilometres across three states. Also known colloquially as the 'dog fence' and with various official names, the wire-and-steel barrier evolved from early attempts to control dingo attacks on sheep in New South Wales, Queensland, South Australia and Victoria. The fence is effectively an unofficial border cutting through states from west to east in an ongoing effort to protect valuable livestock and farm incomes.

While this and other fences slicing through the Australian landscape try to keep a number of predators away from livestock, it is the dingo that has become most closely identified with these structures. Closely related to East Asian domestic dogs, the dingo is now believed to have arrived on the Australian mainland, probably from what is now Papua New Guinea, between five and ten thousand years ago. Dingoes then became part of the local ecosystem, probably by extinguishing the native Thylacines. The dingo became an important element of First Nations peoples' cultures as a hunting companion, guard animal and in traditional mythology and belief. When Europeans introduced sheep, the trouble began.

Dingoes were rapidly seen as a serious problem and shot on sight. Later, they were poisoned with strychnine. 'Death to the Dingo' ran a newspaper heading in July 1868. It was a letter to the editor about the still-vexed topic of wild dog control. The controversy continued and has raged ever since. From early baiting and shooting of dingoes, agriculturalists moved to what they hoped would be the more effective remedy of building long barriers that would fence dogs—and other pests—into their desert habitat and keep them away from valuable flocks. The columns of Australian newspapers were full of articles and letters complaining of the problem or offering solutions, mostly funded by individual pastoralists. Few, if any, of these were part of a coordinated plan, leading to a piecemeal and so ineffective patchwork of varying lengths, heights and designs.

Landholders exerting increasing pressure on governments led to the erection of large fences to stop rabbits in eastern Australia during the 1880s. Despite newspaper cartoons showing rabbits happily playing tennis across the wire, the technique was soon adapted for the control of other native animals considered to be predatory pests. The age of the fence was well underway. A rabbit-proof fence line began in Queensland's Darling Downs in 1893, frequently lengthened and eventually connecting with the Dingo Fence in 1997. Western Australia began building long fences against rabbits, vermin and emus in 1901.

Governments have continued to fund new sections of fence at different times and places. The New South Wales Border Wild Dog Fences, as the line is now known, is being extended along the state borders with Queensland and Victoria from 2020, adding over 700 kilometres to its existing 580-kilometre length. In the same year, the Commonwealth provided $1 million towards a more than 600-kilometre addition the State Barrier Fence in the Esperance region of Western Australia. This project is one of several similar additions to the fences of various states, usually co-funded by the relevant state governments.

As these fences were when they began to be built, so they remain today. Conservationists and environmentalists are generally opposed to them, claiming they are not especially effective, the failure to control rabbits being one, though not the only, example. They are also expensive to build and maintain and can be a danger to non-predatory wildlife. Recent research suggests that the fences cause ecological problems related to the loss of vegetation. This damage is only visible from a satellite and adds another dimension to an already complex problem of balancing the needs of farmers with those of the land.

Some of these conflicts are symbolic rather than practical. The enigmatic image of the dingo in Australia is a fusion of fact and fiction, First Nations peoples' beliefs and the animal's ruthlessly efficient predatory character. Emotion and romanticism have frequently clouded real-life issues concerning dingoes.

Many Australians still have strong memories of the extraordinary events of the Azaria Chamberlain case. Whether or not a dingo took baby Azaria from an outback campsite in 1980 was a question that transfixed the nation and caused perhaps the most egregious miscarriage of justice in Australia's history. It was held by many that dingoes did not attack humans, despite extensive evidence to the contrary from knowledgeable people. Many members of the general public and the media did not wish to believe that an animal so closely associated with Australian cultural identity might kill and eat a baby. They preferred to believe that the mother, with the collusion of her husband, murdered the child. After trials, appeals and massive community discomfort and agitation, Lindy Chamberlain was eventually freed, pardoned and, with her by then ex-husband, compensated.

The Dingo Fence is not only an artefact of Australia's troubled relations with its environment but also cuts through our long and complicated history with the animal it seeks to exclude. It is a wire frontier, dividing the settled agricultural areas from the arid wilderness beyond. A similar approach is also deployed in other locales. The most recent dingo fence is on Queensland's Fraser Island to prevent the resident dingoes, or native dogs, attacking tourists. The battle between nature and what humans want to do in it continues.

The Sheds

We usually think of woolsheds as rough-and-ready buildings, thrown together from bush poles, a bit of corrugated iron and anything else at hand. Their function was limited to one overarching task: getting as much wool off as many sheep as possible in the shortest amount of time. Once the fleece was shorn it could be pressed into large bales for transportation to market. There wasn't a lot else you could do with a woolshed, except for the occasional dance that might be held in one outside the shearing season. Or perhaps to feature in the famous Tom Roberts painting *Shearing the Rams*.

But a few woolsheds were anything but ready-made improvisations. Some were architecturally designed and built with expertise and quality materials. One such is the woolshed at Errowanbang, New South Wales.

Known only to a few heritage enthusiasts and locals until 2012, Old Errowanbang Woolshed was built in 1886. A vast complex of corrugated iron sprawling across a hillside, the shed is supported by a forest of poles set on bluestone foundations. The builders were careful to smooth the rough edges of interior beams so the fleeces would not snag as they were 'taken off' and then carried along the shearing 'boards', as the floor was called.

According to the New South Wales Heritage assessment 'the quality of workmanship in the construction of Errowanbang Woolshed is probably unsurpassed in Australia'.

They might want to argue with that view in South Australia where the astonishing Cordillo Downs Woolshed presents a very different architectural approach to a workaday structure. This shed is unique, with a curved rather than gable roof and built of stone held together by flying buttresses, not unlike a scaled-down medieval cathedral. Built in 1883, just a couple of decades after Burke and Wills passed through the area, Cordillo Downs has faced the same dilemma as Errowanbang. The owners of both properties are keen to preserve and restore their irreplaceable historic structures but face challenges of finance, availability of necessary heritage skills and red tape hampering progress.

Hopefully, they and others with a desire to retain these fast-fading hives of industry, labour and tradition will succeed. Sheds were known to shearers and bush workers by their names and by the tallies clocked upon in them by legendary hand-held bladesmen, or 'guns', like Jackie Howe. Quite a few sheds were immortalised in songs, like the little-known but perhaps finest of all the shearing ballads, 'Goorianawa':

> I've been many years a shearer, I fancied I could shear;
> I've shorn for Rouse, at Guntawang, and always missed the spear.
> I've shorn for Nicholas Bayley, and I declare to you
> That of his pure merinos I could always get a few.
> But, oh! my! I never saw before,
> The way we had to knuckle down at Goorianawa.

The song goes on to boast of the sheds the singer once sheared in, of the bosses who ran them and the fact that he never got 'the spear', or the sack. It ends with the confession that he was sacked at Goorianawa before he had shorn three sheep:

> But now I'm broken-mouthed, my shearing's at an end;
> And, although they call me 'Whalebone,' I was never known
>   to bend.
> I've shorn in every woolshed, from the Barwon to the Bree,
> I got speared, at Goorianawa before I raddled three.
> But, oh! my! I never saw before,
> The way we had to knuckle down at Goorianawa.

Sheep and their shearing are one of Australia's great historical and folkloric experiences. The wool industry was for decades an important source of foreign revenue for the country. The industry employed many people, though none so fabled as the shearers. The tough masculinism and competitiveness of what was one of the hardest and dirtiest jobs in the bush engendered a uniquely colourful working culture and lifestyle. A seemingly endless flow of folk song, verse and yarns extolled the hardships, humour and robust independence of the shearers, travelling from shed to shed, earning a big cheque at the end of the season and, in legend at least, blowing it all on grog, gambling and women. 'Once I rung Cudjingie shed and blewed it in a week', laments one well-known ballad of the roaring days, a theme that appears in many such songs and poems. Then it was back on the track to eke out a slender living until the next shearing season came around and the cycle began again.

Shearers, of course, were master liars. They had an occupational hero named 'Crooked Mick'. He was the largest, strongest and fastest shearer ever known, 'ringing' every shed he sheared in with the highest 'tally' (see Chapter 7). A land of such legendary shearing prowess needed a legendary shed to match. It was known as Big Burrawang (sometimes pronounced 'Burrawong') and probably named after one of the largest sheds in New South Wales, near Forbes. Big Burrawang was so long that the overseer had to ride a bicycle to get from one end of the board to the other in reasonable time.

Seeing the extent of surviving woolsheds like Errowanbang and Cordillo Downs, it's not hard to see how legends like Big Burrawang originated and grew. Shearers told and retold these tales as they digested, or not, whatever the cook dished up and relaxed in the shearers' quarters after a tough day, spinning yarns and singing songs. These ballads and stories are directly linked to the places where shearers earned their daily bread. They are time capsules of history and legend, vignettes of a unique time, of unique places and of the culture that grew there, created and kept by the people who lived it.

The 'roaring days' are long gone. Powered shears, air conditioning and other comforts have improved the work immeasurably but knocking the fleece off a lot of sheep as quickly as possible is still hard work. Not so many follow the shearing these days, but a few shreds of mystique cling to the modern wool workers and their history is alive in places like the Australian Shearers' Hall of Fame at Hay, New South Wales.

A Golden Pipeline

At 4.40 in the morning of 10 March 1902, a well-dressed man rode his horse into the water at Robb Jetty, Fremantle, placed a pistol in his mouth and pulled the trigger. His name was Charles Yelverton O'Connor, Engineer-in-Chief of Western Australia. He had achieved what most thought was impossible: the building of a harbour inside the mouth of the Swan River, removing the limestone bar and sandy shoals that had defeated all previous attempts to destroy them.

Overworked, subjected to vitriolic criticism and baseless allegations of corruption in the newspapers and from some politicians, O'Connor fell victim to despair. He left a poignant note written in pencil but unsigned:

> The position has become impossible. Anxious important work to do, and three comissions [sic] of inquiry to attend to. We may not have done as well as possible in the past, and we will necessarily be too hampered to do well in the immediate future.
>
> I feel that my brain is suffering, and I am in great fear of what effect all this worry will have upon me. I have lost control of my thoughts. The Coolgardie scheme is all right, and I could finish it if I got the chance and protection from misrepresentation; but there is no hope for that now, and it is better that it should be given to some entirely new man to do, who will be untrammelled by prior responsibilities. 10/3/02.

Ever the engineer, he included a postscript directing workers to 'put the wing wall to Helena weir at once'.

Witnesses at the inquest testified to O'Connor's increasingly depressed and deranged state as he was assailed with criticisms in parliament and the press, most of them malignant and ignorant of the engineering issues involved. Mr Moss, a solicitor, said O'Connor visited him a week or so before taking his life. The engineer was distressed and 'his hand was shaking all the time, and he was in a state of high nervous tension'.

The coroner asked, 'Was he rational?'

Moss answered, 'Yes, but his nerves were undoubtedly very highly strung that morning'.

The coronial jury reached the inevitable conclusion: 'That Charles Yelverton O'Connor met his death by his own hand through a bullet wound from a revolver at Robb's Jetty, Fremantle, on March 10, 1902, while in a state of mental derangement, caused by worry and overwork.'

O'Connor's death came before the completion of his greatest engineering achievement, the Goldfields Water Supply Scheme. The pipeline from Mundaring Weir (as it came to be called) near Perth to the distant desert goldfields was completed and water arrived at Coolgardie late in 1902. In January 1903, Premier John Forrest turned on the tap a bit further down the line at the burgeoning township of Kalgoorlie.

At the time, a pipeline of over 310 miles (500 kilometres) in length was thought to be an impossibility, as well as wildly expensive. But O'Connor overcame the obstacles of bureaucracy, political opposition, design, supply of materials and the harsh distance to design and build what has become known as his 'Golden Pipeline'. The pipeline also delivers water to the settlements along its length and to other parts of the goldfields, ensuring the continued existence of the goldmining industry and parts of the Wheatbelt.

In 2020, Water Corporation WA announced that the ageing pipeline was now considered 'not fit for purpose' as leaks and ruptures have been increasing. While the design of the pipes that carry water on an eleven-day journey from Mundaring to Kalgoorlie were groundbreaking technology in the 1890s, new materials and construction methods are far superior.

However, as it was when first proposed and budgeted, building a pipeline of such length is extraordinarily expensive. Water Corporation WA has not put a figure on what they see as a fifty-year replacement project. The pipeline stretches over 550 kilometres all up and the budget for just a single planned new section of around 3 kilometres runs out at $8 million. Do the sums and it's easy to understand why the engineers don't want to mention the cost.

Whatever the eventual fate of the Golden Pipeline, C.Y. O'Connor will always be celebrated as a towering figure, even a martyr, in the history of the state, with an impressive statue in his honour as well as educational establishments and an Australian electoral division among various places named after him, including the beach where a brilliant man was driven to end his life.

Landing the sub-marine telegraph cable from Java to Port Darwin in 1871.

2
DANGEROUS PLACES

The Eye of the Needle

With water lapping the lower hatches, Captain Guy Hamilton ran the *Sydney Cove* onto rocks south of Preservation Island on 9 February 1797. Out of Calcutta with supplies bound for Sydney and a crew of mostly Indian seamen, the ship had been leaking for weeks. Now the seas of the eastern reaches of Bass Strait finally overwhelmed the pumps. Nobody was lost, but they were far from the nearest settlement at Sydney.

Leaving around thirty survivors on the island, Clark and seventeen crew sailed for rescue in the ship's longboat, but they were wrecked on Ninety Mile Beach (now Victoria) and began walking the 435 miles (700 kilometres) to Sydney. With little food and less protection, they encountered Aboriginal groups who were sometimes friendly, sometimes not. One of the sailors was killed and most of the others died along the grim trek.

Only three of the group reached Wattamolla, New South Wales, in mid-May: Clark and two crewmen, emaciated and exhausted. Fortunately, they managed to attract the attention of a fishing boat and were delivered to Sydney, just 50 kilometres to the north. The group on Preservation Island was picked up by two small ships, the *Francis* and the *Eliza*. The *Eliza* was wrecked on the return journey with the loss of all hands and eight of the *Sydney Cove* survivors.

Safely back in Sydney, Clark reported that Preservation Island, then little-known, was in a passage between the mainland and Tasmania. George Bass was making his famous voyage of discovery at this time and set a course for the wreck site himself. He didn't make it but he was able to confirm that Tasmania was an island on the southern side of the strait that now bears his name.

The *Sydney Cove* was one of the first ships wrecked in the treacherous waters between the Australian mainland and Tasmania. Mariners know the relatively narrow seas between the western end of Bass Strait and Cape Otway as the 'eye of the needle' and passing through it is known as 'threading the eye of the needle'. In the days before modern navigational instruments, it was very easy to sail too far north or south and come to disaster on the Victorian coast or on the many islands to the south. King Island was especially notorious for wrecks.

In the early hours of 4 August 1845, the 800-ton barque *Cataraqui* entered Bass Strait with over 400 passengers and crew. Most of those aboard were English immigrants, including many families, who had sailed from Liverpool four months earlier. In high seas and gale-force winds, the ship was blown onto the reef off the west coast of King Island. The passengers were helped up onto the flooded deck but many were washed away. More were lost as the ship lurched to port and began to break up. The masts were cut down but the vessel could not be righted and filled with water, drowning those left below:

> As the day broke we found the stern of the vessel washed in and numerous dead bodies floating around the ship—some hanging upon the rocks. Several of the passengers and crew (about 200 altogether) were still holding on to the vessel—the sea breaking over and every wave washing some of them away. Thus those who were able, continued to cling to the wreck until about four in the afternoon, when she parted amidships, at the fore part of the main rigging, when immediately some seventy or a hundred were launched into the tumultuous and remorseless waves!

All attempts to rig makeshift life rafts failed and the *Cataraqui* broke in half, drowning many more and leaving about seventy clinging to what was left. By daybreak only thirty-five were left, lashed to the disintegrating structure. As the waves continued to pound the wreck, the survivors were released from the ropes by the remaining crew and given their last chance for life. Of those who braved the roiling sea and jumped overboard only nine survived. Washed ashore, exhausted and surrounded with wreckage and bodies, they were lucky to be found by a settler on the island who, together with an Aboriginal man, saved their lives. It was five weeks before the nine men, eight sailors and one immigrant, were taken off and carried to safety.

The wreck of the *Cataraqui* remains Australia's worst civil maritime tragedy. But she was only one of many more ships that failed to thread the eye of the needle. The *Loch Ard* was wrecked on Mutton Bird Island near Port Campbell, Victoria, in 1878. Cloaked in fog, with faulty chronometers and foul weather preventing accurate readings of the ship's position, the three-masted clipper ran aground and sank in less than fifteen minutes. Only two of the fifty-four people aboard survived by clinging to pieces of wreckage for hours. Ship's apprentice Tom Pearce was washed ashore at the place now known as Loch Ard Gorge. He heard faint shouts for help and went back into the sea to rescue young Eva (Eveline) Carmichael, an immigrant from Ireland. The rest of her family were lost in the wreck and she was near death herself when Tom pulled her from the heavy swell. With great difficulty he managed to climb the cliff in search of help. Fortunately, a local farmer was mustering sheep in the sparsely populated area and found the 'much scarred' boy.

On a brighter footnote, when the wreck of the *Sydney Cove* was finally relocated, archaeologists discovered well-preserved bottles of beer. The yeast was still alive and has been used to brew a flavoursome beer, some of which was released as 'Preservation Ale' in 2018 by James Squire, modern bearers of the name of Australia's first beer brewer.

B LXV

For heroic folly and tragedy, the tale of the ill-fated Burke and Wills expedition is hard to top. The disaster that slowly unfolded across the northern reaches of eastern Australia between 1860 and 1862 left an indelible mark on the history of inland exploration and in popular consciousness.

Robert O'Hara Burke was a well-born Irishman with a military and policing background. The more cautious English surveyor and astronomer for the expedition, William Wills, would eventually be Burke's lieutenant in the Victorian Exploring Expedition. This was intended to be the culmination of a frenzy of exploratory journeys that had become a major Australian preoccupation by the middle of the nineteenth century. Inspired by the derring-do of imperial—British and other—adventurers around the world, young and middle-aged men were keen to try their own hands at forging new trails across the wilderness, achieving renown—and probably financial reward—for their efforts in unravelling the riddles and puzzles of new places.

Explorers needed many resources and attributes, especially money and confidence. Burke's faith in himself amounted to fatal arrogance. The money that paid for this debacle came from the overenthusiastic Royal Society of Victoria and the colonial government. The expedition was never well thought out, its basis being greed and a misplaced desire to forge a north–south trail across the continent ahead of its rival, South Australia's stoic explorer John McDouall Stuart.

The handsomely equipped party of men, camels, horses and wagons was farewelled by an enthusiastic Melbourne crowd on 20 August 1860. The trouble began early. By the time the expedition reached the Darling River in October, there was already quarrelling and bad feeling. Burke's second-in-command was either dismissed by Burke or resigned, and Wills was promoted to that position.

Burke and Wills pushed further north with a smaller group, eventually establishing a depot at Cooper('s) Creek, Camp LXV. Burke, Wills, Gray and King made what was intended to be a dash for the Gulf of Carpentaria, over 1500 kilometres north. The remaining three men were to wait at the depot for at least three months, giving the lead party time to reach their northern goal and return. The Camp LXV group remained there four months with no sight of the forward party. Finally, at 10 am on 21 April 1861, they departed the site. They blazed messages on a Coolabah tree they had already marked with 'B LXV', indicating that this was the sixty-fifth camp made by Burke's group. The date 'DEC-6-60' was carved over 'APR-21-61' indicating the days of arriving and leaving the camp. Then 'DIG'.

The exact wording of the famous 'Dig' inscription is debatable as sources differ and bark has mostly regrown over the markings. It might have been 'DIG under', 'DIG 3FT N.W.', 'DIG 40 FT N.E.', 'DIG 21 APR 61' or some combination of those. Whatever the lettering, the meaning was clear. Beneath the ground the Camp LXV party had buried large stores of rice, flour, oatmeal and sugar.

As they were so long overdue, there was no real expectation that Burke and the others would ever return to Cooper Creek. But probably only nine or so hours later, three of the four missing explorers and two surviving camels staggered into Camp LXV. Burke, Wills and King had reached the Gulf and, unbelievably, made it back to the depot, though they lost Gray along the way.

By now, several groups of rescuers had set out from Victoria, Queensland and South Australia in search of the long-overdue explorers. One of these reached Camp LXV but by then Burke,

Wills and King had left again. They buried a note beneath the blazed tree telling of their intention to travel over 200 kilometres west to a remote station near Mount Hopeless in South Australia. Unfortunately, they made no new indication on the tree to let their would-be rescuers know they had buried the letter. Believing there was no point in staying, the rescuers departed, also without leaving a message.

Burke, Wills and King failed to reach safety in South Australia. Lack of water twice pushed them back to Cooper Creek. Wills made a final return visit to Camp LXV alone but because the now long-departed rescue party had left no word, assumed he and his companions had been given up for dead. He buried his diary and notes at the site and returned to Burke and King.

Supplies had run out by now and the three men were eating ground nardoo, at first provided by the local Yandruwandha people who also showed them several methods of preparing it for consumption. The food, as Wills noted in his diary was 'by no means unpleasant' but it lacked calories and may have exacerbated the scurvy they probably suffered from by then. Together with the effects of hypothermia, their fates were sealed.

Wills died alone, left at his request by a waterhole. Burke died a few days later further upstream, after sending King to seek assistance from the Yandruwandha. They helped him survive until a rescue party found him in September.

Burke's egotism, as well as incompetence, miscommunication and seemingly cosmic bad luck combined to kill three explorers and endanger the lives of many others who had to try to rescue them from what was, to Europeans, at least, an unknown vastness. But the expedition had accomplished its aim. Settlement quickly followed in the trail made by Burke, Wills and their companions.

But few people ever sighted Camp LXV. The tree was known but does not seem to have been called 'the Dig Tree' until Frank Clune's popular book about the Burke and Wills expedition, *Dig*, was published in the 1930s. Despite the historical significance of the tree and the scale of the tragedy it marks, little was done to protect it until the early 2000s when it was entered onto the Queensland State Heritage Register. It was not recognised on the Australian Heritage Database until 2016.

The same year, some doubt was raised about whether the 'Dig Tree' was authentic. A researcher found evidence in one of the rescuers' diaries that another tree was the famous icon. If so, generations of visitors have been taking snaps and selfies beneath the wrong tree. But whatever the truth of this suggestion, the blazed trees that make up Camp LXV on Cooper Creek are an evocative memorial to the tragic Burke and Wills expedition.

The famous trees are located on Nappa Merrie station a twenty-hour drive west from Brisbane. Around 5 kilometres from the homestead there is a stone cairn and plaques commemorating the disastrous events. The Royal Historical Society of Queensland is trustee of the Dig Tree Reserve and maintains visitor facilities and signage in conjunction with Bulloo Shire, Nappa Merrie Station and government grants. The once remote site is nowadays visited by over 35,000 people each year.

Stringybark Creek

Deep in the high country of north-east Victoria is the gully and watercourse known as Stringybark Creek. Only one incident marks the place out as different from innumerable similar locations along the east coast of Australia. In October 1878, bushranger Ned Kelly shot three policemen dead among its tall trees. The only survivor of the police party sent in pursuit of the Kelly gang was Constable Thomas McIntyre, who told his story at Kelly's committal hearing several years later.

McIntyre said that he had been left to look after the police camp site while Sergeant Kennedy and constables Scanlan and Lonigan went to search for the bushrangers. Consummate bushmen, Kelly, his younger brother Dan, Joe Byrne and Steve Hart easily surprised and captured the constable. In the conversation with Kelly, McIntyre asked what Kelly would do with them if he couldn't get his three companions to surrender.

'You had better,' Kelly had replied. 'If they get away, we will shoot you; if they surrender, we will not shoot you. We don't want their lives; we only want their horses and firearms.'

As evening came on, McIntyre knew the other three officers would return to camp. He again said to Kelly that he 'would try to get them to surrender if he would promise not to shoot them. He said he would promise'. Just then, Kennedy, Scanlan and Lonigan came out of the bush. McIntyre called out that they were surrounded and should surrender. Kelly stepped forward and cried out, 'Bail up: hold up your hands!' Kennedy went for his revolver and Kelly fired, missing him. All four bushrangers advanced with their guns on the three policemen. Kelly picked up a second, loaded rifle. Four shots were fired by the bushrangers. One hit Scanlan beneath his right arm. Fearing for his life, McIntyre grabbed the horse Kennedy had dismounted and fled. He heard nothing other than two shots as he rode into the bush, where the horse later threw him.

The fortunate policeman spent the night hiding and made it to the nearest police station at Mansfield at three o'clock the next afternoon.

The dreadful news sent the region into pandemonium. More police were mobilised to hunt the Kellys down. When they reached Stringybark Creek, they found the bodies of Scanlan and Lonigan. Later, another search party found the body of Sergeant Kennedy at some distance from the fatal camp site. Wild rumours circulated that the dead man had been handcuffed to a tree and his ears cut off.

Ned Kelly's version of events that day was quite different. He said that Lonigan was not in the bush but in camp with McIntyre. Lonigan fired at Kelly, who shot him dead. Kelly then told McIntyre he would not kill anyone else if McIntyre could convince Kennedy and Scanlan to surrender. He had nothing against the two officers and would let them live if they promised to leave the police force 'as it was the meanest billet in the world'. Kennedy and Scanlan then appeared, both mounted:

> I called on them to throw up their hands. Scanlan slewed his horse around to gallop away, but turned again and as quick as thought fired at me with the rifle and was in the act of firing again, when I shot him. Kennedy alighted on the off side of his horse and got behind a tree and opened hot fire. McIntyre got on Kennedy's horse and galloped away. I could have shot him if I choose as he was right against me but rather than break my word I let him go.

Kennedy was retreating, firing as he went, with Ned and Dan pursuing him. He took shelter behind a tree and fired his revolver at the bushrangers. Ned Kelly shot him in the armpit. He dropped his revolver and ran to another tree where 'he slewed round and I fired with the gun again and shot him through the right chest as I did not know that he had dropped his revolver and was turning to surrender'. Kennedy was in a bad way: 'He could not live or I would have let him go,' said Kelly. He then laid the policeman's cloak over his body 'and left him as honourable as I could'. He claimed that 'if they were my own brothers I could not be more sorry for them, with the exception of Lonigan'. He denied mutilating Kennedy's corpse.

Dan Kelly, Steve Hart and Joe Byrne were all killed in the firefight with police at the Glenrowan Hotel in June 1880. Badly wounded, Ned Kelly survived the battle and was subsequently found guilty of the murder of Sergeant Kennedy at Stringybark Creek. He was hanged in the (now-Old) Melbourne Gaol on 11 November 1880.

Today, Stringybark Creek is a historic reserve in Toombullup State Forest, open to visitors who can walk the marked trail and view a memorial to the murdered policemen. There is a larger memorial at Mansfield:

> To the memory of the three brave men who lost their lives
> while endeavouring to capture a band of armed criminals
> in the Wombat Ranges near Mansfield,
> 26th October. 1878.

Outside the Victoria Police and the descendants of the dead officers, few remember them, but Ned Kelly's controversial legend continues to grow.

The Street of Evil

It had to be somewhere. No city has been without a red-light district of some kind and Melbourne was no different. There, it was an area more or less between Lonsdale, La Trobe, Spring and Stephen (later Exhibition) streets.

Little Lonsdale Street and its network of narrow laneways was recognised as the city's main location for prostitution, gambling, crime and slum living as early as the 1850s. *The Argus* complained of 'females of the lowest and most disreputable class, who pursued their calling with the lowest and most filthy language and conduct'.

Perhaps the most prominent of the many brothelkeepers in the area was 'Madame Brussels', a German woman named Caroline Baum, who also called herself Mrs Hodgson. She ran a number of mostly high-class establishments catering to the more expensive end of the sex market and was said to have been the 'sweetheart' of the Duke of Edinburgh when he visited Melbourne in 1867. Her income from the business was rumoured to be £3 or £4 a week, a very substantial amount at the time. Madam Brussels was quite open about her affairs and advertised her brothels in the Melbourne directories.

Her high profile attracted the ire of evangelicals crusading against the sins of 'Little Lon', as it was known, and everywhere else. Henry Varley, a sensationalist reformer, led the charge and the Wesleyan Methodists managed to have Madame Brussels brought to court in 1889. She was found not guilty of procurement, despite Varley's claims that she openly paraded young virgins for sale along Collins Street. The court also found that her house was well conducted.

Madame Brussels' high-end and well-connected clientele kept her mostly out of trouble for a good many more years. But pressure to clean up Little Lon was building and attitudes were shifting against the roistering days and nights of old. After Melbourne's *Truth* newspaper exposed her financial relationship with the mayor and parliamentarian Sir Samuel Gillott and new legislation against disorderly houses was enacted, Caroline Baum gave up the game and closed up shop in 1907. She lived in her primary Little Lon brothel premises until her death the following year.

Although Madame Brussels was gone, the sex, crime and drugs that characterised Little Lon simply carried on. It was not until the 1930s that a serious effort was made to eradicate prostitution from the area. The biggest vice raid in the city's history was mounted in 1932, followed by amendments to local by-laws that would soon end Little Lon's red-light reign. Subsequent redevelopment completed the clean-up.

The area was by then home to a cosmopolitan collection of poorer folk, small businesses and factories. Latter-day research and archaeology have revealed a Little Lon different from the sink of iniquity painted by the moralising reformers and *Truth*. Chinese, German, Jewish, Italian and other immigrant family groups mingled with the remnants of the earlier British inhabitants, forming a bustling and mostly industrious urban community in which many were happy to live.

Tess (Bridget) Hayes, born in 1890, lived in a small lane off Little Latrobe Street, also part of the Little Lon district. Shortly before her death in 1955 she recalled: 'This area used to have a bad name. Some of these streets were not pleasant, but everyone has always been kind to us. No one has ever molested us, or even made us afraid. When you have lived so long in the heart of the city, you want to stay here always.'

The image of Little Lon as a den of vice had been convenient for a number of interests in Melbourne. First and foremost, the place provided services that were clearly popular, with a lot of people prepared to pay for them. Whether these were sexual or otherwise recreational such as gambling and drugs, they were in demand. These circumstances provided the opportunity for the moralistic elements of the city to rail against the perceived immorality of the area and campaign for its reform, a struggle that went on for many years and ensured a high public profile for their beliefs. *Truth* also found the degraded image of the area useful for selling newspapers, frequently publishing exposés and articles critical of the place and its people and calling loudly for it all to be shut down.

Some poets found it convenient, too. For C.J. Dennis it was the ideal locale for his celebrated ballads of the larrikin Sentimental Bloke, his girl, Doreen, and his mate Ginger Mick. Here, 'the Bloke', as the main character is usually called, reflects in enhanced larrikin slang on his life fighting with policemen, getting drunk with Ginger Mick, and losing his money at two-up, all in Little Lon:

> Me, that 'as done me stretch fer stoushin' Johns,
> An' spen's me leisure gittin' on the shick,
> An' 'arf me nights down there, in Little Lon.,
> Wiv Ginger Mick,
> Jist 'eadin' 'em, an' doing in me gilt.
> Tough luck! I s'pose it's 'ow a man is built.

In another poem, the bloke compares Shakespeare's *Romeo and Juliet* with the larrikins of Little Lon. His unusual interpretation of the famous play pointedly questions the difference between the dagger brawls of the Montagues and Capulets and the boots and all 'stoushes' of the larrikin pushes:

> This Romeo 'e's lurkin' wiv a crew—
> A dead tough crowd o' crooks—called Montague.
> 'Is cliner's push—wot's nicknamed Capulet—
> They 'as 'em set.
> Fair narks they are, jist like them back-street clicks,
> Ixcep' they fights wiv skewers 'stid o' bricks.
>
> Wot's in a name? Wot's in a string o' words?
> They scraps in ole Verona with the'r swords,
> An' never give a bloke a stray dog's chance,
> An' that's Romance.
> But when they deals it out wiv bricks an' boots
> In Little Lon., they're low, degraded broots.

Dennis provided a highly romanticised version of Little Lon, but one that appealed strongly to many Australians of the early twentieth century. *The Songs of a Sentimental Bloke* is probably the most commercially successful book of Australian poetry ever published. This and many of his other books were major bestsellers. For several generations, the Bloke, Doreen and Ginger Mick were household names, celebrated on stage and in early movies.

Dennis and his literary creations are now mostly forgotten, as is 'the street of evil'. Little Lonsdale Street is now a respectable precinct within Melbourne's CBD, full of shops, restaurants and offices and thronged with city workers and visitors keen to experience a little of Melbourne's fabled inner-city vibe. A few of the old buildings survive to give a faint impression of the way it must have been when Madame Brussels and her workers entertained the gents in opulent brothels and larrikins pimped their girlfriends in the dark alleys outside.

Windy Gully Candles

The miners and their families usually called the place 'Windy Gully'. Officially it was the Mount Kembla Colliery at the southern end of the company's land around Kembla Heights, in the Illawarra region of New South Wales. It was the scene of Australia's worst industrial accident and the place where many of its victims were laid to rest.

Coal had been quarried at Mount Kembla since the 1860s but Mount Kembla Colliery began a greatly expanded operation in 1883. The first fatality occurred three years later when a miner died under a collapsed stone roof. Miners died from similar causes with depressing frequency through the 1880s and into the 1890s. In October 1890, over 250 armed police and military personnel shepherded a large group of non-union workers to the mine during the widespread industrial disputes that began in the maritime industries and eventually led to the shearers' strikes and other union actions over the next few years. The Mount Kembla strike was long and bitter: 'scabs' were tarred and feathered and the Illawarra miners were the last of the nation's strikers to return to work.

Although the strike was over, working conditions in the mine continued to be a problem. At 2 pm on 31 July 1902, the Mount Kembla Colliery exploded, spewing a large red fireball out of the mine entrance. The explosion was felt 11 kilometres away in Wollongong. As well as taking out the No. 1 shaft, the explosion destroyed almost all the workings and buildings on the surface and blocked the mine entrance with tonnes of stone, iron and earth.

A total of 261 men were thought to be underground when a roof section collapsed, forcing a mix of methane and air through the main tunnel. The gases shook highly flammable coaldust loose into the air. The miners were not equipped with safety lamps and the dust was quickly ignited by a naked flame, destroying the main tunnel and filling parts of the mine with noxious carbon monoxide.

Miners lived in the company town with their families at the northern end of the colliery land. All rushed to the pit, to be faced with what could have been taken for the consequences of an earthquake. Rescue efforts began immediately under the direction of Major Henry MacCabe, a mining surveyor. He entered the mine with nightshift deputy William McMurray, but both were fatally overcome by carbon monoxide.

Down in the mine, hell had risen. Some men died of burns, some from rockfalls, but most from the poisoned air. Big Joe Wilkinson from Lancashire refused to yield to the gas. He tore his clothes off and raged through the darkness. They found his naked body with a broken leg and a hole in his temple. He was due to be married in a few days. No one came to claim his body, as his surviving mate bemoaned, and 'poor Joe' was laid in an unmarked grave at Windy Gully.

In No. 6 shaft, the miners were so deep underground they did not hear the enormous explosion above them and had to be told about it by other miners attempting to escape the pit. As soon as they were, deputy day manager David Evans and wheeler's overman Mat Frost rushed to No. 1 shaft, saw the smoke and managed to open a door in the ventilation system to prevent it pouring through the mine. But they were trapped. Evans and Frost then gathered about ninety surviving miners together. The two men told them that they knew of old tunnels and workings that might take them to the surface. Around seventy of the miners followed them through deeper levels and shafts they had to crawl through. After three hours they all reached the surface safely. The twenty miners who stayed behind were all killed by carbon monoxide.

Heroism, tragedy and grief were the human outcomes of that day. Inquests, inquiries and a royal commission began soon after. The company claimed there had never been methane in the mine. After taking evidence and visiting the mine themselves, the commissioners decided otherwise, agreeing with the findings of an earlier coronial inquest.

Sanctions against the management were short-lived and by September the mine was back in operation. Despite the findings of the royal commission, the antiquated ventilation system in the mine was not modernised until 1925 and flame lamps were in use until the 1940s. From 1905, individual fatalities continued until the mine closed in 1970.

Ninety-three men and boys were killed underground. Two rescuers died and another miner with shocking burns lingered for two years before he died. A commemoration is held at

Windy Gully each year at the cemetery created on half an acre of company land to hold many of the victims. Ninety-six candles are lit to honour the dead.

One of them, young Michael Brennan, was never found. For two years his widower father searched the mine for his body without success, later drowning himself in Wollongong harbour. It was said his ghost haunted Mount Kembla Colliery until it closed down.

Apart from an elaborate memorial and a heritage trail, there are few physical traces of the disaster remaining today. But the event lives on in the enduring industrial traditions and community memory of the Illawarra region.

The Fatal Railway Station

In 1921, an impressive South Australian railway station 94 kilometres north of Adelaide was the scene of a bloody murder. The reason for this crime is as enigmatic today as it was when radical unionist and New South Wales MP Percy Brookfield was shot to death by a mysterious man with a pistol and seventy rounds of ammunition. Was it a political assassination or was the unfortunate Brookfield just in the wrong place at the wrong time?

Percy Brookfield, almost 2 metres tall and not afraid to vent strong opinions, had no shortage of enemies. One was the diminutive Labor politician and wartime prime minister Billy Hughes, who called him a perjurer, a liar and possibly a traitor. Brookfield had referred to Hughes as a 'traitor, viper and skunk', so there was clearly no love lost between Brookfield and many other politicians and unionists on his own side.

Originally from England, Percy Brookfield was a seaman who arrived in Australia aged about nineteen. He carried his swag and scrabbled hopefully for gold in New South Wales and Victoria before joining the Amalgamated Miners' Association in Broken Hill. He was elected for the ALP in 1917 as a fierce opponent of Billy Hughes's push to introduce conscription and a radical supporter of the Russian Revolution then taking place. He was also in strong sympathy with the 'Wobblies'.

The Industrial Workers of the World (IWW), known as 'the Wobblies', formed in America in 1905, mainly through organising unskilled labour in mines, on farms and in factories. They were a militant organisation that espoused workplace sabotage and, if necessary, civil violence. The Wobblies were seen as a serious threat to industrial stability and to law and order, and were severely repressed in the United States. In Australia, the organisation was also viewed with suspicion by the authorities but had a strong appeal to unskilled and semiskilled workers in the bush and the city.

It also appealed to Brookfield, who was vocal in his support of the radical Wobblies. His enthusiasm for the cause included campaigning for the release of IWW members convicted of conspiracy and sedition in Sydney. The IWW saw World War I as a capitalistic class war and strongly opposed Australia's participation in it. Wobblies were loud and provocative in their protests, leading to police raids in which materials for starting fires were 'discovered', together with seditious literature. It was claimed that the unionists planned to set Sydney alight.

Eventually, twelve Wobblies were charged, tried and imprisoned with lengthy sentences. Brookfield used his political influence to bring about an inquiry that exonerated six of the twelve and found another four guilty of seditious behaviour but recommended them for release. Of the remaining two, one was found to have been rightly convicted of sedition and the other of arson. They too, were shortly released from their punishment for largely trumped-up charges.

By this time, Brookfield had resigned from the ALP and joined an independent Socialist Labor Party, continuing to be a thorn in the side of the middle-of-the-road Labor movement. In March 1921, he was travelling on a busy train to Broken Hill. Another of the passengers was off-duty policeman Constable Edmund Kinsela. The train stopped at Riverton for refreshments Here, Kinsela began a meal he never finished, interrupted by the actions of another passenger, a 36-year-old Russian immigrant known as Koorman Tomayoff or Tomayeff:

> I was having breakfast in the Riverton refreshment room when I heard two reports. A woman rushed in and said that a man was firing a revolver and had shot a man and a woman.
>
> Someone shut the door, but it was opened again, and I walked out onto the platform. Tomayeff was then in a paddock at the north end of the station and he went to a bag which he had with him and evidently recharged his revolver. I could see that discretion was required to deal with such a situation. Tomayeff did not stop firing, and I then went to the compartment in which I was travelling for my revolver. It was loaded in five chambers. Someone said, 'Let him have it', and I fired but only three of the cartridges went off and they took no effect. The man kept firing at me, and I went to the other side of the train with a view of coming up behind him.

While Kinsela and Tomayoff were blazing away, the train pulled away. Kinsela returned to the refreshments room, where he found Percy Brookfield:

The Russian came along the platform and fired at the door. One shot nearly hit Mr Brookfield. I suggested that our only chance was to wait until he had emptied his revolver, and then rush him. Mr Brookfield said to me 'Give me your revolver, and let me have a go at him.' I told him it was no good, as the two cartridges in it would not go off.

Mr Brookfield started out as the man appeared to be manipulating his weapon, and was going towards his bag. Tomayeff turned round when he saw us coming, and fired two or three more shots. The Russian was directing his attention to Mr Brookfield, who was holding my revolver in front of him, and I was on the outside, thinking to come up at the side of him. We struggled for some time, and the Russian freed himself. I succeeded in felling the Russian to the ground, however, and then I punched him on the face. When he was overpowered some civilians came to my assistance, and somebody with a rifle arrived and hit the Russian with the butt of it.

When Kinsela looked around he saw Brookfield lying on the ground—'I'm done, I'm done' he groaned, 'he has shot me.' He later died in hospital. Kinsela was understandably grateful:

I have to thank poor Mr Brookfield for my life. We both went out with our lives in our hands, but the Russian evidently concentrated on Mr Brookfield because he had the revolver. Nobody is more sorry at Mr Brookfield's fate than I am.

The motive for Brookfield's death has remained a mystery. Assassination seemed unlikely as Tomayoff did not have any strong political leanings. Was it a personal issue of some kind? No evidence of any prior contact between the victim and his killer was ever found. Or was Tomayoff simply a deranged shooter? We will never know. The killer was deemed insane and confined to a mental institution for the rest of his life. When he died a quarter of a century later, his body went to the anatomists, presumably for dissection and inspection. What, if anything, they found nobody knows.

Razorhurst

Sly grog, drugs, prostitution and extortion. These were a few of the main ingredients in the stew of crime that bubbled through Sydney's inner eastern suburbs in the 1920s and 1930s. Reigning over the vice and corruption were two queens, each controlling a separate slice of the action.

Kate Leigh, as she was mainly known, was born at Dubbo, New South Wales, in 1881. From a difficult childhood and adolescence, she became involved in crime through the first of what would be four marriages to criminals. Although Kate concentrated on sly grog, her growing network embraced all forms of illicit and illegal activity. She soon came into competition with others seeking a share of the lucrative black markets and rackets, especially with another crime queen of the era known as Tilly Devine.

Born in England in 1900, Tilly Devine, as she came to be known, worked as a prostitute in London before and after marrying digger James Devine in 1917. After the war, Tilly followed Jim to Australia where they worked together to build a criminal business that made them both rich. Their marriage was violent and stormy, ending in the 1940s, by which time Tilly was established as the 'Queen of Woolloomooloo', competing directly with Kate Leigh.

Tilly and Kate each had the assistance of a crowd of lovers, husbands, pimps and assorted henchmen who were up for whatever violence was required. Handguns were the main tool of the trade until legislation in 1927 mandated the licensing of pistols. The preferred weapon then became the cutthroat razor. As well as their low cost and ease of concealment and disposal, the possibility of having one's face sliced open was an effective deterrent in the turf wars that raged between Kate's and Tilly's thugs. So frequent and blatant were slashings that the suburbs of Kings Cross, Surry Hills, Woolloomooloo and Darlinghurst were dubbed 'Razorhurst'.

The press was outraged, especially the colourful crusading Sydney rag *Truth*, which called Razorhurst the 'Cesspool of the Southern Hemisphere' in one of its more restrained headlines. A more typical response was 'Clean up Razorhurst! *Truth* Demands Ruthless War on Denizens of the City's Plague Spot Where Drink and Depravity Reign Supreme':

Dangerous Places

> Thugs and Parasites of Razorhurst
> CLEAN UP THIS PLAGUE SPOT
>
> CENTRE of vice and headquarters of iniquity in the great city of Sydney, the place that was once Darlinghurst, but is now known as 'Razorhurst,' cries aloud for the strong hand of officialdom to clean it up, once and for all. 'Truth' has urged this in the past; it demands it now.
>
> UNDER the very eyes of the police it has grown from a respectable suburb to be a cesspool of vice and immorality—a miniature Chicago, Men and women of the very lowest type resort there, and crime in all its hideousness stalks abroad. Houses that to outward appearance are respectable, harbor individuals who do not hesitate to draw a razor or revolver to avenge some fancied wrong, and who make their living by trading upon the depravity of their fellow men and women.

And that was just for starters. The article trumpeted on:

> DAILY the ranks of these vile parasites are strengthened by fresh recruits; men and women who have drifted into the criminal class, are drawn there as by a magnet, and soon they are striving to outdo their teachers.
>
> No city with such a plague spot can hold up its head amongst its sisters of the Commonwealth. Not only is it a cancerous growth on society, but it threatens to overflow into neighbouring suburbs and win them to Its foulness.
>
> 'Truth' demands that it be cleaned up; and no interests, however powerful, must be allowed to stand in the way. The police must dean up Razorhurst, and the Bavin government

must give them wider powers to enable them to effectively deal with the crooks of every hue who abide there.

The crusading newspaper pledged itself to pursue the problem until it was solved:

> Not until these criminals and vagabonds, parasites and wallowers in vice have been rooted out will 'Truth' allow the matter to rest. Razor slashers, bottle bashers, men who live on the earnings of unfortunate women, racecourse pests and parasites, confidence tricksters, dope peddlers, room letters, sly groggers, keepers of assignation houses, thieves, women of notorious characters, and the vile riff raff of the underworld are all to be found In Razorhurst.
>
> At night the wolf pack is to be seen at the tram stop at King's Cross, jeering and insulting every woman that goes past. At night these vultures of the shadows venture out to rob and sin, often assaulting law-abiding citizens with brutal violence.
>
> They have declared war on society, and made their home in its very midst. It is society's turn to attack them with the strongest weapons at Its command. Gaol for those convicted of crime, and also for their associates, is the only way to deal with them. This cesspool can only be cleaned up by the police and the Government, and their neglect to tackle the problem seriously is one of the black marks against the Bavin Government.

Kate and Tilly were the public face of these gangland wars. They were both smart, tough characters who used violence whenever necessary—or not. They both appeared in public, frequently at court, in jewels and finery. Occasionally, they brawled with each other personally and their gangs fought pitched battles in the streets of Razorhurst. Both continued to prosper through the Depression years of the 1930s, though World War II dried up the flow of cocaine from overseas and the extension of public drinking hours to 10 pm in 1955 ended the sly-grog business: 'The bloom has gone off the grog', as Kate famously put it.

Together with better policing and legislation, the high lives of Kate and Tilly faded to tawdry. Tilly, who had attended the coronation procession of Elizabeth II in London festooned with rings and jewellery insured for the equivalent of $40,000, fell foul of the taxman and died in poverty in 1970. Kate died in similar circumstances in 1964. By then, they were both long-forgotten folk heroines of Sydney's seedy past, though their exploits have since been the subject of books and wider audiences became familiar with them after 2011 through the popular television series *Underbelly*.

Escaping the Island

It was front-page news in the Brisbane *Truth* newspaper. 'Crooks Need Him Outside' brayed the headline on 7 December 1924, describing the daring escape of gunman Charles Leslie from the 'joke gaol' of St Helena.

Situated in Moreton Bay, the 75-hectare island of St Helena is only 5 kilometres from the mouth of the Brisbane River. Named for Napoleon's famous isle of exile after an Aboriginal man was exiled there in the 1820s, the island was later used as a base for hunting and processing dugong. From the 1860s it became a penal establishment for criminals sentenced to hard labour, usually for violent crimes. The prison developed a contradictory reputation. On the one hand it was noted as being a place of brutal punishment and control. On the other, it was regarded for a while as a model of its kind and was known for prize-winning Ayrshire cattle and olive oil, industries based on the labour of the inmates.

It was also known as a difficult place to escape from. A few had tried, braving the water and the sharks, but very few had succeeded by the time Charles Leslie and his accomplices gave it a go. As the crusading popular news sheet told the tale, 'the dour, determined-visaged crook' had escaped from two earlier bouts of imprisonment and should have been under close guard on St Helena. Instead, he was not treated as a prisoner but 'as a returned boarder who had accumulated to himself quite a host of privileges, owing to his previous association with this slipshod prison farm colony'. Leslie was said to more or less please himself about which tasks he would and would not perform and under what level of security.

Leslie had no trouble communicating with cronies on the outside and it was not long before a couple of southern identities turned up at Wynnum and hired a launch. On the day determined with 'the coterie of Southern crooks that needed him', Leslie and another prisoner were erecting a fence 'about three quarters of a mile away from a warder'. Leslie went into the bush and did not return. It was some time before anyone realised he was missing and although warders made a search of the mangroves fringing the island they did not find him. He hid out uncomfortably in the mud with the mosquitoes until darkness. Then, as *Truth* colourfully painted the picture:

> Quietly, but with but a whispered conversation amongst the men on board a dark grey launch creeps out towards Mud Island heading in the direction of the south side of St. Helena.
>
> It might be an ordinary fisherman's cruise, with a harmless looking dingey [sic] attached to the back of the launch—and then again it might not.
>
> There are no lights and soon the launch has been swallowed up by the darkness of the night.
>
> A pair of anxious eyes are straining to penetrate the darkness over on the southern shore of St Helena and a keen pair of ears are especially attuned to catch the first sound of a pair of oars being through the shallow water close into the shore.
>
> Suddenly he catches the sound for which he has waited so long and about which he has been mistaken so often during the previous hour or so.
>
> His pulse beats faster, and, throwing all further caution to the winds, he races over the intervening open space, and calling one word, in a low voice, wades out into the water.
>
> It might not be his friends—still, 'tis worth the risk—then back comes the answering word—it is all right.
>
> Not another word is spoken as the boat rocks dangerously as he climbs in, dripping wet, but away at last.
>
> Willing hands pull that dingey out to the waiting launch, the shadow of which can only be picked up after some search.

Silently, he is taken on board the launch, the dingey is made fast and away they go.

The Southern crooks have got the man they want as an associate.

The launch landed Leslie in the Wynnum flats from where he walked an hour or so to his friends. From there he went to the 'Gabba where 'people may see things that the police would like to know, but they are not given to talking about them'. With potential informers' mouths sealed by money and well-founded threats, 'a dangerous criminal is loose again to prey upon society'.

The rest of the article went on to analyse the many failings of the St Helena prison, a 'systemless system', and demanded a government inquiry. As usual, *Truth* sided with the workers, in this case the warders and the police, whom the prison administration tended to blame for escapes. The anonymous journalist finished with a flourish: 'Never mind talking about his having made food for the sharks in an endeavour to swim to the mainland from St Helena—CATCH HIM!'

Over time, the mostly wooden prison structures deteriorated, along with the administration of the facility. Its isolation made it unpopular with warders and public opinion also turned negative. It was mostly dismantled and closed by 1932. Since then, the island has become a popular leisure and tourist location and is now a heritage-listed national park.

And Charlie Leslie, armed robber and professional crim, also known as Ryan, Deacon, Deakin and Hayes? He got clean away and was never found.

Greased Lightning Let Loose

That was how they billed the Olympia Speedway in 1926. Daredevil motor car drivers battled motorcycle stars in the Great Challenge Race. There was a 'Spectacular Flying Race' and you were 'missing a treat' if you didn't make it to the 'Dazzling Night Races' by 8 pm for two hours of motorised mayhem. A 'Big Night' for only two bob. And on Saturday it was even better when 'The Demons of the Dirt . . . Conquered the Concrete Wall at 100 mph'.

Where were all these thrills to be had? The Olympia Speedway was at the Sydney beachside suburb of Maroubra. Opened with great fanfare in 1925, the banked concrete course between what were then sandhills attracted a reputed 70,000 spectators to watch men and women risk their lives in overpowered machines. Among them was an early woman racer, Marie Jenkins. Marie only managed a second place that time, but the next year in her Bugatti Brescia she took out the 5-mile handicap against noted male drivers. Described by *The Australian Women's Mirror* as 'a little under average height, slim, with gloriously dark eyes and clear brunette complexion', Marie was a star of Melbourne racetracks and a serious contender in any race she entered. Sadly, she seems to have been mostly forgotten by history, apart from a few photographs and an interview.

Despite its auspicious opening and the fascination with motoring at a time when few people owned automobiles, the Olympia Speedway had a troubled history. It had been thrown up in a hurry and the banking angle on the wall was so dangerous that some cars, including Marie's, had to carry a passenger who risked death by hanging out of one side of the car to keep it on the track, like yacht sailors. For Marie, this was her brave mechanic, 'Bob'. Both of them seem to have survived, but not all the competitors were so fortunate.

The noted racer Reginald 'Phil' Garlick was born in Blayney, New South Wales, probably in 1887, just in time to catch the first exciting wave of speed that the automobile allowed. Garlick managed a company that specialised in fast cars and raced various customised versions of an Alvis sports car, which he called 'Lucky Devil' with the number 13 painted on its rear. He held the record of 98 miles (160 km) per hour at Maroubra and was keen to reach the century. In 1926 he won the 'Lucky Devil Cup' at Maroubra as well as just about every other event in which he competed. Sadly, his luck didn't last.

On 8 January 1927, just as he was catching up to the Sunbeam of another pioneer woman racer, Hope Bartlett, during the final high-speed handicap, the emerald green 'Lucky Devil' disappeared over the north-east curve of the banking. According to one newspaper report:

> To the horror of his onlookers, his car, in the fraction of a second, flicked over the edge of the track into the darkness beyond. It dropped 20 feet (6 m) and turned somersault after somersault.
>
> On its way over the embankment, the car hit a telegraph pole supporting the lights on the track, and snapped it off like a carrot. The crowd was struck dumb with horror and dismay. There was hardly a murmur, though here and there could be heard the muffled scream of a woman.

> Garlick was frightfully injured. There was a large hole in his head, he was covered in blood, and his clothes were torn.

Phil Garlick's family buried him at South Head Cemetery in Vaucluse with a striking marble headstone depicting the racer at the wheel of his supercharged Alvis, completely destroyed in the fatal accident.

There had already been fatalities. Shortly after the speedway opened, Leo Salmon and his riding mechanic Albert Vaughn died at the same spot as Garlick during a practice run. A motorcyclist also died in another accident shortly after. It was not long before the press dubbed the giant concrete doughnut 'the Killer Track' and from 1927 the venue continually closed and reopened as successive owners took over and tried to recapture the early success. They never did and the track quickly deteriorated, leading to calls for its closure. That finally happened at the end of the 1930s.

Today, most of the area where the Olympia Speedway once resounded with the roar of powerful engines and excited crowds has long disappeared beneath houses. The Coral Sea Park is the only remaining area of the track in the desirable seaside suburb.

The Woman Who Ran the Radio

Admiral William F. Halsey was the United States Commander of the South Pacific in 1942. Nicknamed 'Bull', supposedly due to a misspelling of 'Bill' in some official correspondence, he was a determined and direct character, well suited for the task of repelling the Japanese naval advance through the region. One day, he walked unannounced into the home of Ruby Boye on the small island of Vanikoro.

'My name's Halsey,' he said, 'I just want to meet the marvellous Australian woman who runs the radio.'

Born in Sydney in 1891 tall, dark-haired Ruby Jones married Skov Boye in 1919. A few years later they moved to the island of Vanikoro in the British Solomon Islands Protectorate, where Skov managed a timber company. Life was pretty quiet for the family of four until World War II began. The islands around Australia and New Guinea, as it was then known, and out into the Pacific were right in the path of Japan's planned expansion. In response, the Royal Australian Navy installed a teleradio and operator on Vanikoro to relay information and messages to and from Tulagi, capital of the Solomon Islands. When the operator decided to join up with the fighting forces, a replacement was not available. Ruby volunteered for the job. The departing operator gave her a few basic lessons and then she was left to work things out as best she could.

Unwittingly, Ruby had become the only female coastwatcher of World War II. But she was not a member of the military group known mostly as 'M Special Unit'. They were trained soldiers who pursued a dangerous form of intelligence gathering, training locals in guerrilla warfare and rescuing allies. The unit had its origins in an earlier group known as 'Coastwatchers', which was scaled up significantly in World War II under the initial direction of Commander Eric Feldt. They were complemented by a more informal group of strategically located civilian teleradio operators, also known as 'coastwatchers', who reported to the military on weather conditions as well as any potential enemy movement in their areas around the Australian coasts, in New

Guinea and on many islands in the South Pacific. Both groups played highly dangerous roles in the war, but because they were not serving in uniform, the civilian coastwatchers like Ruby were liable to be treated as spies and probably killed if discovered.

As the Japanese advanced south and the Allied American and Australian forces geared up to confront them, Ruby's reports and relaying of coded messages became increasingly important elements of Allied intelligence in the South Pacific, especially in relation to the Battle of the Coral Sea in May 1942. This engagement, the first between aircraft carriers, weakened the Japanese navy and contributed to the decisive Allied victories at Midway and Guadalcanal over the following months. Whatever threat Japanese sea power might have posed to Australia and the broader region no longer existed, but that did not mean the war was over.

Ruby continued her dangerous work on the teleradio using Morse code, a more secure form of communication than voice transmission. Nevertheless, the Japanese became aware of her activity and she was in great danger, once being directly threatened over the airwaves. To provide some protection if she was caught by the enemy it was decided to make her an honorary member of the Women's Royal Australian Naval Service, the WRANS, and a RAN Commander made a special visit to Vanikora to appoint her a Third Officer. This made her a uniformed member of the armed forces, and so not liable to being considered a spy if caught by the Japanese. The all-important uniform to go with the rank was parachuted to her. Other civilian coastwatchers were also given military status.

As well as the Japanese, Ruby braved crocodiles every day after her equipment had to be moved elsewhere for safety. When she developed shingles, Ruby was taken off the island through Admiral Halsey's direct intervention—he was also a shingles sufferer—and flown firstly to the American base in the New Hebrides, where she was treated 'like royalty', then to Brisbane for further care. After recovering, she went straight back to work in Vanikoro, where her teleradio and her bravery created a tiny but vital part of wartime Australia. Admiral Halsey later declared: 'The Coastwatchers saved Guadalcanal, and Guadalcanal saved the South Pacific'. He was referring to the military unit, but he undoubtedly had Ruby and the other civilians in mind as well.

Ruby's work was recognised with the award of the British Empire Medal and she remained on Vanikoro until 1947, when she returned to Sydney. Skov Boye died there from leukaemia soon after and Ruby later married Frank Bengough Jones, becoming known as Ruby Boye-Jones. She died at the age of ninety-nine and is remembered in the name of a building at the Australian Defence Force Academy and by the Ex-WRANS Association in the Garden Island Chapel Remembrance Book. But her story is little known elsewhere.

Nor is the larger story of the civilian coastwatchers and the vital service they selflessly contributed to the protection of Australia and its region. There is a memorial lighthouse in Madang, Papua New Guinea, dedicated to 'the small body of men who constituted the Coastwatchers' and Station 12 on the Kokoda Track Memorial Walkway in Sydney's inner west is 'a tribute to the men of that little known force the Coast Watchers'.

Two Up, One Down

A remarkable event hurled the small Riverina settlement into world headlines during World War II. Brocklesby is about 45 kilometres north-west of Albury, New South Wales. It's a pretty place, established in 1870 and growing over the following decades as more people settled and the Culcairn–Corowa railway was opened in 1882. Tom Roberts painted his celebrated *Shearing the Rams* in the area in 1890 but it would be another fifty years before Brocklesby's next brush with fame.

On 29 September 1940, Leading Aircraftsman Leonard Fuller achieved the almost certainly unique feat of landing two aeroplanes at the same time in a Brocklesby paddock. He was piloting a twin-engined Avro Anson on a training flight from Forest Hill air base near Wagga Wagga, New South Wales. With him was a gunner and accompanying him was another Avro Anson training plane also carrying two men. As the trainers wheeled into a banking turn, both pilots lost sight of each other's plane. Somehow, the two machines became locked together, with Len's Avro pinned to the top of the other aircraft.

The propeller of Len's plane sliced into the cockpit of the plane below, injuring the pilot who managed to bail out, followed by his gunner as well as the gunner of Len's aircraft. Len was left sitting alone in the cockpit with no power, locked to the top of another aeroplane, which was still flying on full engines. He should have bailed out also, but he stayed in his seat as the two planes began to circle aimlessly in the sky.

A remarkably cool character, Len began playing with his controls and found that he could use the flaps and ailerons to more or less control the speed of the throbbing machine directly beneath him. After flying for about 8 kilometres, he looked around and saw a place where he just might be able to land his conjoined aircraft. He came in as best he could and was able to put the two planes down in a belly landing with no harm to himself and not much to the planes. They were later repaired and went back into service. When interviewed about his amazing feat, Len reportedly said that 'he thought it was a pretty rough old landing, but it was better than the ones he'd been doing the day before'.

Who was this young man with nerves of steel?

Leonard Fuller was born in 1918 into a pioneer aviation family from Cootamundra, New South Wales. His mother had 'looped the loop in some of the earliest, rattliest old planes in Australia', according to Leonard's father.

'I loved it', she said in an interview with *Australian Women's Weekly*. 'I'd find it very dull to fly in these luxurious modern planes. They would seem like slow trains in comparison.'

As well as singing his wife's praises, Len's father also described his son as a 'normally high-spirited youngster' who had 'always been mad on pulling engines apart and putting them together, and, like all youngsters, he liked cars, and has been interested in planes since he was a tiny kid.' Len had already won his civilian flying licence prior to joining the Royal Australian Air Force about five months before his unusual aviation experiment.

For his skill and gallantry, Len was promoted to sergeant. He later went on to further, uneventful, training in Canada as part of the Empire Air Training Scheme. He flew Wellington bombers in the Middle East and was awarded the Distinguished Flying Medal (DFM) for action in Sicily, where he set an enemy ship on fire. Not satisfied with that, he returned to base, refuelled and again attacked the ship, remaining behind as it burned and harrying crews trying to contain the damage he had inflicted.

Later, Len returned to Australia as a flying officer instructing trainees at East Sale, Victoria. Riding his bicycle along Heart Road in East Sale on 18 March 1944 he was killed in a collision with a bus.

A monument and plaque commemorate Len Fuller's unusual niche in aviation history near the site of the landing, and a section of one of the aircraft can still be found in Blacksmith Park, Brocklesby.

There is a slightly spooky coda to Leonard Fuller's story. His uncle—also named Leonard—had been a World War I pilot who made a freak landing of his own. But in his case, he was already dead. Killed in the air over enemy lines, his plane continued flying for around twenty minutes towards the British position at Arras. Then it made a perfect landing, reportedly without human intervention.

Saving Silver Town

In the summer of 2019–2020, the ghost town of Yerranderie, New South Wales, was a very dangerous place. The one-time silver mining community between Oberon and Goulburn was encircled by raging flames for days as the Green Wattle Creek bushfire swept through the area. The few residents were evacuated early while the New South Wales Rural Fire Service (RFS) fought to save the historic settlement from complete destruction.

Like many other communities savaged by flame in that disastrous summer, people were often lucky to escape. One local reported having to slice his way out with a chainsaw. When it was over, the bush was so devastated that returning residents would have to cut their tracks back in the same way.

Three times RFS fire trucks beat the flames back. One crew logged a shift of more than twenty-two hours as firefighters struggled to contain the fire that eventually destroyed nearly 280,000 hectares of bush. Across New South Wales and Victoria, other crews were carrying out similarly heroic actions in the fiercest fire season Australia has ever known. Many properties could not be saved but the historic ghost town had one unusual advantage.

When Yerranderie passed into the hands of the Lhuede family from the late 1940s, the new owners developed it as a tourist attraction and built an airstrip to facilitate access to the town. This allowed the RFS to establish a base and barrier against the fires. Even though Yerranderie was saved, the roads and bush were so dangerous that locals were unable to return for weeks afterwards. They found their unique town intact, though the February floods that followed caused further damage to this historic place.

Established in the 1890s to mine the Burragorang Silver Field, the settlement eventually grew to a population of around 2000. They were served by shops, churches, hotels, a post office, banks, a courthouse and a school. By 1906 there was a town brass band and all the usual social and sporting activities of the time were available, including a masonic lodge, a rifle club, lawn tennis, bicycling and—the miners' traditional favourite—boxing.

Bush fires and accidents were not infrequent, though the town prospered on silver ore extraction and the company regularly paid good dividends to investors.

A visitor to Yerranderie described the place in 1909:

> The township is about a mile from the hotel, so, after having a spell and getting rid of our luggage, we went down to town. My first impression was that this was a very small town indeed, for there seemed to be only about a dozen houses altogether, including two or three stores, a bakery, a tailor's shop, a hairdresser and tobacconist's shop, a post office, a Bank of New South Wales branch, a small hall and a few private, houses. I learned afterwards however, that these few places were not the only signs of habitation. My walks among the hills taught me otherwise. Everywhere one went there appeared to be a few huts or houses, and if they were more congested they would form a fair sized village. But the miners have evidently built their shanties as near as possible to their work, and so made the township scattered. The public house and police station are situated about a mile from the main portion of the town. The population of the township and district is about 1000, so that it is not such a small place as might be imagined...

The big news that year was the discovery of another rich silver lode 8 kilometres from Yerranderie, bringing more investment to the area, which by then was also being mined for lead and gold. This was balanced by the observation of Eight-Hour Day, confirming the town as a union stronghold. There had already been trouble at Yerranderie as early as 1901 when miners struck, unsuccessfully, for a wage increase. A union branch was formed at Yerranderie in 1908, joined by around half of the 250 or so miners working there. The scene was set for one of the longest actions in Australian industrial history, a decade later when the town was already in decline and the payable ores were mined out.

In 1919 the miners joined the Broken Hill strike for better working conditions. The action lasted into 1920 over a period of almost eighteen months, resulting in a royal commission. More industrial unrest in 1928 led to the miners being locked out and by the 1930s Yerranderie was largely abandoned. The last bus departed in the early 1950s when the flooding of the Burragorang Valley left the town with only one approach via the Colong–Oberon stock route.

In 2011, the then 89-year-old owner, Val Lhuede, gifted the village to the New South Wales Minister for the Environment and the Yerranderie Regional Park was created the following year. Now under the control of the National Parks and Wildlife Service, Yerranderie's history is being brought to a wider public with new works and walks to expand those already in the area.

There seems to be some doubt about the meaning of the town's name. Val Lhuede said she did not know what it meant. Old-timers believed that it meant 'sharp peak' in the language of the various peoples who occupied the Burragorang Valley and surrounding area, including the Dharug, Dharawal, Wiradjuri and Gundungurra. Whatever its exact origins and meaning, Yerranderie must be one of the most mellifluous place names in the country.

The Field of Thunder

In its art collection, the Australian War Memorial holds a poignant image that speaks of a still unsettled story. Painted by Pitjantjatjara man Jonathan Kumintjara Brown, the earthy pigments on the rectangular canvas depict a large crater framed within four bora, or ceremonial rings. The stark simplicity of the painting is well suited to its subject, the discovery of a First Nations family camped on the crater left by an atomic bomb a few months after its detonation at Maralinga, South Australia.

'Maralinga' is said to mean 'thunder', a word from a Northern Territory language rather than that of the traditional owners of the test site, but it has been adopted in the term 'field of thunder', a fitting name for the 1950s atomic blasts carried out at the remote location. After several inquiries, a royal commission and years of squabbling between the Australian and British governments over responsibility for cleaning up the nuclear mess, exactly what happened at Maralinga remains controversial. Officially, all the traditional owners of the Maralinga area were removed and resettled, mostly to Yalata, South Australia, before the atomic tests began. Persistent accounts to the contrary have been unearthed ever since the tests ended. The most startling evidence for an incomplete clearing of the land prior to the tests is the subject of Jonathan Kumintjara Brown's painting.

On 14 May 1957, John Hutton, one of the soldiers monitoring radioactivity following the Marcoo ground explosion the previous October, was in an area known as 'Pom Pom' when he was approached by an Aboriginal man in a loincloth carrying spears, dingo pelts and a billy can. Recalling this incident many years later, Hutton said, 'We ran the counter over him and he was red hot (with radioactivity)'. The man's name was Charlie Milpuddie, head of a family of two children and his pregnant wife, Edie. 'They were hot as well. We gave the man and the boy a shower but his wife was pretty shy and only let us wash her hair'. Hutton and a sergeant shot two of the family dogs which were lethally contaminated and drove the Milpuddies to the Yalata Mission. Edie later had a stillborn child.

It is estimated that as many as 1200 First Nations people may have been affected by the Maralinga tests, either directly or down the years as the health consequences of radiation exposure became apparent. Veterans of the project, their families and descendants have also reported a variety of medical issues, including cancers and the birth of children with deformities. Infant mortality rates among these groups and early deaths seem to have been more common than in the general population.

Jonathan Kumintjara Brown became entwined with the field of thunder story late in his life. He was born at Yalata in 1960 but was separated from his parents and raised in New South Wales by a non-Indigenous family. Before Kumintjara Brown died in 1997 aged thirty-seven, he had managed to locate his birth family and reconnect with them and the culture of their traditional lands. Sadly, there was no fairytale ending. The reunion was difficult, hampered by language difficulties and the impact of the relocations on the family and their community. Jonathan heard for the first time their stories of rupture and loss. They affected him deeply and inspired his art. As he said of his painting on the subject, *Maralinga Aftermath, Crater Where Four Bodies Were Found*: 'Over the last few years I have visited my homeland and talked with the Elders and others. I have also taken the opportunity to visit Maralinga, the field of thunder, and the result is that I have produced a number of works that comment on the atomic tests.'

He also spoke of the double social and health damage of the tests: 'Much of my Ancestral land is now inaccessible to me as a consequence of the testing in the Maralinga region in the 1950 and 60s. As well as this my community is suffering many of the social and physical ills that occur in other Aboriginal communities that have been dispossessed.'

Since the 1980s, the traditional lands of the Maralinga Tjarutja people have been gradually returned to them, following intense remediation of the soil. The last 3000-square-kilometre area, known as Section 400, was returned in 2009. The land is now deemed to be very low radiation by the Australian Radiation Protection and Nuclear Safety Agency (ARPANSA), although one area known as 'Kuli' could not be decontaminated. And while most of the traditional owners are happy to be back on their country, some are not so sure. Maralinga Tjarutja Council Mima Smart said: 'I know it's still dangerous. The radiation is still around on the trees and plants and buildings and the cement. Everything you touch you are going to get infected because the radiation is still on this land. It is a happy and a sad day.'

Even today, a 1-kilometre circle of sterility means no plants can grow around ground zero and globules of desert sand fused into green glass by the blasts lie all around. No wonder the Maralinga Tjarutja call it 'Mamu Pulka', or 'big evil'.

Photographer John (Jack) Bailey captured the magnificent presence of Uluru in 1930.

3
SACRED PLACES

The Rock

Even the bare facts are impressive. The coarse sandstone monolith known as Uluru is well over 500 million years old. It towers more than 300 metres over the desert, is over 3 kilometres long and almost 2 kilometres wide. It is the world's largest single rock, or monolith. Most amazingly, it extends beneath the ground for over 2 kilometres. It's not surprising that it has long been known colloquially as 'The Rock'.

Uluru is in the traditional territory of the Western Desert peoples known collectively as Anangu who have lived there for over 30,000 years. These groups include the Ngaanyatjarra, Pitjantjatjara and Yankunytjatjara. Uluru is a central feature of their traditional knowledge, known collectively as Tjukurpa. A Pitjantjatjara women named Nganyinytja described Tjukurpa:

In the land, the footprints of our Creation Ancestors are on the rocks. The hills and creek beds they created as they dwelled in this land surround us. We learned from our grandmothers and grandfathers as they showed us these sacred sites, told us the stories, sang and danced with us the Tjukurpa (the Dreaming Law). We remember it all; in our minds, our bodies and feet as we dance the stories. We continually recreate the Tjukurpa.

The significant ancestors for Uluru are three groups of Mala (hare wallaby) people. They came to Uluru from the north and two of the groups travelled on to locations in what is now South Australia. The female python, Kuniya, came from the east to stay at Uluru where she fought with venomous snakes known as Liri or Liru. The Rocks themselves also have sacred significance:

> Anangu are not just talking about rocks as being 'like' people or representing them; they 'are' the person. They act towards these rocks as relatives. They respect, sing to, care for and interact with particular rocks as sentient beings in the landscape that can affect their lives. The rocks can watch, listen and get angry and shake people off their backs, as Nellie Paterson says of the Devil Dingo in Uluru, 'He shakes off tourists'.

Uluru's recent history began when the rock was first sighted in the distance by explorer Ernest Giles in the early 1870s. He finally reached the rock in 1873 and described it in his book *Australia Twice Traversed*, as 'ancient and sublime'. Another explorer, William Gosse, sighted the monolith that same year and named it after Sir Henry Ayers, frequently a premier of South Australia. Gosse also found the rock 'the most wonderful natural feature', as he wrote in his expedition diary after becoming the first recorded climber to reach the summit. As pastoralism and mining expanded through the area there were conflicts between the Europeans and the traditional owners that continued even as the rock began to attract a few tourists from the 1930s on. The traditional owners were frequently sidelined in decisions about the management of the rock and surrounding country as it became an increasingly popular tourist destination, promoted by clever marketing.

Through these years, Anangu were discouraged from visiting the area but persisted with their claims, and in 1985 Uluru formally passed back into traditional ownership with a 99-year leaseback arrangement that sees The Rock and surrounding area jointly managed by the Anangu and Parks Australia. While this has been an overall success, problems persist.

A major issue is the climbing of the rock. Its sacred character means that the Anangu do not climb it and over decades they have asked that others not do so either. However, scaling the monolith had become a tourist tradition and tourists continued to ignore requests to respect the site, despite many deaths and accidents. In 2019 Uluru was finally closed to climbing.

Uluru is perhaps the most significant site in Australia. It has geological importance, profound spiritual meanings for the Anangu in its location, its stories and its rock art. It also has a unique natural beauty and deep appeal for Australians and international tourists seeking an authentic outback experience. Its association with the Azaria Chamberlain disappearance in 1980 added another layer of intensity to a tangle of competing and contradictory meanings.

Yet from these difficult considerations a positive force has developed. Uluru has become a powerful symbolic focus for reconciliation efforts. The 2017 Uluru Statement from the Heart spoke directly to all Australians, requesting a First Nations peopes' say in laws affecting them as well as a written treaty, or 'Makarrata'. Although the Statement was rejected by the sitting government, it has found traction with many others, including the federal Labor government elected in 2022, and shows no sign of going away.

It seems likely that this unique place will continue to be both controversial and compelling for a long time to come.

The Wurrwurrwuy Stones

One of Australia's most unusual places is at Yirrkala in northeast Arnhem Land, home of the Yolgnu people. In an area roughly 80 by 70 metres lie three groups of stones picturing scenes from the interactions between the Yolgnu and Macassan trepang traders.

Long before Lieutenant Cook voyaged along the east coast of Australia, fishermen from the port of Makassar in what is now South Sulawesi, Indonesia, voyaged to Arnhem Land for the annual trepang season. The Makassans in the area fished and then dried the prized marine creatures usually referred to as 'trepang', establishing good relations with the Yolgnu, many of whom worked with the visitors in preparing the delicacy. Some Yolngu journeyed back to Makassar with their new friends, sometimes establishing families there. A few even sailed further to Singapore. Elements of Islamic belief and languages spoken by the visiting fishermen remain in Yolngu custom today.

The first hint European settlers had of this two-way cultural traffic seems to have been in 1803 when Matthew Flinders circumnavigated the continent and came across a fleet of Macassan praus near the Wessel (sometimes also 'and English Company's') Islands. The leader of the first group of ships he encountered was named Pobassoo.

> [Saturday, 19 February] According to Pobassoo, sixty prows belonging to the Rajah of Boni and carrying a thousand men, had left Macassar with the north-west monsoon, two months before . . . The object of their expedition was a certain marine animal called 'trepang' . . . Pobassoo had made six or seven voyages from Macassar to this coast, within the preceding twenty years, and he was one of the first who came . . .

Flinders was both surprised and impressed by the size and intensity of the trepanging operations and the trade that passed along it and named the route 'the Malay Road'. It connected to China, where the trepang was highly valued as a food and medicine. For their part in these arrangements and local products traded with the trepangers, Yolngu received a variety of cloth, glass, ceramics and foodstuffs, including alcohol, betel nut, tobacco and even opium. They also received iron tomahawks, knives and the related technology of hollowed-out tree trunk canoes, more stable than those made of bark.

It seems that this trade had been going on for at least a century, and probably much longer, when Flinders stumbled across it, despite Pobossoo's claim to be 'one of the first'. For the Yolgnu it was a valued and influential dimension of their recent history. This was the impetus for a Yolgnu father and son, Yumbul and Dhatalamirri, to create the scenes depicted in the Wurrwurrwuy Stones, some time around the middle of the nineteenth century, at Macassan Beach (Garanhan). According to Yolgnu oral tradition, the two men were concerned that the knowledge gained from the links with the trepang trade route might be lost. Forming the pictures with stones of varying size and shape provided a permanent reminder of the relationship.

The northern group of stones represents aspects of Macassan life, as does the group to the south. The western array combines both Macassan and First Nations subjects. The pictures include praus, canoes and houses, as well as tools and techniques of trepang processing. There are also detailed representations of the structure, layout and sailing parts of the praus.

First Nations stone arrays are usually associated with ceremonial activities and spiritual beliefs, so these stones seem to be unique. They are considered to be of outstanding heritage value and were inscribed on the National Heritage List in 2013.

The Devil's Marbles

The devil man, Arrange, came from Ayleparrarntenhe. As he travelled, he was twisting a belt of the kind men wore in their hair from the time of their initiation. Scraps of hair fell from the belt onto the ground as he went, transforming into the singular rock arrangement of Karlu Karlu, or 'the round boulders'.

When survey party leader John Ross came by this remarkable feature in 1870 during preparation for the construction of the Overland Telegraph, he drew on British traditional names for such rounded rocks as the 'devil's marbles'. This became the name by which the granite boulders, situated between Tennant Creek and Alice Springs, were officially known for many years.

Karlu Karlu is sacred to the traditional owners of the area: the Kaytetye, Warumungu, Warlpiri and Alyawarra language groups. The site features in their traditions, in other stories that remain secret and is also an important ceremonial meeting place for the various language groups of the surrounding country:

> In the Dreamtime Traditional Owners used that place for ceremony. They came from four parts of the land to spend their time together for three to four weeks, dancing and singing to the spirit people, giving praises to them so that they would bless the land and give them what they need.
>
> Each tribe came and performed their ceremony. The tribes were Warlpiri, Warumungu, Kaytetye and Alyawarra. Women were separated from the men, when the ceremonies were finished they came together and waited for the sign that everything was finished. They then went their separate ways . . .

The history of the area since colonisation has been deeply troubled. Traditional culture was undermined through massacres at Barrow Creek in 1874 and at Coniston in 1928. By the 1930s, local inhabitants were living in or being moved to official reserves. There was further desecration in 1953 when one of the boulders was removed to form the memorial to John Flynn's Royal Flying Doctor Service in Alice Springs. Fortunately, the boulder was restored to its original location in 1999 where it continues to play a role in traditional spiritual practices.

The area was declared a reserve in 1961 and registered as a sacred site in 1982. It was the centre of several land rights claims and after many setbacks an agreement was reached for the reserve to become First Nations freehold land in 2004. In 2008 the site was returned to the traditional owners and is jointly managed with Parks and Wildlife under a 99-year lease to the Northern Territory government.

When Arrange finished making the initiation belt, he returned to where he had come from: Ayleparrarntenhe, the twin-peaked hill to the east of the reserve. Along the way, he spat on the ground, creating the granite formation that is a distinctive local feature and which, like all the other landforms of the area, has a role in the beliefs of the traditional owners. Ayleparrarntenhe is also the Alyawarre name for the whole area in which local people hunted, found water and collected bush tucker and medicines. Traditional owners are now involved in the management of the reserve and in passing on their knowledge to the younger generation. Karlu Karlu is one of the most popular tourist destinations in the Barkly region and is recognised as a symbol of the Northern Territory, in Australia and around the world.

Hallowed Grounds

It is often said that Australians are 'sports-mad'. It is true that we are a nation that enjoys outdoor activities and a variety of mostly competitive sports. But a few games have become hallowed icons of national identity.

Cricket is foremost nationally, while a number of football codes have become, depending on which state you live in, the most revered by their many fans. These are Rugby League, Australian Rules Football (often abbreviated to AFL after the overarching Australian Football League) and 'soccer', or association football, as it is properly titled. The extremes to which players, administrators and fans of the various football codes went to ensure that games were played during the COVID-19 pandemic was testament to their significance in the lives of many people and communities.

The places in which these and many other sports have been played have also attained celebrity status. None more hallowed, perhaps, than the MCG, the Gabba and the Waca.

Locals simply call it 'the G', but to the rest of the country the Melbourne Cricket Ground is usually known as the 'MCG'. Whatever it is called, the sports stadium in Yarra Park has seen many of the most memorable moments in Australian sport—which means the place has seen quite a lot.

Since its establishment in 1853, the grounds have hosted cricket, Rugby League and Rugby Union, Olympic and Commonwealth Games events and, of course, the AFL Grand Final, the culmination of the annual Aussie Rules wars. As well as these mighty matches, Victoria's first official tennis game was played here in 1878 and some of Australia's earliest bicycle races were held there in the late nineteenth century. Concerts have been staged there and other major events attracting record crowds. The highest attendance still stands, at the time of writing, at over 130,000 for the Billy Graham evangelical Christian crusade in 1959.

The Melbourne Cricket Club, which owns the ground, was established in the 1830s and moved several times before settling on the current site. Originally a First Nations meeting area, the ground was used by mounted police and as a public recreation area until the club took it over and began its long history of development and redevelopment to keep pace with the changing demands of fans and players. The mythic origins of Australian Rules Football are usually dated from 1858. On that momentous day, Scotch College and Melbourne Grammar played a game with a semblance of the rules we now associate with Aussie Rules on Richmond Paddock near the MCG.

Records of all sorts have been made and broken at the MCG. So too have many legends of Australian sport, official and unofficial. There are recollections of young ladies spending the night at 'the G' when American soldiers slept in the stands during World War II. And no one knows exactly how many goalposts and point posts were quietly sawn down and driven away on dark nights as souvenirs, pieces of the 'true cross'.

Located in the Brisbane suburb of Woolloongabba, the Brisbane Cricket Ground is affectionately known to all as 'the Gabba'. Like the MCG, it has hosted an array of sporting events, including baseball, athletics and even greyhound and pony races. Today it is home to men's and women's domestic cricket, as well as AFL. Cricket was first played here in 1896 and the ground featured in the 2000 Olympic Games. Since winning the right to hold the 2032 Summer Olympics, Brisbane has been considering a complete rebuilding of the Gabba, increasing its capacity to 50,000.

On the west coast, East Perth is home to the Western Australian Cricket Ground, or 'the Waca', after the owners, the Western Australian Cricket Association. The site opened in 1893 and has been redeveloped many times. Since the 1980s it has been a multi-sports venue, hosting AFL, Rugby League, Rugby Union and even baseball. Plans are in hand for further development.

Like all the hallowed grounds of Australian sport, the Waca can boast a roll call of great moments, legendary sporting heroes and record performances. The 'Miracle Match' of December 1976 has never been forgotten. Western Australia was playing Queensland in the semifinal of the Gillette Cup. The visitors bowled the local side out for 77 runs. Not a great outcome, especially in front of a home crowd. Captain Rod Marsh rallied his players to fight for it. Fast bowler Dennis Lillee responded: 'Make 'em fight for it be buggered. We're going to beat these bastards!' The Queenslanders were bowled out for 64 runs, giving the West Australians a stunning victory snatched from the jaws of defeat.

Through the many changes in sports and their audiences, as well as financial ups and downs, the MCG, the Gabba and the Waca have become revered sites of turf, wood and, latterly, concrete. Fans have flocked to their sometimes spartan facilities for well over a century with a tribal—almost religious—fervour that has made them cathedrals of Australian sport and national identity.

The Tree of Knowledge

The price of wool had dropped. The station owners wanted to cut the shearers' wages. They struck. The pastoralists brought in non-union or 'scab' workers to cut the wool. Always a difficult relationship, shearers and their employers were never likely to agree, even in good times. As the economic depression of the 1890s took hold, relations quickly deteriorated. The bitter industrial warfare of this period resulted in the formation of a unified union movement, the birth of the Australian Labor Party—and the seeding of a legend.

Established in the 1880s, the Central West Queensland railhead town of Barcaldine is 1000 kilometres north-west of Brisbane and almost 600 kilometres west of Rockhampton. The town quickly became the centre of the strike, with thousands of shearers and other bush workers, sometimes with families, setting up a tent city. Out of the ugly years of naked class war that followed came the modern labour movement of trade unions and the electoral party. Many of the most significant debates and decisions leading to this took place beneath a ghost gum outside the Barcaldine railway station.

That tree had been a meeting place for travelling bush workers for some years. It was also where the local Salvation Army band played and preached, leading to the local name of 'the Hallelujah Tree'. It was called by this name until the 1930s when it began to be referred to as the 'Tree of Knowledge'. This was possibly a reference to the Biblical story of Adam and Eve being forbidden to eat from the 'Tree of Knowledge of Good and Evil' in the Garden of Eden. Or it might simply have been an acknowledgement of the information shared by unionists beneath the tree. Or a bit of both. Or neither. Myths are fluid things, especially as they evolve over time. But whatever the tree was called, its status as the accepted foundation place of the Australian Labor Party is firm.

Bush workers had been forming trade unions for some years before the trouble began, leading to the pastoralists forming an association to further their interests. As strikebreakers came into Barcaldine on the train, they were met at the station by unionists who gathered at the tree, some armed. The unionists burned woolsheds and fields, as well as threatening pastoralists and scabs. Other unions struck in sympathy with the shearers and the government sent in the police and a military force.

The strikers enjoyed the support of many writers, including William Lane, a radical who penned newspaper articles in sympathy. He also wrote a novel titled *The Workingman's Paradise*, putting the socialist side of the argument. Henry Lawson wrote fiery prose and equally incendiary poetry on the topic, notably the famous 'Freedom on the Wallaby', which celebrated a republican view of the strike as a final breaking of the colonial chains with Britain, and ended:

> Our parents toiled to make a home,
> Hard grubbin' 'twas and clearin',
> They wasn't crowded much with lords
> When they was pioneerin'.
> But now that we have made the land
> A garden full of promise.
> Old Greed must crook 'is dirty hand
> An' come ter take it from us.

So we must fly a rebel flag,
As others did before us,
And we must sing a rebel song
And join in rebel chorus.
We'll make the tyrants feel the sting
O' those that they would throttle;
They needn't say the fault is ours,
If blood should stain the wattle!

The strike was broken and the leaders charged with sedition and conspiracy. Thirteen men received sentences of three years on St Helena Island prison in Moreton Bay. But that was only the beginning of the story.

Over the next few years, industrial unrest spread. There were violent attacks on property and armed confrontations between strikers and pastoralists. While these events played out on bush stations, along the Murray River, on the docks, on the railways and in the mines, there were rapid developments at the political level. In 1892 the first Labor representative was elected to the Queensland parliament and in September that year the manifesto of the Queensland Labor Party was read out beneath the ghost gum in Barcaldine. Subsequently, the Australian Labor Party was formed and, in conjunction with the trade unions, continues as a major force in Australian politics today. The 'Hallelujah Tree', later the 'Tree of Knowledge', was celebrated as the birthplace of the movement.

But while the ALP flourished, the fabled tree did not. In 1990 it was found to be suffering from insect damage. Treatment restored the tree to reasonable health but in 2006 it was poisoned by unknown parties. It has since been cloned for posterity and the trunk of the original tree still stands on the site as part of a commemorative sculpture erected in 2009.

Mer

To the people of Mer, or Murray, Island in the Torres Strait, the shark-headed Malo is the protector and lawgiver. He sailed with his three brothers from New Guinea in a canoe in search of his uncle, the supreme being, Bomai. There are many other versions of the story, but the voyage brings the customs by which the Meriam people live and the rules they must follow to ensure peace and social harmony.

The Meriam fished, traded and followed a system of land ownership involving small-scale farming of yams and other subsistence crops on pieces of land allocated to each of the eight clan groups. They had been following these traditions for probably well over 2000 years when Captain Edwards of HMS *Pandora* arrived in 1791 and renamed their home Murray Island. Two boys shipwrecked from the *Charles Eaton* in 1834 were captured by other Torres Strait peoples and sold to the Meriam for two bananas. The boys were cared for until recovered almost two years later.

Traditional life continued unchanged until the 1860s with the establishment of the trepang and pearling trades. The Queensland government annexed the island in the 1870s and the London Missionary Society arrived around the same time, an event known as 'The Coming of the Light', still celebrated on Mer and throughout the Torres Strait today.

The spectacular masks, costumes and dances of the Meriam have long attracted the admiration and attention of anthropologists and collectors of exotic artefacts. In the 1880s and 1890s, the Cambridge University anthropologist Alfred Court Haddon acquired island costumes, crafts and other objects, and documented Mer culture with film, sound recordings and on paper. These records would be crucial in the momentous consequences of the Mabo case a century later.

In the meantime, the usual story of official oppression played out on Mer, as it did elsewhere in the country. There were forced removals to missions and reserves elsewhere in the state and government regulation became increasingly galling for the original inhabitants throughout the Straits. In 1936 there was a long strike, leading to some reforms. In World War II, men from Mer served in the Torres Strait Light Infantry, though were only paid a third of the wages given to other soldiers. Once again, there was a strike, ending with the Mer soldiers having their pay raised to two-thirds of the pay of other members of the armed services. The men were not compensated fully for this financial discrimination until the 1980s.

Around that time, another long battle fought by the people of Mer began.

Born on Mer in 1936, Edward (Eddie) Koiki Mabo grew up with a knowledge of the myths and customs of Mer. When he discovered that the island did not belong to his people but to the Queensland government he began advocating for legal recognition of their land. Many years of legal cases involved an exhaustive examination of claims to ownership of Mer. Alfred Haddon's work was vital, as was Eddie Mabo's knowledge of Mer tradition and belief.

A final determination was handed down by the High Court in June 1992. Perhaps the most important single piece of legislation ever passed in Australia, 'the Mabo Act', as it is popularly known, confirmed the rights of the Mer Islanders to their land and also overturned the doctrine of *terra nullius*—the empty or unoccupied land—upon which the British colonisation of Australia was based. All Aboriginal and Torres Strait peoples could now make a case for the return of their traditional country under the *Native Title Act 1993*.

The perseverance of Eddie Mabo, his family, friends and other Torres Strait Islanders returned Mer to its traditional owners and opened the way for others to make similar claims. Eddie Mabo died before seeing the culmination of his efforts, but his single-minded pursuit of justice has earned him a unique place in Australian history as the man who got his country back.

More recently, Mer traditions have featured in the continuing struggle for the return of sea rights. While the Mabo case covered land rights, it did not necessarily cover fishing and other maritime activities. By demonstrating the connections between Mer and another island, Mabuiag, through song and dance, Torres Strait Islanders were able to prove their ancient beliefs and practices to the satisfaction of the legal system. In 2013 the High Court unanimously upheld native title rights to commercial fishing and related rights in around 44,000 square kilometres of Torres Strait waters. This precedent has opened the way for other First Nations groups to make similar claims around Australia.

Sad Waterlilies

The Henry Lawson Bicentennial Park at Walloon, Queensland, features beautiful bronze statues of two young girls dancing hand in hand on a mosaic of waterlilies. Nearby, signs tell the sad story of 'the Babies of Walloon', together with Lawson's poem on the tragedy reported in a local newspaper in March 1891: 'A sad mishap occurred at Walloon on Saturday afternoon last, when two young daughters of Mr. Patrick Broderick, a lengthsman on the Southern and Western Railway line, were drowned in a waterhole . . .'

Nine-year-old Bridget and six-year-old Mary Broderick had been sent to get some butter from a neighbour's home. But the house was empty when they arrived and they must have been attracted by the lilies in the nearby waterhole. When the sisters did not return to their home, a search was mounted and their bodies were found by a group of local people including their father. It seemed that the girls had reached for the pretty flowers. They either both fell in, or one did and the other went to her rescue. Both were drowned. The grieving family was well known among the fifty residents of Walloon and many mourners attended the funeral to pay their last respects to the girls.

Henry Lawson composed some hasty but heartfelt verses on the tragedy, first published in the journal edited by his mother, Louisa:

> He was lengthsman on the railway, and his station scarce deserved
> That pre-eminence in sorrow of the Majesty he served,
> But as dear to him and precious were the gifts reclaimed so soon
> Were the workman's little daughters who were buried near Walloon.

Sacred Places

Speak their names in tones that linger, just as though you
    held them dear;
There are eyes to which the mention of those names will
    bring a tear.
Little Kate and Bridget, straying in an autumn afternoon,
Were attracted by the lilies in the water of Walloon.

All is dark to us. The angels sing perhaps in Paradise
Of the younger sister's danger, and the elder's sacrifice;
But the facts were hidden from us, when the soft light from
    the moon
Glistened on the water-lilies o'er the Babies at Walloon.

Ah! the children love the lilies, while we elders are inclined
To the flowers that have poison for the body and the mind.
Better for the strongly human to have done with life as soon,
Better perish for a lily like the Babies of Walloon.

For they gather flowers early on the river far away,
Where the everlasting lilies keep their purity for aye,
And while summer brings our lilies to the run and the lagoon
May our children keep the legend of the Babies of Walloon.

Lost children are a recurring reality of Australia's history and folklore. Sometimes they are found but frequently they are not, or found too late. And while the memory of these incidents usually fades from local communities with the generations, the family is left to bear the burden. Down the years the stories are told and retold, sometimes losing details in the telling. In the case of the two girls, not only was their final resting place forgotten but so was the location where they died.

It was not until the 1990s that the Babies of Walloon story was rediscovered. A children's book about the incident was written by Judith Baker, leading to the establishment of a poetry festival and eventually to a hunt for the lost graves. Using ground radar, the local council located the graves in 2012. They also located thirty-two descendants of the Broderick family and arranged for them to attend the site at Ipswich Cemetery, the waterhole where they died and the statues in the park. Ninety-year-old Joan Busby from Rockhampton was a niece of the girls and she recalled: 'We never knew about the poem, but my mother always warned us to stay away from waterlilies . . . All this time, members of our family believed that the girls had drowned somewhere up in Rockhampton.'

Three years later, the council organised a ceremony marking the erection of a headstone on the girls' grave. Mrs Busby again attended, together with other descendants to witness a blessing of the site by a Catholic priest.

Once notable as the first stop on Queensland's first railway line, Walloon is today a rural commuter suburb 9 kilometres west of Ipswich. Matthew Tobin's evocative sculpture was installed in 2006 as part of the rediscovery and commemoration of a sad but important part of the town's history. It was vandalised in 2012.

Places in the Heart

As the Great War of 1914–1918 drew to a close, people at home grew used to the many newspaper columns naming the heroic dead. On the anniversary of the event, when the empty place at the table or the unworn clothes in the wardrobe were still bringing tears, it was customary to place a memorial item in the death notices section of local newspapers. Over 60,000 Australians who fought in the Great War lie buried in distant lands, each resting place becoming a small piece of home for loved ones and for the country as a whole.

It was an age of poetry and many mourning parents, brothers, sisters, wives and sweethearts turned their hands to tear-stained verse to express their grief in the public memorials that newspapers had now become. If they were unable to fashion their own tributes, they could select from something already written, as many did, their sentiments no less genuine for that. In the brief confines of a newspaper death notice, under headings like 'Heroes of the Great War', were the otherwise untold stories of those who had 'made the supreme sacrifice'. Entries like these began shortly after Gallipoli, continuing throughout the war and after. For the bereaved, the war would never end.

On just one day in 1919, in one issue of one South Australian newspaper, these tributes were just a few among the many.

Lieutenant Thomas Corcoran M.C. died of wounds on 30 May 1918. He was still remembered in one heart:

> In fond memory of Lieutenant T.L. Corcoran, R.I.P. Always remembered.—Inserted by his loving friend, Annie.

Ern Cooper died of wounds, in France, 31 May 1918. His sister and brother-in-law wrote:

> He went with hope of returning,
>   Along with his comrades so brave;

> But with many a hero he's sleeping
> > In a soldier's honored grave.

Careful to note that he had died facing the enemy, Ern Cooper's father, sisters and brothers also turned to verse: 'In loving memory of our dear son and brother, Private E. R. (Ern) Cooper, who died of gunshot wounds (face) in France on May 31, 1918:

> He was a soldier, noble and true,
> > Died with his colors, white and blue;
> No matter how we call,
> > There is nothing to answer,
> But your dear photo on the wall.

Private L. Chapman, 43rd Battalion, died at Villers-Bretonneux in June 1918. Like many, his wife and children called on the divine to help them bear the unbearable in a verse often used in these remembrances:

> Absent from each, yet close to him,
> > Holding the selfsame hand;
> No anxious thought or weary sigh,
> > But he will understand.
> He knows the ties we hold so dear,
> > Each wish of thine and mine,
> The love made purer, stronger still
> > By His great love divine.

His daughter remembered her father more prosaically but no less affectionately:

> A life made beautiful by kindly deeds,
> A helping hand for other's needs,
> > But open converse is there none.
> So much the vital spirits sink,
> > To see the vacant chair, and think
> How good, how kind, and he is gone.

Corporal 'Ham' Healey DCM also fell at Villers-Bretonneux, on 1 June 1918. A year later his parents began the many notices from his family:

> To you, and such as you, we kneel;
> > You were so brave we dare not weep;
> Our hearts go out in mute appeal
> > Towards where you rest, war tired, asleep.
> Not farewell, dear Ham; only good night.
> > —Mother and father.

His sisters wrote: 'To the memory of Ham, who deemed it no sacrifice to give his life for a noble cause':

> So shall it be at last, in that bright morning,
> > When the soul waketh, and life shadows flee;
> Oh, in that hour, fairer than daylight dawning,
> > Shall rise the glorious thought, he is with Thee.

So did his brothers:

> When honor looked you squarely in the face.
> > You met her, eye to eye;
> And true unto the birthright of your race,

> Showed how the brave can die.
>> You chose the nobler, the better part.

There were other tributes to Ham from brothers and sisters-in-law. Lastly came the simplest:

> In loving memory of Ham, who fell in action in France, June 1, 1918. Greater love hath no man than this.—Inserted by his loving girl, Dorrie.

Ray Jones's Aunt Jennie remembered that he had been killed on 31 May 1918:

> In many Australian homes to-day:
>> There's a vacant chair, there's a boy away;
>
> There's a falling tear and a hungry yearn,
>> For the soldier boy who will never return.

The Newlands family remembered their 'dear son and brother, Leslie, who died of wounds in France on June 1, 1917':

> In a soldier's grave he is sleeping,
>> One of earth's bravest and best;
>
> In our hearts we shall miss him forever.
>> Though we know he is only at rest.

Private Bill O'Donnell died of wounds on 31 May 1918. His 'loving brother and sister-in-law Beat and Jim' remembered him:

> Always happy and cheerful,
>> With a heart that knew no fear,
>
> He stood to face life's battle

> For the one he loved most dear.
> In France now he is lying;
> He answered his country's call,
> And died an Australian hero.
> Fighting to save us all.

And the grief never ended. The 'loving mother, sisters, and brothers of Corporal W.A. Snell MM, 3rd Field Company Engineers (Anzac)' remembered their son and brother, who died of wounds in France on 31 May 1918:

> Days of sadness, still come o'er us.
> Hidden, tears they often show;
> Memory keeps our loved one near us
> Though he died one year ago.

Some, like Frank 'Cherry' Smith, were recalled with a few simple words from a friend:

> He will always live in the hearts of those who knew his worth.
> —Inserted by his mate, Jimmy Turner, North Unley.

'Here is their spirit'

It is a place of many meanings. A memorial to Australia's wars and those who fought in them; a shrine of memory; a museum of wartime artefacts; an archive of mostly irreplaceable official and personal records; and one of the country's leading tourist attractions. Deliberately aligned with Parliament House in Canberra, the Australian War Memorial is a complicated place, performing many important national tasks.

Not surprisingly, the Memorial is often the focus of controversy, as different constituencies seek to have their stories told or to have the larger story told differently. Should the Memorial feature the frontier wars against Indigenous Australians? Yes, say many. Others point out that the colonial wars were not officially declared conflicts and so were not military in nature.

Should the building be bigger, with more space for displays? A proposal for a half-billion-dollar redevelopment divided opinion but was approved in 2021. Should the Memorial accept funding from companies involved in the arms trade? Should it be less military-focused and give a broader picture of war, including the experiences of women, children, the home front? But while the nature of the arguments and controversies shifts from generation to generation, disquiet about the Memorial goes back to its germination in the thinking and writing of a man named Charles Bean.

As Australia's only official war correspondent during World War I, Bean was on the spot for many of its most momentous events. He was in the Middle East; he was at Gallipoli; he was on the Western Front; he was in 'Blighty', as Britain was known. He was also one of the first people to return to Gallipoli after the war, walking the bloodied and now fabled hills, trench lines and dugouts to retrieve relics, memories and information for preservation and memorialisation. He wrote and edited books about the war, including the *Official History of Australia in the War of 1914–1918*.

Through his wartime journalism, Bean was largely responsible for creating the image of the digger—the volunteer private soldier, careless of military authority and protocol, rolling up his sleeves to get the job done with a high charge of larrikin humour and hijinks. Bean heroised the men of the First AIF as typical Australian blokes who went to war to defend their country. Already the story was a selective one. We hear little about sailors, airmen, medical staff or others who served in this pantheon. For Bean, the diggers were the highest form of Australian, embodying the virtues of the idealised bushman and they deserved to be venerated in an appropriate shrine.

Bean knew that Australian soldiers were great collectors of souvenirs and mementoes of battle. He also knew that some other countries were planning to construct museums of the Great War and suggested that Australia should do something similar. A War Records Section was established in 1917 to locate and preserve the records of the war. Headed by John Treloar who would later become the Memorial's first director, this was the basis on which the Australian War Memorial was founded. By this time Bean was referring to the relics of war as 'sacred things' and in his mind a memorial would be a kind of secular shrine as well as a repository of the detritus of war.

Despite some resistance and the impact of the Great Depression, the Australian War Memorial was eventually built, opening on Remembrance Day (then known as Armistice Day), 11 November 1941, in the midst of another war. Bean's dream was largely realised. As he would later say: 'Here is their spirit, in the heart of the land they loved; and here we guard the record which they themselves made.'

The War Memorial soon became a central institution of Australian life, military history and its associated mythology. It has only become more so in the decades since. The numerous ongoing stoushes about its roles and functions are testament to the passion Australians hold for the place. It is more than the sum of its parts and, for better or for worse, still holds the heart of a nation whose history and mythology have largely been determined by wars, mostly fought somewhere else.

Misery Hill

The Anglican church of St Mary in the small Wiltshire village of Codford holds a special piece of Anzac in its soft green embrace. The church cemetery is a very English place, but it is one of many overseas locations that is now a part of Australia and New Zealand. Arrayed around a tall white cross are the neat lines of regular white headstones that signify the work of the Commonwealth War Graves Commission. Sixty-six of the graves are of New Zealanders, thirty-one of Australians from World War I and one from World War II. They are beautifully kept.

During World War I this area and the surrounding Salisbury Plain was the location of a massive military base for housing, training and healing soldiers of Britain and its empire. The plain was dotted with settlements of tents and wooden huts. Codford had at least fifteen camps in its immediate vicinity, with many more not far away. Through these encampments passed tens of thousands of Australian and New Zealand troops. Some never left.

With the fighting in France and Belgium, Australian and New Zealand forces began to use the Salisbury Plain facilities from 1916, initially for transfers, training and related activities and then, increasingly, for the care of wounded and sick soldiers. No. 3 New Zealand Hospital at Codford produced its own magazine written and published by the patients and staff, aptly named *Codford Wheeze*. It was said to be the successor to the efforts of previous soldier journals known variously as *The Wiltshire Wangler, The Wylye Wail* and *The Salisbury Swinger*.

Down the road in the village of Sutton Veny, an agricultural training program was established for Australian troops after the war ended in late 1918. Two thousand soldiers were taught useful skills for the many postwar soldier settlement schemes that developed in Australia. Gradually, the huts and camps disappeared as soldiers returned to their home countries. Before they left, the Australians continued a local Salisbury Plain tradition of carving pictures into the chalk hills that surround the area. Soldiers were put to work carving a giant Anzac hat badge on a hill above Sutton Veny. It doesn't seem to have been a very popular job, as the soldiers called the place 'Misery Hill'. But the carving has left a very visible reminder of the Anzac presence during the war.

Many Australians had to wait until well into 1919 before going home, sometimes on the same ships that had taken them to the war. Large numbers became infected with the Spanish flu, the influenza pandemic that broke out in 1918, and were isolated on their ships or in quarantine stations set up around the country.

Australia's history of fighting wars in other parts of the world has given the country many 'little Australias' like Codford. The body of only one Australian soldier was repatriated from World War I—Major General William Bridges—and few from World War II. The places where more than 100,000 others lie are highly significant for descendants and for the nation. As well as noted memorial sites like Gallipoli, Villers-Bretonneux, Tobruk and Kokoda, there are many smaller memorial sites in the eighty-three countries in which Australian servicemen and women are buried. There are also 'memorials to the missing' that remember those who have no known grave.

Each Anzac Day since 1997 the little churchyard of Codford St Mary has been the focus of a small but intense Dawn Service. In 2015, at the centenary of the Gallipoli landings, the event closely followed the usual structure of the Dawn Service, with hymns, prayers, readings on the meaning and significance of Anzac and the laying of wreaths followed by the Ode, the Last Post, one minute's silence and Reveille. At Codford the ceremony also includes reading a Roll of Honour with the names of all the Australian and New Zealand dead in the cemetery. On this special occasion, a singer rendered Eric Bogle's well-known song 'And the Band Played Waltzing Matilda', then a piper led the crowd down the lane to the village hall for a Gunfire Breakfast. Around 200 guests sat down to a meal that included tots of rum for those who wished to take it in their tea.

Among the guests were a number of expatriate Australians who had lived and worked in the area for ten years or so. They were among the local volunteers who keep the Anzac hat badge on 'Misery Hill' clear of grass. The carving is on private property, but with the cooperation of the owner, the council and the Australian High Commission in London, an annual recutting of the badge is carried out. Visitors to the area enjoy the sight as one of the numerous historical chalk drawings that surround Salisbury Plain remembering, if they wish, the bravery, sacrifice and futility of war.

'I am the last of the Tasmanians'

A weatherboard hall with a corrugated iron roof, the former Methodist church at Nicholls Rivulet, Tasmania, isn't very imposing. Apart from the Gothic church windows and front door, and some wooden decoration on the front bargeboard, there's not much to suggest a church. It could be just another of the many places of worship scattered around the country, thrown up by local communities of the faithful in the colonial era. But this one has a special story.

In 1899, one Horace Watson prepared an Edison phonograph and its wax cylinders for what would be a momentous recording. Standing close by the large brass horn of the primitive machine was a Tasmanian Aboriginal woman.

'I'm Fanny Smith. I was born on Flinders Island. I am the last of the Tasmanians,' she projected loudly and proudly into the horn. Then she sang. The scratchy recordings made that day and those from a repeat session made a few years later are the only ones ever made of a First Nations language from Tasmania.

Fanny Cochrane Smith was the name of this early recording star. She was born in 1834 and spent much of her childhood in the none-too-gentle care of church and state institutions, experiences that helped develop her independent spirit. In 1854 she married an ex-convict named William Smith and they began raising what would be a family of five boys and six girls, as well as farming, shingle splitting and doing it pretty tough, as people usually did in those times.

One of the things that sustained Fanny was the Methodist faith she had learned in childhood. Despite her ill treatment by Christians, Fanny found that the basic elements of Methodism accorded with the traditional spiritual matters she had also absorbed. With her husband, she conducted Methodist services in her kitchen and became a widely respected member of her church and community, known for her cooking skills and for singing the traditional songs of her people.

As an ex-ward of the state and possibly the last Palawa—she was close friends with the older woman Truganini, also a claimant to the title—Fanny received an annuity from the government. She was eventually recognised as the last surviving 'Tasmanian Aboriginal' and granted over 120 hectares of the land that once belonged to her people at Oyster Cove.

By 1900, the Methodist gatherings were becoming too large for Fanny's modest house and it was decided to build a church. She donated a parcel of her grant for the construction of the building. It took just six months and the first services were in May 1901.

Fanny died in 1905 but is not forgotten. Although the church eventually lost its congregation as people moved away and was at one stage used to store hay, it is still there today. Known as Fanny Cochrane Smith Church, the building has been restored by members of the local First Nations community and was operated until its closure as a museum of First Nations history and culture.

Horace Watson, the man who had the foresight to etch the songs and language into wax cylinders was an entrepreneurial Hobart businessman who heard one of Fanny's concerts and asked her to record with the then very new phonograph. He became one of the first to make field recordings, which became a primary source for the recent reconstruction and revival of

Tasmanian Aboriginal languages into a new version known as palawa kani. It seems that Fanny was more than happy to contribute her singing to the new technology and on one of the recordings you can hear Horace say, 'We had a real excellent time here'. In 2017, the recordings were inscribed on the UNESCO Australian Memory of the World Register.

There is another contemporary resonance of these events. Horace's great-grandson songwriter Bruce Watson and a descendant of Fanny's, the late Cape Barren musician Ronnie Summers, recorded and performed Bruce's song about Fanny and Horace. It ends with Bruce singing his final verse, followed by one written and sung by Ronnie:

> (Bruce) There's a photo on a wall in a museum in Hobart,
> It was taken in October of 1903;
> Of a man and a woman and an Edison phonograph,
> Recording her songs of the land and the sea.
> And the man had a son, who in turn had a son,
> Who in turn had a son, who was me.
>
> (Ronnie) And the woman had a son,
> Who in turn had a daughter,
> Who in turn had a son, who in turn had a son,
> And the next one was me.

The Star of Taroom

One of the consequences of Australia's colonisation has been the removal of First Nations peoples' human remains and sacred artefacts. Sometimes these were taken for what were then considered to be scientific purposes, but also because there was a thriving world market for such objects.

Most of the artefacts ended up in British museums, but also in some Australian collections. There has been increasing pressure for the return of these objects to their rightful owners and in recent years a number of important items have been repatriated. Although the removal of Indigenous cultural property is now illegal, it still occurs.

In the 1970s Jim Danalis, an outback veterinarian, often visited the town of Taroom, Queensland. On one of his farm calls he came across a large, rounded sandstone boulder, deeply grooved in a strangely tactile star pattern. A keen collector of artefacts, he convinced the farmer to drag the stone from its nesting in the earth and took it home to his Brisbane garden.

Growing up, the vet's son John used to run his fingers through the grooves in the mysterious rock. 'I used to imagine it was a stone star that fell from the sky,' he recalled on ABC's *7.30* program in 2021. 'It was a bit of a time machine because when you sat with it, with your hands on it, it took you back. You could imagine the people that sat around that stone centuries ago.'

And so they had. The rock that Jim had taken home was sacred to the Iman people of southern and central Queensland. With the multiple functions that characterise many Indigenous Australian objects, the Iman used the stone to sharpen their hunting tools, as a waypoint for direction finding and as a marker of the traditional boundaries of their country.

Before his father died, John convinced him to return items from his collection. A skull was returned to its rightful place with descendants of the Wamba Wamba people of Victoria, documented in John's book, *Riding the Black Cockatoo* (2009). This act generated so much goodwill from those who received it that Jim decided to also return the stone. He died before he was able to do this but, in his stead, John made a remarkable journey of repatriation and reconciliation. With the help of friends, he had a special cart made in which to carry the stone back to its proper place in Iman country. John and a dozen others pulled the 160-kilogram stone 500 kilometres from Brisbane to Taroom.

Why go to what might be considered extreme lengths to return an object that could have easily been loaded into a ute? John and his supporters wanted to highlight the importance of giving back stolen cultural property. 'There are treasures all over Australia that need to go back, they need to go home,' he told *7.30*.

The return of the rock was a big event in Taroom, a dusty outback town with a fraught colonial history of First Nations resistance and settler reprisal. Hundreds turned up, including many Iman people. A smoking ceremony and singing greeted the rock and its carriers. John Danalis was embraced and made an Iman man. Referring to the spiritual significance of the stone, Elder Heather Tobane said, 'It's healing a lot of our people and a lot of the people who live around us, and that's what it's meant to be'. She said that it was especially important for the younger generation in 'rekindling that sense of place . . . Now the rock has come back, it has brought us back to where the roots are, and it means a lot'.

For John Danalis, the return of the stone is 'healing for everybody'. In honouring his promise to his late father, he feels pride—and some relief—to have successfully carried out a significant and high-profile act of reconciliation. Perhaps other individuals and institutions holding First Nations artefacts will follow his lead.

A Plait of Hair

It wasn't only the thousands of artefacts in Western Australia's Juukan Gorge rock shelters that made them so important. Archaeologists also found a few strands of human hair, twisted into a plait. When analysed, the 4000-year-old hair contained DNA that was a match for direct descendants and current custodians of the shelters.

The Juukan rock shelters in the Pilbara region have been in human use for 46,000 years. Their wanton destruction in May 2020 reverberated around the world and has been compared to the destruction of Afghanistan's Bamiyan Buddha statues by the Taliban in 2001. A combination of faulty heritage legislation and inadequate internal and external corporate communication processes resulted in the rock shelters being blasted to rubble. Urgent requests to stop the blasting had been made by the Puutu Kunti Kurrama and Pinikura people (PKKP) and the company had been repeatedly advised that the caves were of the highest Australian and global scientific value.

The Rio Tinto company mining the area apologised, corporate heads rolled and bonuses were withheld. Condemnation from heritage, archaeological, anthropological and other organisations was swift and official inquiries were established by various Australian governments. One of the astonishing admissions made by the company was that the destruction of the caves could have been avoided. There were options that preserved the site but these were ignored in favour of a decision to 'access higher volumes of high-grade ore'.

Burchell Hayes, spokesman for the PKKP Aboriginal Corporation explained the significance of the shelters to the inquiry set up in the aftermath of the incident:

> Juukan Gorge is an anchor of our culture, with a number of individual cultural sites that makes it unique, an important place . . . The Juukan Gorge is known to be a place where the spirits of our relatives who have passed away, even recently, have come to rest. It is a place that the very, very old people still occupy. Purlykuti has been specifically referred to by the old people as a place of pardu, which refers to the special language only spoken during ceremonies in the Pilbara. Our elders state that it is certain that the spirits are very disturbed, and their living relatives are also upset at this. This is why Juukan Gorge is important. It is in the ancient blood of our people and contains their DNA. It houses history and the spirits of ancestors and it anchors the people to this country.

He went on to say that 'The loss of Juukan Gorge rock shelters is also a loss to all First Nations peoples and the community within Australia and internationally'.

Working with the traditional owners, archaeologists and anthropologists have been investigating and documenting the Juukan rock shelters for many years. Artefacts had been removed for further study and are, fortunately, preserved. These include tools of stone and wood, as well as the plait of hair. But the treasures have been held in containers at the Rio Tinto office in

Dampier, Western Australia, rather than in the proper facilities for such ancient objects. The traditional owners have requested that the artefacts remain on their country in a 'keeping place' controlled by the Puutu Kunti Kurrama and Pinikura people.

After the destruction of the rock shelters, efforts got underway to amend faulty laws covering ancient sites of cultural significance. The Senate inquiry into the incident released an interim report in 2021 that was scathing in its criticism of state and Commonwealth heritage legislation, and of corporate behaviour, which was characterised as:

> A self-interested reliance on outdated laws and unfair agreements containing gag clauses prohibiting PKKP from critiquing the operations of the company and restricting their rights to access state and federal heritage protections without first obtaining the company's consent.

The report also pointed out that 'For the PKKP the destruction was personal and visceral—and a sharp reminder of how vulnerable their culture and heritage are to the imperatives of governments and corporations'. In late 2021 the Senate inquiry into the incident presented a final report that recommended new and improved Commonwealth legislation to better protect sacred sites.

The Juukan rock shelters fiasco was not the first example of the destruction of such sites in pursuit of mineral wealth. North of Juukan Gorge is the Burrup Peninsula (Murujuga), part of a precinct thought to hold the world's most ancient rock art, including what may be the oldest representation of a human face. Some of these works were destroyed in 2009 and there are now fears that industrial pollution from mining emissions are causing a 'Juukan Gorge in slow motion', further endangering the estimated one million petroglyphs on the peninsula. Other such sites around the country have also been damaged by insensitive, though usually legal, vandalism. It is likely that sacred places like these will continue to be at risk due to conflicting and confusing state and federal heritage laws.

The Botteri family standing with a friend (left) under a sign at Bonegilla in 1955.

4
UNSETTLING PLACES

Hell's Gate

For a place that only operated for little more than a decade, Tasmania's Macquarie Harbour Penal Station on Sarah Island had a fearsome reputation. Established on the west coast of what was then Van Diemen's Land, the penal station was intended mainly to punish convicts who had committed further crimes in the colony or on the way there. Thieves, fraudsters, escapees and mutineers did extra time there, almost 1200 of them in total, almost all men. Convicts were mainly employed in timber-getting from the rich Huon pine resources in the area and fashioning the lumber into ships.

From its earliest days, Macquarie Harbour was feared by convicts as a place of hard work, difficult living conditions and flogging. Men worked in chains, often neck-deep in water to fell and raft logs to the work areas. The place soon gained the name 'Hell's Gate', a reference to both the brutal existence there and the dangerous sea entry into the harbour to reach the main base on Sarah Island. Prisoners began trying to escape within months of the first arrivals, and over 150 attempts were made in the first six years of the station's existence. Few succeeded. If they were not recaptured, usually starving and desperate, fleeing convicts simply disappeared into the wilderness.

Of the many escapes, the most notorious were those including Alexander Pearce. On both occasions he killed and ate some of his companions. Later, a group of convicts including James Porter managed to steal a newly built ship in the final days of the station's operation. They sailed it across the Pacific Ocean to Chile in one of Australia's most daring convict escapes. After settling in Chile for a while, they were recaptured, returned to England, tried and re-transported to Van Diemen's Land.

Macquarie Harbour's most famous escapee was Matthew Brady. Transported for seven years from Manchester in 1820 after stealing some food and a basket, Brady often defied authority and was frequently flogged. After escape attempts and general disobedience in Sydney, he was sent to Macquarie Harbour and in 1824 escaped with several other convicts. Brady and his companions stole a boat and sailed it to Frederick Henry Bay on the south-east coast, from where they established a bushranging gang that became the terror of the island. For the next two years, Brady and his accomplices raided and robbed settlers and settlements, proving elusive despite the efforts of the colonial authorities.

Brady's gang grew to the point where they became a serious threat to authority. Lieutenant Governor Arthur issued a reward of £25 and a conditional pardon for anyone who could capture the bushrangers. Famously, Brady replied by issuing a reward for the capture of Arthur:

> It has caused Matthew Brady much concern that such a person known as Sir George Arthur is at large. Twenty gallons of rum will be given to any person that will deliver his person unto me. I also caution John Priest that I will hang him for his ill-treatment of Mrs. Blackwell at Newtown.

Arthur also tried to infiltrate Brady's gang with convict undercover men. One, Thomas Kenton (sometimes known as Kemton), lured Brady to his hut where the bushranger was ambushed and wounded. He escaped and returned to take his revenge, though not before another daring raid in March 1826:

> On Saturday evening last, Brady, with his whole party of fourteen attacked Mr. Dry's house; and, after putting in the necessary centinels [sic] and securing the servants in an inside room, proceeded to rifle the house of all its contents—very coolly emptying all the drawers and boxes of their contents of linen, clothes, and every thing valuable, and deliberately tying them up in bundles to be conveyed away on horses' backs.

A servant escaped with news of the attack, bringing a group of troopers and settlers to the scene under the command of Colonel Balfour. They rushed Dry's house where they thought the bushrangers were holed up. In the fierce gunfight that followed, one of the settlers was wounded in the knee, later having his leg amputated. In the darkness, the bushrangers were able to move about with ease, keeping the troops at bay and eventually slipping away.

The defenders of the town suspected there might be as many as nineteen bushrangers in the attack, outnumbering their own forces, and that they were under the command of the feared Brady—'nothing is more remarkable than the generalship observed by Brady', one defender grudgingly admitted. The colony had been in fear of Brady's gang for many months. Such a concerted attack, together with a new level of violence, caused panic. Where were they? How many were there? What were their intentions—possibly a convict insurrection of the kind always feared in colonial Australia?

The press reflected the concerns of settlers:

> The appalling accounts detailed this day of the proceedings of that most diabolical banditti, headed by Brady, are calculated to excite the most serious considerations. Twenty-one months have now elapsed since the escape of Brady and thirteen others from Macquarie Harbour. And several of them are still at large, carrying terror and desolation in their progress, from one end of the Island to the other, which they appear to traverse at their pleasure, without dread or apprehension.

The newspaper told its readers that the island had sufficient civil and military forces to track down the bushrangers and asked 'To what then can be attributed the non-apprehension of this detestable and lawless banditti, whose outrages are now of a character threatening the most serious consequences! There must be something wrong somewhere.' The writer concluded:

> We trust the Executive will turn immediate attention to the necessity of adopting some measures which may be calculated to remove that dreadful state of alarm and anxiety, in which the whole Island is now placed, and which much inevitably produce the most unfortunate results.

The following month, a wounded and demoralised Brady was betrayed and captured. He pleaded guilty to the murder of Kenton and to horse stealing and was sentenced to hang. His gentlemanly reputation made him a criminal celebrity, with ladies bemoaning his fate, well-wishers delivering flowers to his cell and even some of his opponents visiting him before his execution.

Resigned to his end, the notorious bushranger nevertheless violently protested at being held in the same cell as Thomas (Mark) Jeffries. He was another infamous Macquarie Harbour escapee: a rapist, baby killer and cannibal who had briefly been a member of Brady's gang but later informed against him. Brady continued to complain at being unjustly associated with Jeffries when the two Hell's Gate fugitives were hanged together, along with three other bushrangers, on 4 May 1826.

The Massacre Hill

One Easter Sunday in 1854, Italian linguist, writer and revolutionary Raffaello Carboni pitched his tent on a hill above the goldfields near Ballarat:

> Who could have told me on that Easter Sunday, that the unknown hill which I had chosen for my rest, would soon

be called the Massacre Hill! That next Christmas, my mate would lie in the grave, somewhere forgotten: and I in the gaol! the rope round my neck!!

Carboni was one of the thousands of disenchanted diggers on the Ballarat goldfields and a ringleader of the revolt of 3 December 1854. Under the leadership of Irishman Peter Lalor, the diggers raised the now famous flag of stars and swore 'by the Southern Cross, to stand truly by each other, and fight to defend our rights and liberties'. The miners were unhappy with the cost of the government licensing system, the corruption of those who administered it and the oppressive policing that kept the ramshackle arrangement teetering on. Now, in defiance of authority and in defence of what they believed their rights to be, they armed themselves and threw up a rough wooden stockade. Lieutenant Governor Charles Hotham of the recently founded colony of Victoria sent armed troops to quell the insurrection. Together with police, they attacked the stockade at dawn. As Carboni stated, though he was not himself inside the stockade, it was a massacre.

Young Michael Canny and his brother Patrick were among the miners, sheltering with two other diggers behind an upturned dray:

It was bright moonlight, and we saw the redcoats blazing away at us. I had my own rifle and fired several shots. I saw Captain Wise fall, and a couple of soldiers take him by the shoulders and drag him behind a mullock heap. Teddy Moore and John Hines (Hynes) fell dead beside us. Then my brother was hit with a bullet, which splintered his shin bone, and he was stretched out. I had my rifle ready for another shot when a bullet pierced my right arm, went in at my side, and out under the breast-bone. It did not hurt, but the blood spurted out, and scared me, I threw the rifle down and went over the stockade fence like a deer, and ran like a racer over the hill towards Pennyweight Flat where our tents were.

As he flew, he 'saw Lalor stagger and drop his gun, and stoop quickly to pick it up with the other hand, but I did not know till afterwards that he was then wounded'.

Narrowly escaping the troopers, Michael made it back to his tent:

My sister-in-law was in the neighbouring tent and she brought a cloth and a bucket of water, and I pulled off my shirt, and kept bathing the wound in my side with water to try and stop the bleeding. Someone carried word to Dr Carr that I was wounded, and he came along during the morning and dressed the wound.

Patrick Canny was taken prisoner and spent six or seven weeks recovering from his wounds in the camp hospital. Rumours insisted the surviving diggers were to be shot. When the army returned in even greater force, Michael decided his best bet was to run:

Bare-headed and bare-footed as I was, I bolted for the bush, towards Warrenheip. My feet gave me more pain than my side, so I ran breathless into the scrub. I went back in the afternoon to the tent hardly able to walk, my feet were so badly cut. I had a bad time for months with the wound in my side. It was nearly a year before it properly healed, and I was able for work again.

The Canny boys lost their claim, windlass, buckets, ropes, and tools and nearly 2000 wooden slabs they had contributed to the building of the stockade.

The government forces killed at least twenty-two diggers. Six soldiers died in the fighting. More on both sides were wounded and over 100 diggers were arrested. Thirteen of them, including Raffaello, were tried for high treason. Ultimately, charges against one were dropped and the rest were acquitted as no jury could be found in the colony willing to convict them.

While the dramatic events at the Eureka Stockade are well known, they were the culmination of a lengthy period of discontent and public agitation on the goldfields. The year before, in 1853 a petition from the Bendigo miners gathered more than 23,000 names and asked for a reduction of the 30-shilling fee to a more affordable 10 shillings. They also requested land reform, a foretaste of the growing agitation for land settlement that succeeded the goldrushes. Various associations were formed that coalesced into what became known as the Red Ribbon Rebellion. Miners, tradesmen, shopkeepers and others who supported reform wore a red ribbon in their hats to symbolise their defiance of the government. In response to the agitation, there was a temporary suspension of the licence fee that calmed the situation for a few weeks but the system was soon reimposed and the antagonism between the goldfields and their administration finally became the armed confrontation of the Eureka Stockade and its aftermath.

The bloodshed at the Eureka Stockade did bring reform. After an official inquiry, the hated licence fee was replaced with an export duty and an affordable annual 'miner's right'. The goldfields police force was severely purged and the notoriously corrupt goldfield commissioners replaced with a single warden.

As the rush of hopeful diggers inevitably gave way to industrialised mining of the deeper veins, the cry for land that began on the goldfields became a clamour, leading to 'free selection' legislation. Land was opened up to pretty well anyone who could scrape a small deposit together and undertake to 'improve' their block, creating a new social class, the cocky farmer, often struggling on a sub-standard property, bringing up a family on 'pumpkin and bear' (koala) and competing with the wealthier holders of the better land who obtained it during the earlier 'squatting' era. Economic and social tensions between these classes were one of the flashpoints for the Kelly outbreak of 1878–1880.

As for the passionate radical, after his release from custody, Carboni left Australia in 1856, travelled widely, wrote and took significant roles in Italian nationalist activities. Raffaello Carboni died in obscurity in 1875, though he is remembered in Australia as a significant, if enigmatic, figure of the Eureka Stockade tragedy. The event itself, and the Southern Cross flag, have become potent symbols of resistance to authority—a mythology utilised by both the left and right sides of politics.

Cullin-La-Ringo

For several decades, historians have been trying to confirm the incidence of mass violence on the Australian frontier. Usually described as 'massacres'—of either settlers or First Nations peoples—these events are being added to a database and map. The map is already extensive and still growing as evidence of fatal frontier conflict is unearthed or new details about known conflicts emerge.

Why? Because frontier violence has left little official evidence and what there is remains murky at best. There are also persistent oral traditions suggesting that massacres were more frequent and more savage than was generally acknowledged. This emotive topic is also a political one, splitting researchers, First Nations groups and commentators into warring camps that have become known as 'the history wars'.

The subject of massacres and the reluctance to discuss them is central to issues of reconciliation and the recognition of historical wrongs. Getting the facts straight is vital, despite problems with the available records. In 2021, researchers turned up new evidence related to the involvement of a sporting pioneer in a reprisal event.

As settlement pushed further north in the wake of the trails blazed by explorers, those seeking land in north Queensland met resistance from traditional owners. There were many violent confrontations, one of the worst involving an attempt to settle the selection known as Cullin-La-Ringo in 1861. Horatio Wills and a large group of settlers, livestock and wagons camped on the 260 square kilometre property around 320 kilometres west of Rockhampton when they were attacked by a large party of people from the Gayiri language group. Nineteen men, women and children of the settler party died, including their leader. A band of settlers and Native Police tracked those they considered to be the perpetrators and caught up with them at Expedition Range in late November, killing at least sixty and possibly many more. As with other incidents of this type, reprisals on both sides continued for some years.

Horatio Wills's son, Thomas, was a member of the settler party but was, fortuitously, away from the camp when the attack took place. His role in the subsequent reprisals has long been in question. Historians have sought to clarify whether he did commit any related crimes largely because Wills was later prominent in the establishment and development of two of Australia's iconic sports, cricket and Australian Rules Football.

Tom Wills was born in Australia but educated largely at the exclusive English Rugby school, where he displayed outstanding cricketing skills that took him to prominence in the sporting circles of the time. He returned to Australia where he soon became captain of the Victorian team. He was a star, if a controversial one, often refusing to accept official decisions and flitting from club to club. To keep cricketers fit during their winter break, he proposed the formation of a 'foot-ball club' that became the Melbourne Football Club in 1859, the origin of Australian football.

Wills had left Melbourne and his sporting activities to take part in his father's attempt to settle Cullin-La-Ringo. After the massacre he returned to sport, continuing to cause ructions with his aggressive approach and apparently lax attitude to what was then considered to be cheating and unsportsmanlike conduct. Dropped from the team, his life became increasingly unstable through debt, alcohol and probably what we would now describe as depression and trauma related to the massacre.

In 1880, he stabbed himself in the heart three times with a pair of scissors during a bout of delirium tremens.

Until recently, there was only ambiguous evidence about Tom Wills's participation in reprisal killings. He had grown up with First Nations people and was captain and coach of a First Nations cricket team that toured Australia in the summer of 1866–67. Since the 1980s he has been presented as a reconciliatory figure and a hero of Australian sport. Was Tom Wills likely to have murdered Aboriginal people?

In 2021, historian Gary Fearon discovered an article in an 1895 edition of the *Chicago Tribune* that provided strong evidence of Wills's guilt. The author of the article, credited only as 'G', claimed that he was told by Wills in response to a question about the massacre that 'I cannot tell all that happened, but know we killed all in sight,' and described how he shot one man who had stolen his prized cricket jacket—'I emptied the whole six barrels of my revolver into him, the brute.'

Why Wills would give this confession, rendered in the article in a 'boys' own' adventure style, may seem puzzling. But Emeritus Professor Lyndall Ryan, a leading specialist in massacre research, points out that it was not uncommon for those who had carried out such deeds to unburden themselves of guilt many years later, even to strangers. Perhaps Wills did that in conversation with whoever 'G' might have been.

Further research may reveal more. Or it may not. Faced with calls from First Nations organisations to show leadership on such a contentious possibility, at the time of writing, the AFL and Cricket Australia are seeking further advice.

A Troubled Light

There's something about a lighthouse. Whether thrusting straight up from rocky headlands or squatting defiantly on lumps of rock surrounded by boiling seas, these flashing beacons attract tales of tragedy, heroism and the supernatural. Australia has well over 300 lighthouses, nowadays all automatic. But in the past the lights were tended by resident keepers and, often, their families. The isolated locations and difficult access for many lighthouses meant that keepers completely depended on supplies being brought to them and they were often thrown onto their own resources, with potential dangers.

Queensland's Bustard Head Lighthouse began shining its beams in 1868. The white-painted cast-iron structure is 17 metres tall and located around 20 kilometres north-west of Seventeen Seventy, 120 kilometres north of Bundaberg. It seems to have been troubled from the very beginning. One workman died building the lighthouse and others were drowned in nearby shipwrecks. A one-year-old girl born at the lighthouse was scalded to death there in 1898. Sixteen years later the son of a worker at the lighthouse accidentally shot his brother. The boy lived, but with badly damaged internal organs.

Another particularly grisly tragedy occurred in 1887. Assistant Lighthouse Keeper Nils Gibson lived at the light with his wife, Kate, and four daughters. On 5 May 1887, Kate left the home to take a walk. She did not return. After two days searching, the Gibson's eldest daughter, Annie, found her mother's body. She had slit her throat with Nils's cutthroat razor, eventually found beneath a nearby tree root.

That was not the end of tragedy for the Gibson family. Almost exactly two years later, Nils was in a boat with his daughter Mary; Assistant Lighthouse Keeper John Wilkinson and his wife, Elizabeth; and Telegraph Master Alfred Power, when it capsized in stormy seas. Nils kept hold of Mary for as long as he could 'while strength lasted', but by the time he began to swim for the shore, almost 500 metres away, Mary had disappeared beneath the swirling waves. Nils made it to land and Wilkinson managed to right the boat, but his wife did not survive. Power's body was washed up on the beach, but Mary was never found.

Tragedy again visited the light in 1912. Edie Anderson was the seventeen-year-old daughter of the lighthouse keeper at that time. She was returning from a visit to Turkey Station under the escort of 32-year-old stockman Arthur Cogzwell, who had been sent to bring Edie home. According to evidence given at the inquest, Edie was romantically involved with several men, one a young worker on the station named George Daniels.

On Sunday 11 February, Cogzwell and Edie rode off towards Bustard Head. Not too long after, several witnesses saw Daniels leave the station and follow them down the road carrying a Winchester rifle. At around 11.15 that morning, a visitor returning along the same road from Turkey Station came across Arthur Cogzwell sitting on a creek bank by the side of the road. He was moaning and bleeding badly from bullet wounds. At the subsequent inquest the visitor reported their conversation:

'Good God, Arthur, old man, what is the matter?' he exclaimed, and pointing to his stomach, Cogzwell said, 'I'm shot', then: 'That black _____ George . . .'

This was taken to mean Daniels, who was of mixed Chinese and Torres Strait Islander ancestry. The visitor made Cogzwell as comfortable as possible and returned to the station for help. By the time the rescue party arrived at the scene, Cogzwell was dead, his clothing soaked in blood and covered in ants.

Daniels and Edie were long gone and a subsequent hunt and large reward of £500 produced no trace of them. A woman named Kate Leslie claimed to have seen the couple a few days after the murder. She provided them with bread and tea and 'the black-fellow' told her 'he shot the man because he wanted to take his wife'. As the man left, 'a girl came out to meet him; she had something in her hand resembling a rifle; they went up the creek towards Colosseum . . .' Kate Leslie, who was said by another witness to have been 'part imbecile', was later found burned to death in her house.

As other witnesses gave their evidence, a mix of observation and gossip, a tangled tale of Edie and George's relationship emerged. A station worker deposed that 'Edie Anderson and George Daniels got very friendly' and that Daniels aimed to seduce the young woman and that 'Edie would make a good little wife and that he would like to take her away in a boat'.

Edie's father testified that he was aware of his daughter's relationship with Daniels and cautioned her. She replied that she needed to speak with her lover first but promised that would be for the last time. Her father had joined the unsuccessful search party for the missing couple and believed 'that Daniels shot Edie the same day as he shot Cogzwell and then did away with himself'. As if all this was not enough trouble for the Anderson family, only a few weeks after Edie's disappearance one of her older sisters, Ethel, died as a result of an epileptic fit.

That was how things stood for another twenty-three years. In 1935, a stockman found the bones of a man and a woman in a creek in the isolated locality of Cania, Queensland. The male bones were thought to be those of Daniels. The female remains were presumed to be those of Edie. The skull had 'two small holes on the left side and a dent in it about two inches long'.

Ironstone Mountain

Imagine this: you have found and claimed a chunk of a promising mineral location. You form a syndicate of investors to exploit the resource but sell out just before the claim begins to yield riches that will make it the largest gold mine in the world. Oops!

This was exactly what the Morgan brothers of Rockhampton did in 1884. Their impatience cost them dearly and made the remaining investors in the syndicate obscenely wealthy.

After some years of prospecting and pegging various claims around Rockhampton, Frederick, Edwin and Thomas Morgan took out a claim on the unusually red-brown coloured bump known locally as Ironstone Mountain. They immodestly renamed it after themselves and Mount Morgan began its long history of fabulous production and vast wealth—for some. William Knox D'Arcy, a local solicitor and member of the syndicate, is said to have made a massive return on his initial investment, as did the other remaining members—200,000 per cent over ten years. Two of these lucky men would put their wealth to use in very different ways at opposite ends of the world.

William Knox D'Arcy was born in England and came to Australia as a young man. He qualified as a solicitor and did well in Rockhampton, mainly through property speculation. After the Morgan brothers left the syndicate, he remained as a principal shareholder of the Mount Morgan Gold Mining Company formed in 1886. By then, the mine was a proven bonanza. D'Arcy took his wealth and departed for England where he lived the extravagant life his money allowed. He purchased a substantial manor in Middlesex and a London townhouse. But as the nineteenth century ended, he embarked on an even bigger mining adventure that would have profound consequences for much of the world, some of which we are living with today.

Signs of oil had been discovered in what was then Persia (basically modern Iran and Iraq). D'Arcy was convinced to invest in an exploration venture that was troubled from the start. As well as the politics of the time and the greed of Persian officials and the monarch, the drilling operation refused to produce oil. Even D'Arcy could not sustain the enormous costs involved and was forced to mortgage his Mount Morgan shares to keep the project going. He did a deal with the Burmah Oil Company which gave him financial relief and a large parcel of company shares.

But still there was no oil. The company instructed their engineer on site, George B. Reynolds, to close down the drilling, sell whatever he could and return home. But Reynolds was reluctant to abandon all the hard work endured during the years he had struggled to bring the project to fruition. He kept his men working. Six days later their drill bit broke through into the largest oil reserve in the world. Black gold gushed into the sky, staining the desert sand and igniting a blaze of money, politics and religion that ultimately produced the current situation in the Middle East.

D'Arcy was saved from ruin, though. He was a director of a newly formed Anglo-Persian Oil Company until his death in 1917. The company changed its name several times after that, eventually becoming British Petroleum—BP—in 1954.

While the Mount Morgan magnate was living out his financial adventures in England and the Middle East, one of his old partners in the original syndicate would put his money to very different uses.

Walter Hall arrived in Australia as a young man with little money. He prospered, and his Mount Morgan investment and subsequent business activities produced another massive fortune. With his wife, Eliza, Hall practised an unflashy form of grassroots philanthropy, giving small but vital amounts to help people and families in need. Walter died in 1911 and the following year Eliza decided to establish a charitable trust of £1 million. The money was to be used to help those in need but also to fund Australia's first medical research facility for 'rendering signal service to mankind in the prevention and removal of disease and the mitigation of suffering'. The Walter and Eliza Hall Institute of Medical Research quickly developed into a leading provider of medical research, vital work it continues today.

Mount Morgan produced vast and valuable amounts of gold, silver and copper until its closure in 1981. Subsequent working of the tailings yielded yet more wealth up until 1990, and some activity continues today. But what mostly now remains is a large hole in the ground where Ironstone Mountain used to be and vast piles of shattered rock, together with an ongoing environmental remediation challenge. Who will pay for all this? That would be you and me.

Visions Splendid

Kingsley Fairbridge, Rhodes scholar and humanitarian, had a vision. It was a big one. Visiting England from his native Rhodesia (Zimbabwe) in the early twentieth century, Fairbridge was shocked at the number of destitute and parentless children wandering the streets. A man of steely determination, he decided to do something about it. His vision was of:

> Little children shedding the bondage of bitter circumstances and stretching their legs and minds amid the thousand interests of the farm. The aim was to provide children with a sense of self worth, and the training and skills necessary for their future in the sparsely populated rural areas of the British Empire.

In 1909 he gathered a group of his Oxford University chums together and proposed an ambitious scheme to rescue these boys and girls and to send them to farm schools around the world. There, they would be educated, trained in useful skills and, implicitly, boost local populations. His proposal was enthusiastically accepted and the well-connected scholars ensured that financial and logistical support of all kinds, private and government, was forthcoming. The scheme would eventually see Fairbridge Farm Schools established in Canada and, through an offshoot organisation, in Rhodesia (Zimbabwe). But they would begin in Australia.

Kingsley and his wife, Ruby, moved to Western Australia in 1912 and at Pinjarra, south of Perth, eventually established the first of the Fairbridge Farm Schools. Another was later established at Molong, New South Wales. Kingsley Fairbridge died in 1924, but his family and others carried on his vision.

Fairbridge, Ruby and their many supporters were genuinely concerned to help needy children. They were an important part of the child immigration movement that grew after penal transportation to Australia finally ceased in the 1860s. The children were not convicts, of course, but they were in the care of those with complete control of their lives while they remained in institutions like the Fairbridge farm schools, of which there were many. These places were operated by a variety of charitable organisations and religious groups, often sponsored by, or in partnership with, government, and all responding to a social problem with a similar philosophy of care, education and training.

A typical Fairbridge farm school experience saw children arrive in groups from British orphanages and other care facilities. They were met by Fairbridge representatives and taken to a farm school where they entered into the cottage system. The children lived in wooden houses under the supervision of a 'cottage mother' and a routine intended to replicate something of family life. Boys and girls lived in separate accommodation, though all the cottages were named after 'great men', mostly of British origin. The boys were expected to do most of the farm work, which was seen as preparing them for their intended employment in agriculture, and the girls did the domestic work, until they were old enough to enter the mainstream community.

A typical Fairbridge day began at 6 am with showers and chores. Older boys were usually up well before this, bringing in the milking cows at 3 am. Then it was breakfast followed by domestic duties for the girls and farm work for the boys. Church on Sunday was followed by a leisurely afternoon. Primary education was provided, followed by secondary classes at local high schools for the children deemed to have potential beyond farm work.

The goal was that children whose lives would otherwise have been blighted or completely lost would be given the chance of a new beginning through these schemes, and contribute to the development of the nation. After World War II, unaccompanied child immigration gradually declined as mass immigration programs to resettle displaced persons and others wanting to emigrate were fostered by the Australian and British governments. Australia began receiving large numbers of new arrivals, mostly in family groups and often with skills required for postwar reconstruction. Several investigations and reports in the 1950s were critical of the child immigrant institutions and the Fairbridge Society began to accept only accompanied children. Unaccompanied child immigration nevertheless continued through other groups until the 1980s, from which time the now well-known abuses in the system began to be revealed.

These included physical, emotional and sexual abuse of some children, as well as what would now be considered forced labour and inadequate diets for such heavy work. One of the homegrown ditties sung by children in England and Australia used the hymn tune known as 'The Happy Land', adding a refrain on the theme of malnutrition:

> There is a mouldy dump, down Fairbridge way,
> Where we get bread and jam, three times a day.
> Eggs and bacon we don't see, we get sawdust in our tea,
> That's why we're gradually fading away.
>
> Fade away, fade away. Fade away, fade away.
> That's why we're gradually fading away.

The Fairbridge Farm School at Molong closed in 1973 and the Pinjarra operation ceased in 1981. Today, there are remnants of a Fairbridge farm at Molong, though the only intact property is at Pinjarra which lives on as a youth education and training facility as well as the site of a popular folk festival. Its chequered history can be found in official inquiries and reports, public apologies by national governments and the childcare organisations involved and in the recollections of those who lived and worked there. These often make for confronting reading and listening, telling of mental, physical and sexual abuse, malnutrition and forced labour. The consequences of the revelations of the 'forgotten Australians' are still being worked through in the form of criminal charges, compensation and official apologies.

The Country Knows the Rest

> The year was 1929, the place was Rothbury town
> The miners were all locked out and our wage had been knocked down
> From March unto December we lived on bread and dole

'Til the Rothbury mine reopened with scabs to dig the coal
And the country knows the rest . . .

So begins a ballad of the tragic events in the Hunter Valley coalmining community. Things began badly and became much worse as the strike and lockout dragged on, fuelled by decades of bad relations between the miners and the mine owners.

Coal was hewn in the Hunter Valley from the early years of settlement. Convicts were the first miners, working in dangerous and brutal conditions, sometimes chained. Francis MacNamara, or 'Frank the Poet', worked as a convict shepherd in the area. He had seen the conditions in which the prisoners laboured and made it clear in a poem how reluctant he was to be a coalminer. The 'Company' is the Australian Agricultural Company, granted a million acres (400 hectares) of New South Wales which, in part, allowed them to mine Hunter River coal:

When Christ from Heaven comes down straightway,
All His Father's laws to expound,
MacNamara shall work that day
For the Company underground.

When the man in the moon to Moreton Bay,
Is sent in shackles bound
MacNamara shall work that day
For the Company underground.

When the Cape of Good Hope to Twofold Bay
Comes for the change of a pound.
MacNamara shall work that day
For the Company underground.

Great Australian Places

When cows in lieu of milk yield tea,
And all lost treasures are found,
MacNamara shall work that day
For the Company underground.

When the Australian Co's heaviest dray
Is drawn 80 miles by a hound,
MacNamara shall work that day
For the Company underground.

When a frog, a caterpillar and a flea
Shall travel the globe all round,
MacNamara shall work that day
For the Company underground.

When turkeycocks on Jews harps play
And mountains dance at the sound,
MacNamara shall work that day
For the Company underground.

When Christmas falls on the 1st of May
And O'Connell's King of England crown'd,
MacNamara shall work that day
For the Company underground.

When thieves ever robbing on the highway
For their sanctity are renowned,
MacNamara shall work that day
For the Company underground.

When the quick and the dead shall stand in array
Cited at the trumpet's sound,

Even then, damn me if I'd work a day
For the Company underground.

Nor overground.

As the industry grew, so did the communities that worked the mines. Many were immigrants from English, Welsh and Scots mining areas, bringing their skills and their families with them to settle in a new land. While conditions had improved since the convict days, the mines remained hard and dangerous places to earn a crust. Accidents were frequent, disasters not much less so. As in Britain, miners were proud, independent and mindful of their industrial rights and traditions. This frequently led to conflict with mine owners, and the pits were highly unionised.

The Rothbury Colliery, as it was officially called, was 28 kilometres from Maitland and 58 kilometres from Newcastle. It was on the original land granted to James Mitchell, which he named Rothbury Estate, and came into existence early in the twentieth century. It was a mine worked without machinery in the traditional way, with timber supports installed by miners as they cut their way through the black seams. There was a gas explosion at Rothbury Colliery in 1925, and it was considered a hard mine to work.

Early in 1929, colliery owners on the northern coalfields formed an alliance and issued their nearly 10,000 workers with what amounted to an industrial ultimatum. They were to accept a reduction of 12.5 per cent on the contract rates and a lesser day wage rate. They would hold no more pit-top meetings and work stoppages, and managers would be able to hire and fire miners with no consideration of their years of service. As well as cutting their income, the demands trashed traditional work practices with regard to assemblies and the order of promotion. The miners refused to accept the demands and were locked out of the mines by the owners.

In September 1929, the New South Wales Parliament passed legislation empowering the police to suppress gatherings, and in December allowed non-union workers to take over the working of the Rothbury mine. On 16 December, around seventy policemen protected a group of strike-breakers, or 'scabs', as they tried to reach the mine. Around 5000 miners, led by a pipe band, met them near the colliery. Some were armed with guns; most with clubs. There was fierce fighting and then shots were fired—by which side is still debated. Many of the miners were wounded and an unassuming young man who was apparently not involved in the violence was fatally wounded. The Maitland District Coroner carefully declared that 'Norman Laurence Brown . . . died from the effects of a gunshot wound accidentally received at Rothbury . . . during the course of a quelling of a riot by police officers.' Over 7000 miners and their families attended the funeral.

This was the bloodiest industrial confrontation since the 1890s and it shocked the country. Unfortunately, that had no effect on the situation in the Hunter. Supported by miners elsewhere in the country, the Hunter mining community held out as long as it could, but with no income and serious poverty affecting them and their families, they accepted the colliery owners' terms in June 1930, just as the Great Depression began to bring further misery to many workers.

The Rothbury mine was closed in 1974. There is a memorial to the events of 1929 and the death of Norman Brown at North Rothbury:

> At This Site
>
> During The Northern Coal Lockout
> March 1st 1929—June 3rd 1930,
> Miners And Police Clashed
> On Monday, December 16th 1929,
> Over The Use Of Non-Union
> (Scab) Labour
> At Rothbury Colliery.
>
> One Miner—Norman Brown—Was Killed
>
> An Unknown Number Of Miners And Police
> Were Wounded.
>
> This Monument Is Dedicated By The
> Northern District Miners Womens Auxiliary
> To Honour All Of Those Who Endured The Lockout
> And Who Were At Rothbury
> Monday, December 16th, 1929.

A Troubled Triangle

Abandoned buildings often have a strange allure. Houses, churches, factories and other structures that once bustled with human activity now lie empty, broken shells of the places they once were. You will find them in cities and country regions throughout the country, decaying sadly and often the victims of vandalism. Many have unhappy histories and frequently provide a haunt for ghosts and other unexplained events.

Goulburn, New South Wales, boasts three neglected old buildings, sometimes referred to as 'Australia's Bermuda Triangle', referencing the well-known area of unexplained disappearances in the Caribbean. While an exaggeration, there are certainly some powerful tales and supernatural traditions attached to the Goulburn sites.

St John's Orphanage (also known as the Goulburn Boys Orphanage), is a large two-storey brick building with a central balcony fronted with iron railings. Its architectural character was described as 'severely simple Gothic'. Construction began in 1912 and extensions were soon added as demand increased. By the time the building closed after sixty-six years, the Sisters of Mercy who ran it had cared for around 2500 young people, mainly boys but with an occasional family group also taken in. Some child immigrants were housed there, and girls were taken in during its last few years of operation. The building was used for religious training until 1994, when it was abandoned.

As the years and weather have done their work, St John's Orphanage has been vandalised, given heritage status, survived a number of redevelopment proposals and suffered damage from several fires. Some past residents have made claims of physical, mental and sexual abuse. With its troubled past, current deterioration and Gothic appearance, it is no surprise that the orphanage is said to be haunted and has been investigated by paranormal specialists. They reported unsettling voices and the sound of chimes heard deep within the old building when they visited one dark night. The ghost hunters also said they encountered several unhappy child presences.

The Sisters of Mercy ran another local charitable institution, St Joseph's Orphanage, which began in the 1860s in Clinton Street,

Goulburn and moved to the Kenmore area outside the city in 1905. Girls between five and sixteen years of age were cared for there until amalgamating with St John's in the 1970s. The 2000 or more estimated to have lived there during the institution's existence included local children in need, as well as child immigrants and children from the Stolen Generation. St Joseph's finally closed in 1987 and at the time of writing the imposing brick building was being renovated by its current owners.

Former residents remember a harsh life at St Joseph's, with early rising and a steady stream of menial tasks, like scrubbing the parquetry floors with a toothbrush. In later life, past residents came to feel that their experiences 'affected them emotionally, psychologically, and socially—being at the hands of those who they looked upon for guidance, compassion and understanding only to be punished and shown cruelty, wearing the ever-growing feelings of being judged, never belonging or ever fitting in'. Despite this, they also recall good times involving sport, the movies, visits to the beach and the circus and even 'the occasional Mr Whippy treat'.

The third abandoned building in Goulburn's ghostly triangle is Kenmore Insane Asylum. Another imposing example of institutional Gothic architecture, it opened in 1895 and continued, in one form or another into the early 2000s when it was sold into private hands. The site was placed on the New South Wales State Heritage Register in 2005.

While it operated as an asylum there were several suicides and murders, as well as natural deaths including from the Spanish flu in 1919. James Claxton, a widower in his late sixties, had been at Kenmore for around five years when he hanged himself from a tree in the grounds. He had been discharged for a few months the previous December but was back again in April 1917. He was described as 'a quite sociable, well-behaved man' who gave no sign that he intended suicide. But that day was the anniversary of his wife's death and, according to Dr Hogg, medical superintendent at the asylum, that 'might have caused a fit of depression'. He was survived by three daughters.

A few years later, in 1920, Alston Broome was tried for murdering his wife, an inmate at the asylum, by poisoning her with strychnine. His motive was related to his relationship with another woman. He was sentenced to death.

Incidents like these gave the Kenmore asylum a dark local reputation of the sort often associated with older mental health facilities. Not surprisingly, Kenmore is said to be haunted.

More earthly troubles are also part of Kenmore's story. In 2016, the site was purchased by a company with plans to redevelop the site for residential and tourism uses. Despite plans and promises there has been no further progress and the property, now known as Kenmore Gardens, is deteriorating rapidly through vandalism, neglect and a damaging fire in late 2021—'a dishonour to Goulburn's history', declared the local MP.

Unexplained Ipswich Phenomena

They are no longer called 'Unidentified Flying Objects'. UFOs are now officially known as 'Unexplained Aerial Phenomena' or 'UAP'. By whatever name we choose to call them, UFOs/UAP have been reported around the world since the 1940s. One of the earliest sightings in Australia was in the vicinity of Ipswich, Queensland. Since then, the area has become a bit of a hot zone for UFO sightings.

Unsettling Places

On 27 July 1948 a flash was seen in the sky, followed three to five minutes later by a loud explosion. Startled witnesses spoke of a 'fireball', 'lightning' and even a 'flying saucer'.

At Redbank it was reported to have passed 8ft. [2 m] over two children, and to have gone under electric and telephone wires. It shook houses and rattled windows throughout Ipswich and was seen by hundreds who were dazzled by the brilliant glare for a few seconds. Two explosions, the rumble of thunder, and a trail of smoke are reported to have followed the phenomenon.

Mrs Ward and her children saw the object as it 'zig-zagged like lightning' through the backyard of the Commercial Hotel at Redbank, flew beneath the telephone wires and made off rapidly into the sky northwards. It left a rubbery smell behind on the kids' clothes. The milkman's horse reared, the ground shook and the blinding light from the object, visible for a good ten minutes, 'was like a large star with a trail about a mile long, brightly coloured like a rainbow', said Mr R. Rea of Junction Road, Lower Tivoli.

Locals rang the press and the university. The scientists said it was a meteor and asked for help in locating fragments. Twenty-two-year-old Mr D. Bevan of East Ipswich, a perhaps overenthusiastic member of the Interplanetary Rocket Society of America (all the rage in those years), thought it was an interplanetary reconnaissance saucer. He did make a good argument against the possibility of it being a meteorite though, pointing out that '. . . if the object came to within a few feet of the ground then rose into the sky again it definitely could not have been a meteorite'. A meteorite, he said, would have come to earth and would not have risen again. He theorised imaginatively that the burned rubber smell clinging to Mrs Ward's kids' clothes could be 'the gamma ray of an atomic blast would have had that effect'.

A couple of years later, in December 1950, residents of Maryborough also saw one:

> About 8 o'clock a bright blue object was seen travelling at a great speed to the north and returned at a low level. Approaching River Heads direction the phenomenon moved almost perpendicularly to an estimated 8000ft. Maryborough R.S.L. Sub-branch President (Mr. S. Bryant-Smith) said he estimated its speed at 400–500 m.p.h. [650–800 km/h]

And there have been other sightings in recent years in Ipswich, elsewhere in Queensland and at the remote Wycliffe Well in the Northern Territory, another place where many UAP have been reported since the 1940s.

After decades of denying their existence and ignoring the many sightings around the world, the Pentagon released a 'preliminary assessment' allowing the possibility that strange objects might fly through the air. Examining reports made by military pilots between 2004 and 2021, the Director of National Intelligence found that:

> Most of the UAP reported probably do represent physical objects given that a majority of UAP were registered across multiple sensors, to include radar, infrared, electro-optical, weapon seekers, and visual observation. In a limited number of incidents, UAP reportedly appeared to exhibit unusual

flight characteristics. These observations could be the result of sensor errors, spoofing, or observer misperception and require additional rigorous analysis.

The history of UFOs is intriguing. People have been seeing odd things in the sky since ancient times, including sailing ships, shapes, optical effects, angels and spectral packs of hellhounds, among others. But massive popular interest in UFOs began in the 1940s and lasted until the late 1990s, coinciding with the Cold War. This fitted well with the prevalent explanation that UFOs were a kind of mass hysteria generated by anxiety about the likely nuclear extinction of humanity. As these fears faded—mostly—the media became less fascinated with the subject and, it seems, so did the public. From the 1990s, relatively few sightings had been reported and flying saucers and aliens were on their way to a place in the well-stuffed dustbin of faded fads and delusions.

Until 2017.

That year, secret UFO research being carried out by the American military was publicised. Revelations that the US government was, as many had suspected, taking flying saucer yarns seriously kicked off the UFO craze once again. The government has admitted that it has secret UFO investigations, as well as clandestine weapons projects that might be one cause of the many reported sightings. As well as the release of its preliminary report, in which it appears to accept the existence of Unexplained Aerial Phenomena, some scientists are reportedly willing to accept the possibility of other lifeforms out there, somewhere.

Whatever the truth about UAPs, aliens and extra-terrestrial intelligence, our own Ipswich UFO hot zone will have an honoured place in the annals of one of the world's most intriguing beliefs. And it seems that we may be in for another bout of UFO/UAP spotting.

Recent developments in space technology have allowed large numbers of small satellites to be launched into orbit around the earth at the same time. As these are deployed, they appear in the night sky as a long, straight line of glowing points, like a gigantic spacecraft. At least, that's how they have been described by those who have been startled by them. A resident of Northern Beaches near Mackay, Queensland, expressed his amazement at sighting a lighted chain of mini satellites to an ABC reporter in November 2021: 'It definitely wasn't a plane. It wasn't a satellite. I don't do drugs or anything like that. What the hell is it?'

A professor of astrophysics provided the answer, also noting the mostly unregulated proliferation of space junk above the planet. It seems that people will be seeing strange things in the night sky for a very long time to come.

'Populate or Perish!'

'Populate or Perish!' That was the slogan of Australia's post-World War II immigration program. Centres, also known as 'camps' or 'hostels', were set up around the country to house the hundreds of thousands of 'new Australians' brought here from an austere United Kingdom and a shattered Europe.

Established in 1947 at an army base near Wodonga on the border of Victoria and New South Wales, the Bonegilla Migrant

Reception and Training Centre was to become the largest centre, and one of the most troubled. It was built and run very much like a military camp, with over 800 rudimentary huts, each with associated facilities. Catering, supplies and the general routine of the camp were military in the first few years and although the accommodation and regime slowly improved, Bonegilla always retained something of its military origins right up until its eventual closure.

The original mass immigration plan assumed that large numbers of British people would migrate to Australia. But over the first few years of the schemes, far fewer arrived than anticipated. The government was then forced to look to continental Europe to satisfy the labour and population needs of the postwar economy. Since the colonial era of convict transportation and the influx of Chinese and other nationalities during the goldrushes, the arrival of large numbers of 'others' has been a difficult issue in Australia, as it remains today with much smaller numbers of asylum seekers. As well as a variety of racial and ethnic prejudices, there has always been a concern that large numbers of newcomers would undercut wages.

These concerns played into attitudes towards postwar immigrants from the Baltic states, Italy, Greece and elsewhere in Europe. Derogatory terms developed to describe the new Australians, such as 'Balts' for those from Baltic countries like Latvia and Estonia, 'reffos', from 'refugees' and 'DPs' for 'Displaced Persons', the official term used by the International Refugee Organisation for the millions made homeless and often stateless by the war.

Wherever they originated, those who came to Australia shared many of the same experiences. They began with official processing and paperwork at their point of embarkation, followed by a month or more aboard crowded ships. The men, women and children were finally disembarked at various Australian ports, were processed again and eventually sent to one of the camps, where there was yet more processing. Sadly, due to the inadequate facilities at many of these places, families were often separated, a point of great frustration.

Other issues included the arrangements for integrating immigrants into Australian society. Generally, they were expected to undertake directed work for two years. This often meant being sent to rural and regional locations, with further family traumas. Even though many immigrants had advanced trade and professional qualifications, these were usually ignored, with men being classed as 'labourers' and women as 'domestics'. Some became staff members at the camp, enjoying better accommodation and, if not able to speak the language, being required to learn English.

While many ex-residents and workers remember their Bonegilla time as positive and helpful in starting their new lives, there were some serious incidents at the camp. Thirteen children died of malnutrition in 1949. Blame was cast in many directions—poor conditions in European refugee camps and on the ships, and the quality and amount of food available at Bonegilla. Some tried to blame the parents, and medical care at the hospital was criticised. The final report found that the food at the centre was adequate and fresh but that there were hygiene problems with the huts, kitchens and the latrines, which were simply 'long drops'.

In 1952 Italian immigrants burned buildings and protested at not being able to get work, as well as the quality of the food and basic facilities. Their actions brought improvement but in 1961, Italian and German arrivals again protested about the same problems, forcing an embarrassed government to rethink immigration policies. Ten years later, Bonegilla was quietly closed and the army returned.

Today, around twenty-four of the 834 huts that once made up the centre remain. Block 19 is a recognised national heritage site and operates as an interpretation and memory centre for the many who visit the place each year, including many ex-residents who often remember their difficulties with tempered affection. A German woman recalled: 'There was always plenty to eat, but every now and then it got boring. You only had to look at your plate to know what day of the week it was.'

Others found that Bonegilla was a rite of passage from their old lives to a new Australian identity: 'I was a Bonegillian before I understood I was Australian,' said a woman who came to Bonegilla as a child.

Estimates vary, but around 300,000 people went through the centre and it is said that more than 1.5 million Australians have family connections to Bonegilla immigrants and their bittersweet transition to new lives in a new country.

The Spirit Stones

They were later dubbed 'spirit stones' but nobody really knew what they were. The rocks fell from the sky or materialised at various times and places over a period of sixteen years. Nobody could explain them then; nobody can explain them now.

In 1955 people on the Hack family's farm at Mayanup (also known as Keninup), Western Australia, reported stones falling from the sky—or being thrown by an unseen hand. There was no natural explanation for these peculiar events and so the supernatural was invoked to solve the mystery.

One of the Aboriginal workers on the farm had become gravely ill and a local spirit catcher, Freddie Winma, was called in to save his life. Local belief was that when the sick man had first collapsed some weeks before, his spirit had departed. It needed to be caught and returned to his body, or he would die. The falling stones were a result of the life force—'a very wild spirit and hard to catch', said Freddie, after trapping the spirit beneath a blanket and carrying it back to the sick man's bed. Once returned to the body, the stones would stop falling.

With 'the light of a full moon shining down on the gathering', around 150 people assembled to witness this ceremony. The spirit was restored to the man and the next day he felt better. A few more stones fell, then ceased. But a few days later, they began to rain down again.

Freddie Winma stoutly defended his actions and beliefs. Regardless of the stones returning, 'In my own funny way I know I have helped the old man; I don't care what people say', he declared, and offered £5 to anyone who could prove the stones were cast by human hands. The stones continued falling for several years, but Freddie kept his money.

More strange events began at nearby Pumphrey's Bridge in 1957. A group of First Nations people fencing for a local farmer were camping on the property when they were pelted by stones of various sizes, one said to weigh 19 kilograms. Some of the mysterious missiles were seemingly thrown, some seemed to fall from above and some simply appeared with no apparent source. Some were warm to the touch. Disturbed, the workers reported the incidents to their employer, who'd also witnessed the materialisations, as did a number of other folk in the area. The stones kept falling and the workers asked to be relocated.

In the meantime, their vacated campsite was visited by curious locals who also witnessed the falling stones. The press and police soon arrived, observing, interviewing and reporting. Journalists and policemen confirmed that the stones were real, common to the area, and that they had not been thrown or propelled by any human or mechanical means. They were not meteorites, either.

So, what was going on in this otherwise unremarkable part of south-western Australia? It seems that the area had been the focus of unexplained phenomena over many years. Stones or sandalwood nuts reportedly fell from the sky in several other locations, while oral tradition told of similar events at Boddington in 1946 and at Borden in 1962. Various theories were suggested.

The local First Nations tradition explained the falling stones are involving the presence of evil spirits, known as the Jannick, or the malign influence of the Widgecarra. These small male creatures are invisible, though they can be heard. If a grave is disturbed, even inadvertently, they can attack anyone in the vicinity.

Others blamed the incidents on ghosts or poltergeists. Although some of the reported events did occur around adolescents, there seemed to be little suggestion of the usual psychic or tragic events that are said to produce such apparitions and disturbances. Many thought it was all a hoax and went to considerable lengths to catch the culprits, including nocturnal shotgun parties. None was successful.

Scientists have also been unable to offer rational explanations for the falling stones which, to the present at least, do not seem to have returned. The events in the south-west between 1946 and 1962 remain in the large category of unexplained phenomena, ranked by ghost hunters as the best-evidenced instance of poltergeist activity in Australia.

Mysteries within Mysteries

Strange happenings have been reported on northern Sydney's Wakehurst Parkway for decades. They are mysterious enough, but there is an even bigger puzzle about these hauntings that continues to perplex.

Late-night drivers on the bushy Parkway have reported seeing a woman dressed in what is often described as a nun's habit or sometimes a wedding dress. As they stop or swerve to avoid her, 'Kelly', as the shade is known, simply vanishes. Who was she and why does she play chicken with cars on the Parkway? Unusually for spectres of this kind, there seems to be no tale of tragedy or violent death surrounding the ghost.

Research by local filmmaker Bianca Biasi has come up with a possible explanation. The Parkway is one of the most direct routes to Manly's old Quarantine Station, which sits on a promontory about 7 kilometres from the where the Parkway ends in Seaforth and which is also said to be haunted by the spirits of those who died there during the station's long history, including the Spanish influenza outbreak at the end of World War I. The nun's habit—also sometimes described as a 'wedding dress'—is very similar to the uniforms worn by nurses at the Quarantine Station. Photographs of the nurses certainly match the descriptions given by motorists unlucky enough to have encountered Kelly.

As if this wasn't enough to get the shivers going, there is also another ghost, or possibly another manifestation of the same one, along the Parkway. Drivers have reported an ethereal figure, much like Kelly, suddenly appearing in their back seat. At a certain spot on the road, the figure disappears. Others say they have picked up a blood-covered woman and driven her to hospital, only to have her disappear as soon as they arrive.

Again, there does not seem to be the usual narrative of accidental death or cold-blooded murder. 'White Woman' or 'White Lady' traditions of this kind are known around the world and have been reported over many centuries. They tend to be experienced in rural or lonely areas and have supporting tales of tragedy such as murder or suicide, all localised to their particular areas, which are frequently trails, tracks or roads of some kind.

The disappearing hitchhiker or road accident victim is also an old and widespread yarn. Its modern form is an urban legend in which a male motorist picks up a young woman on a lonely road one night. She asks to be taken to a local address. When they arrive, the gallant driver gets out of the car and knocks on the door of the house. An elderly woman answers and the man tells her that he has picked up the passenger in his car at a certain spot along the road and she has asked him to bring her here. The elderly woman's face collapses in shock and she stammers out that her daughter was killed at that exact spot on this very night twenty years before.

Why do people report these unexplained and unexplainable experiences without a narrative rationale?

It is possible that the apparitions are connected with the history and character of the road. It was built by unemployed workers, beginning at the end of the Great Depression of the 1930s and completed after interruption by World War II. Although there seem to be no tales of hauntings by workers who died on the job, the road itself is isolated, dark at night and notorious for accidents.

The area is also associated with a number of violent crimes, in particular the kidnap and murder of young Graeme Thorne in 1960. The boy's clothing was found along the road and, eventually, his body was discovered at Seaforth. There have also been stories of people smelling blood at the isolated Deep Creek and it's often said that there is something unsettling about the route, even though no one seems able to put a finger on what that might be.

Toxic Town

The headlines are alarming. 'Australia's Chernobyl'; 'Largest contaminated site in the Southern Hemisphere'. Even the town's name has an ominous ring: Wittenoom.

The trouble began billions of years ago beneath the Kimberley country of north-western Australia when geological processes began forming a mineral that would come to be called 'crocidolite', more commonly known as blue asbestos.

The asbestos deposits were first identified in 1908 but it was not until the 1930s that mining at what was by then known as Wittenoom Gorge began. Colonial Sugar Refineries became the owner and operator of the lease and expanded mining. A town known as Wittenoom was built near the entrance to the gorge from the late 1940s. It grew to include an open-air cinema, stores, a pub, bank, schools and churches as miners moved there with their families.

This was the era of the 'fibro frontier'. The postwar baby boom and immigration, combined with a new-found affluence, created a generation of residential owner-builders around the country. They usually began with a block of land in one of the many suburbs being developed around major cities. If funds were tight, they often built a habitable garage for the family and worked on their homes at weekends and holidays, often with the help of friends and neighbours. The cheapest and fastest material to use for these structures was 'fibro', a solid sheet containing large amounts of asbestos. Although said to be quite safe in this form, as soon as it was cut, sawn or sanded, fibro gave off potentially deadly fibres of asbestos.

As well as these residential time bombs, many commercial and industrial buildings also used the widely available fibro, as did schools, hospitals and other structures. As a result, Australia has the highest rate of asbestosis, the often-fatal lung condition, in the world.

Wittenoom was ground zero for the extraction of the mineral. Despite the known dangers, few precautions were taken by workers in the mining, handling and transportation of the raw material bound to be turned into fibro and, even more deadly, insulation. Children in Wittenoom played on the tailings dumps of raw asbestos, trucks spread it along roads as they transported it, not only in their tyre treads but through bags of raw asbestos falling on to the road, splitting and spreading their contents across wide areas, blown by the wind. Much more has been washed through the gorge and beyond by rain and flowing water.

As well as its use as a sheet construction product, asbestos was widely used to insulate buildings and as 'lagging' around pipes in industrial and maritime works. In this wool-like form, the fibres are far more dangerous. Plumbers, waterfront workers and others who came into contact with this material in the course of their work have a high rate of contracting mesothelioma or other lung diseases. Overall, at least 2000 people have been killed by Wittenoom, according to the Asbestos Diseases Society of Australia. People are still dying. It is likely that these statistics are underestimates as many of the conditions caused by exposure to asbestos can take decades to appear.

As the frightening health potential of asbestos mining at Wittenoom became apparent in the late 1970s, activities were phased down and residents were encouraged to leave. The town was 'deproclaimed' in 2007, utilities were disconnected and the town was removed from maps. Only a few residents remained by 2019, and in 2021 the Western Australian government finally legislated to clear the town and remove the remaining residents. They were reluctant to leave what is beautiful country, attracting hundreds of curious tourists each year, despite large warning signs and an official ban on visitors.

It is also the traditional country of the Banjima people who want the 50,000-hectare site remediated. They and other First Nations peoples were among the mine workers, and many have died as a result. As well as posing an ongoing health risk, the site cannot be accessed for traditional activities.

The outlook for the area is not bright. It is estimated that there are approximately three million cubic metres of tailings scattered through Wittenoom Gorge. Responding to the comments of traditional owners and residents, Tony Buti, the Minister for Lands in Western Australia, said in 2021: 'There is no question that this area is one of the saddest chapters in WA history . . . However, we must be realistic, and the fact is it's unlikely Wittenoom will ever again be a safe place to live or visit.'

A group of hikers around a campfire in the Victorian high country in about 1937.

5
WILD PLACES

Ghost Gum Dreaming

Eucalyptus trees are synonymous with Australia and its unique environment. They even have their own National Day on 23 March. Known generally as 'gum trees', these distinctive Australian natives are among the world's greatest arboreal survivors. Able to grow on minimal rainfall, they are found across the continent and have been here for millions of years. Over the last 60,000 years or so they have provided for the environment, as well as many of the needs of the First Australians and of settlers.

Said to be the tallest flowering plant on the planet, they can grow to almost 100 metres, as with the *Eucalyptus regnans*, found in Victoria and Tasmania. Hardy survivors of this arid continent, eucalypts can thrive after bushfires and are highly efficient recyclers of the greenhouse gas carbon dioxide.

Gum trees, in all their great variety, provided the land's tradition custodians with medicinal treatment for a wide range of inflammatory diseases. The Dharawal people of the Illawarra and Sydney regions used the trees 'for the treatment of inflammatory conditions, for example, asthma, arthritis, rheumatism, fever, oedema, eye inflammation, and inflammation of bladder and related inflammatory diseases'. Eucalyptus preparations were also useful as a leech repellent and for the relief of burns. The wood of the trees provided tools such as digging sticks, spears and boomerangs, as well as eating bowls; fibres for cordage and weaving, as well as firewood.

At first, European settlers only used eucalyptus leaves for brewing peppermint-flavoured tea. Later, they learned to use eucalyptus oil for antiseptics and as cures for colds, cramps, chest pain, toothache and diarrhoea. Eucalyptus was also found to be useful for household cleaning and as an infusion for clearing blocked noses.

It was not until 1853 that Yorkshire emigrant pharmacist Joseph Bosisto started brewing his famous distilled eucalyptus oils. He asserted that the eucalypt was a 'Fever Destroying Tree' and advertised a 'Syrup of Red Gum' that delivered the user a 'delicate mucilaginous astringency [that] renders it effectual in all affections of the mucous membrane of the Stomach and Bowels, inducing a feeling of repose and tranquillity'. The logo of a parrot on a yellow label became known in households across the country and in many parts of the world, and Dr Bosisto's Eucalyptus Oil and related products can still be purchased today. Sadly, Bosisto sems to have been better at chemistry than business. He lost control of his thriving company and ended his life in difficult circumstances in Richmond, Victoria, in 1898.

As well as their practical value, eucalyptus trees have spiritual significance for many First Nations peoples. In some traditions, the trees are associated with creation stories involving the Southern Cross constellation and the Milky Way. The Arrernte (Aranda) people of Central Australia regard ghost gums as ancestral beings, featuring in traditional stories and lore. Arrernte artist, Albert (Elea) Namatjira (1902–1959) painted many eucalypts in his work, the best-known being a pair of ghost gums just outside Alice Springs. In 2013, the trees were, it is thought, deliberately burned down by persons unknown.

The tallest ghost gum recorded in Australia grows in Trephina Gorge, about 85 kilometres east of Alice Springs in the Northern Territory. The National Register of Big Trees includes many other imposing monarchs of the eucalyptus genus. The Register is always looking for more nominations and it may be that there is a ghost gum taller than the Trephina Gorge tree near your place?

The Great Divide

It's said that around three-quarters of the Australian population lives within it or either side of it. The precise official prose of the *Year Book Australia* for 1910 indicates the extent of the Great Dividing Range:

> The chief mountain system of Australia runs parallel with the eastern and southern coasts of the continent. The main Dividing Range, which forms its central chain, can be traced

from New Guinea across Torres Straits to Cape York, and thence southward through the States of Queensland, New South Wales, and Victoria to Wilson's Promontory. From that point it is continued by the islands of the Flinders group to Tasmania, while a second spur traverses Victoria in a westerly direction.

The Range is among the world's largest mountain ranges and the most extensive in Australia, running for over 3500 kilometres. Formed around 300 million years ago, it is a labyrinthine interconnection of smaller ranges, each with their own characteristics and names and with climatic regions varying from the alpine environment of the Snowy Mountains to tropical rainforest at Cape York.

Nowadays, we tend to take the natural beauty of the Great Divide for granted, even though it is a vital source of drinking water and location of a myriad of productive activities, from agriculture to tourism. But the mountain chain has been an important element in the development of the east coast and is a rich source of history and legend.

Early colonists spread north and south along the coast, but the mountains were seemingly impenetrable. Many attempts were made to find a way through their forests, peaks and gullies but few were known to have succeeded. Convicts tried to escape across the ranges, usually dying or returning half-starved to their punishment. One or two probably succeeded with the help of the traditional owners, the Gundungurra, Dharawal, Wiradjuri, Wanaruah, Dharug and Darkinjung peoples, who had been crossing the ranges for thousands of years. But it seems that they were rarely consulted. When the much-lauded Blaxland,

Wentworth and Lawson expedition of 1813 finally found a way across the ridges to the plains beyond, they benefited from the help of at least one local guide.

The explorers were often taken aback by the savage splendour of the country they traversed. Wentworth wrote in his journal that they saw country that:

> could in my opinion only have been produced by some Mighty convulsion in Nature—Those immense unconnected perpendicular Masses of Mountain which are to be seen towards its Eastern Extremity towering above the Country around, seem to indicate that the whole of this tract has been formed out of the Materials of the primitive mountains of which these masses are the only parts that have withstood the violence of the concussion

Blaxland similarly noted that: 'The broken rocky country on the western side of the cow pasture has the appearance of having acquired its present form from an earthquake, or some other dreadful convulsion of nature.'

In addition to the unsettling character of the country, the exploration party was shadowed by the traditional owners. They did not attack, but the explorers were continually afraid that they might. The track that the expedition blazed over the ridges was quickly followed up by surveyors, road-builders and settlers hungry for the grazing and agricultural lands of the Western Plains. They were resisted by the Wiradjuri in what is known as 'the Bathurst War', culminating in a military campaign in which at least six and possibly as many as 100 members of that group were killed in 1824.

Other sections of the Great Divide were traversed as the colonial population increased and spread, mostly with unacknowledged assistance from First Nations peoples. In 1824, Hamilton Hume and William Hovell journeyed to present-day Geelong, crossing the Murray, Murrumbidgee and several other rivers. Allan Cunningham found the passage known as 'Cunningham's Gap' in 1828, opening the Darling Downs to settlement. Major Thomas Mitchell explored into what is now Victoria during the 1830s, setting off a land rush when he reported that he'd found rich grazing lands.

These explorations 'opened up' the country. Various roads and railways would gradually cross over and through sections of the range, but there is no single overall route or connection and some areas are still isolated even today. The tiny settlement of Woodenbong is one of these. Home to the Githabul group of the Bundjalung people, Cunningham and other explorers first reached the area in the late 1820s. Pastoral settlement was underway in the 1840s and Woodenbong was declared a village in 1908. The area has become famous for an unusual reason.

The first ape-like creature we now know as a 'Yowie' was first reported by settlers in the 1890s. It is said that the Bundjalung people held stories of the Yowie among their ancestral traditions but it seems that the next reported sighting of the creature was not until 1928 at Palen Creek in Queensland's Border Ranges. The being was said to be over 2 metres high with a human-like face and a body covered in thick brown hair. It had large feet and moved very quickly.

Several sightings were reported in the 1970s. In one of these a pet dog was mauled by an unmistakably male Yowie and later died. A large footprint found near the scene was cast in plaster and sent for scientific analysis. The results were inconclusive. There were several sightings in the early 2000s and timber workers have also reported Yowies, all more or less fitting the general description of tall men covered with hair and fleeing quickly from human contact. With the exception of the unfortunate dog, Yowies in this part of the Great Divide seem to be shy rather than aggressive. This accords with most of the many encounters with similar beings reported throughout the range since early colonisation.

Even though a large number of people live on and around the Great Dividing Range and its ridges and gullies have been breached by explorers' trails, stock routes, roads and railways, its vast wilderness still has the power to confound us—and perhaps hide mysteries yet to be revealed.

'A Small, Woody Island'

History records the remarkable English mariner William Dampier as a pirate, hydrographer, explorer and author of the famous book *A New Voyage Around the World*. Dampier's life was one of contradictions, successes and failures, all tied loosely together by his seemingly insatiable curiosity. His need to know and understand the places and people he encountered on his epic voyages drove him to observe and record information that is still relevant 300 years later. How he came to be on an uninhabited island at the far end of the earth in 1688 and writing in his journal about red crabs is a typically convoluted Dampier yarn.

Born in 1651, Dampier went to sea as a young man, firstly in the merchant fleet and then in the Royal Navy. From 1686 he was with a group of privateers—authorised pirates—aboard the *Cygnet*. The ship voyaged through the Pacific from the Central American coast. In the Philippines the crew mutinied and took over the vessel with Dampier as navigator. Whether Dampier was a willing participant in the mutiny and piracy of the *Cygnet* is, like many things about the man, not very clear. They sailed to China and into what is now Indonesia and then to the west coast of Australia. After spending some months in or near what is now known as King Sound, making some of the first scientific and anthropological observations of the Australian environment and its people, the *Cygnet* sailed for the Cocos Islands.

Soon beset by heavy weather, the winds did not favour the *Cygnet's* planned course and the ship was blown further east than they intended. At the end of March, they came in sight of 'a small woody island', as Dampier described it in his *A New Voyage*. He does not name the island, but it had been called Christmas Island since 1643, when a British East India Company vessel had sighted it on that day. *Cygnet* found no anchorage but sent two boats, or 'canoas', as Dampier called them, to find fresh water and cut timber for a new pump. The sailors also returned with 'as many Boobies, and Men of War Birds as sufficed all the Ships Company, when they were boiled'.

While there, Dampier observed the island's famous robber crabs:

> . . . a sort of Land-Animal, somewhat resembling a large Craw-fish , without its great Claws. These Creatures lived in holes in the dry sandy Ground, like Rabbits. Sir Francis Drake in his Voyage round the World makes mention of such that he found at Ternate, or some other of the Spice

Islands, or near them. They were very good sweat [sic] Meat, and so large that two of them were more than a Man could eat; being almost as thick as ones Leg. Their Shells were of a dark brown; but red when boiled.

Dampier also noted the island's cliffs, heights and fertile soils then, waiting no longer, sailed away 'about one-o-clock in the afternoon'.

Around 1500 kilometres from the Australian mainland, Christmas Island was first sighted in 1615, but sailors from the *Cygnet* were the first people known to have walked upon it. The island was visited mainly by explorers seeking information about its plants and animal species. One of these expeditions discovered the island was rich in phosphates in 1887 and the island was swiftly annexed by the British in 1888. The deposits were worked by indentured Chinese, Malay and Sikh workers who laboured in poor conditions. During World War II the phosphate deposits attracted the Japanese, who occupied it and relocated a large percentage of the population to Java. After the war the island passed through several administrative arrangements until 1958, when it became an Australian territory.

Since 2001, Christmas Island has housed asylum seekers and been the location of a number of related debacles, including the *Tampa* incident of 2001 and the loss of a boat and the majority of the asylum seekers aboard in 2010. Controversies concerning asylum seekers have continued to the present, particularly in relation to the 'Biloela family', the family of Tamil asylum seekers who had settled in Biloela, Queensland, and were detained there for nearly two years. The island was also used briefly for quarantine purposes during the COVID-19 pandemic.

For a 'small, woody island', this place had already experienced a tumultuous history when it also became connected with the solution to one of the nation's saddest wartime mysteries.

HMAS *Sydney* (II) was sunk with all hands off the Western Australian coast in 1941. Before the eventual discovery of the wreckage in 2008, the only physical evidence of the event were the remains of a sailor washed up at Christmas Island on one of the ship's life rafts. Locals buried him and the grave was forgotten until 1950 when it was photographed by navy veteran Brian O'Shannassy. Brian gave the picture to researcher Glenys McDonald, whose work eventually involved the Royal Australian Navy and led to the rediscovery of the grave and reburial of the remains in the Commonwealth War Graves cemetery at Geraldton in 2008. But the identity of the 'Unknown Sailor' remained a mystery.

Following DNA testing of well over 100 descendants of *Sydney* crew members, the 'Unknown Sailor' was at last made known late in 2021. He was Able Seaman Thomas Welsby Clark. Thomas was twenty-one years old when the German raider *Kormoran* destroyed the *Sydney* and was the only known survivor of the brief battle. The ABC reported that his niece Leigh Lehane had contact with her uncle shortly before he joined the *Sydney*. 'He came and held me as a little baby, so that's a very pleasurable thought,' she said. 'I don't think anyone else is alive now who knew Tom.' Other descendants of those lost from the *Sydney* also expressed their happiness.

Able Seaman Tom Clark, castaway and buried on Christmas Island, then exhumed and reburied on the mainland with full honours, now represents all the sailors lost with the *Sydney*.

Dark Emu in the Stars

One of the quietest places on earth is the Murchison region of Western Australia. Near Boolardy Station is the Murchison Radio-astronomy Observatory (MRO), ground base for what will be the largest and most powerful space telescope on the planet, the Square Kilometre Array (SKA). This remote but scientifically important base is located on the lands of the Wajarri people and is a unique collaboration between the traditional owners and international astronomers.

Established in 2009 by the Commonwealth Scientific and Industrial Research Organisation (CSIRO), the MRO is part of an international collaboration with another base in South Africa and the project headquarters at England's Jodrell Bank Observatory. The MRO will be a vital part of the powerful radio transmitters that will make up the SKA, a device that will be fifty times more sensitive than previous equipment, allowing scientists to survey the stars more than 10,000 times faster than previously possible. Among the many complex scientific projects and problems to be addressed by the SKA will be the perennial quest for extraterrestrial life.

To function effectively, this expensive and impressive array of technology needs radio silence, or as close to that as possible. The remote location of the MRO provides this. In order to proceed, the astronomers required the agreement of the Wajarri traditional owners, a process of negotiation that has provided powerful insights into the significance of the stars, planets and galaxies that are the target of the SKA.

First Nations sky patterns do not depend on joining the dots of stars to form a figure, as in European tradition. Instead, shapes and patterns are perceived in the dark clouds visible between stars. The widespread emu pattern in First Nations interpretations of a section of the Milky Way is an example of this and one with great significance across the continent. Stretched between the Southern Cross and Scorpius (Scorpio) is a distinctive dark cloud shaped like an emu, with a long neck, oval body and long, thin legs trailing behind.

To the First Australians, the emu was an important source of food and feathers for clothing, as well as providing medicine in the form of fat or oil and tools and weapons from the bone. These important practical functions underlie the cultural meaning of the emu which, in some traditions, features in creation stories and may be important in kin systems governing marriage. The Dark Emu in the night sky is closely connected with the availability of water at different times of the year and so possibly with some aspects of male initiation customs. Depending on the position of the Emu in the night sky, First Peoples are able to tell when it is the right season to collect emu eggs or to hunt for the birds themselves.

The collaboration between the oldest way of seeing the stars and the newest has fuelled a creative burst of cross-cultural storytelling and art. The Ilgarigiri—Things That Belong to the Sky exhibition was established in the 2009 International Year of Astronomy as a partnership between Indigenous artists and astrophysicists. One of the coins released by the Royal Australian Mint in 2020 featured the bird in its Wiradjuri (New South Wales) version at the time of year when the image is spread across the sky with other images that tell the story of the Dark Emu.

The SKA is scheduled to begin operating from 2029.

The Burning Mountain

Mount Wingen, near Scone in New South Wales, has been burning for five or six millennia, maybe many thousands of years longer. Acrid fumes rise from fissures in the yellow, red and white ground, seared of all vegetation and collapsing under the 1000-plus-degree Celsius heat 20–30 metres below. The fire is not volcanic but is burning its way southwards through a seam of coal at a rate of about 1 kilometre a year.

There are several traditions about the origins of the burning mountain. The traditional custodians, the Wonnarua people of the hills and plains, as they describe themselves, tell of a battle with a party of raiders from the north who were seeking wives. The warriors went to fight them, and all returned but one. His wife sat on top of a cliff above the valley, waiting and worrying. She waited a very long time but eventually had to accept that her husband must have died in battle. Distraught and no longer wishing to live, she asked the sky god, Baayami (Biami), to end her misery. Baayami was unable to kill the woman and instead turned her into a stone. As she transformed from her human to her stone form, the woman wept tears of fire that rolled down the cliff, setting the mountain alight. A local mountain cliff with a rock formation suggesting a woman leaning back into the cliff and gazing forever down the valley is identified as the spot where the woman was fossilised.

Another tradition tells of a man setting a fire on the mountain when he was captured by an evil being and taken deep beneath the ground. Knowing his fate was sealed, the man used his firestick to ignite the mountain so that the resulting smoke would be a warning to others to stay away from the evil place.

Scientific explanations for the phenomenon are more prosaic. The first explorers and settlers to encounter the mountain assumed that it was a volcano. But in 1829 a geologist noted that the area consisted mainly of sandstone and other non-volcanic rock with no evidence of volcanic lava or other activity. The fire may have been ignited by a lightning strike or, less likely, by firestick burning or by something else: we don't know. But it is known that Wingen was part of an extensive system of traditional pathways and trade routes and was also a boundary marker between the territories of the various First Nations groups inhabiting the Hunter Valley and surrounding areas.

The mountain became a popular picnicking place in the late nineteenth century and is still a featured walk in the Burning Mountain Nature Reserve. As well as the natural beauty and history of the area, Wingen is the world's longest burning coal-seam fire and the only naturally burning example in Australia. Truly a unique place.

The Coral Kingdom

Far out in the Indian Ocean, halfway between Australia and Sri Lanka, lie the Cocos (Keeling) Islands. Few are aware of the long history of this far-flung fragment of Australia, but it has often played an important part in our history.

The little collection of pristine coral atolls was probably first discovered in 1609 by William Keeling. Other voyagers visited, but it was not until 1825 that it was claimed for Great Britain by merchant trader John Clunies Ross. He planned to bring his family from Scotland and settle there. Before he could return, an unusual character named Alexander Hare, an English colonial administrator, settled the islands with an apparently voluntary harem of Malay women. When Clunies Ross and his entourage arrived, there was conflict, which was eventually resolved when the Malay women increasingly deserted Hare in favour of males in the Clunies Ross group. Comprehensively rejected, William Hare left.

Clunies Ross recruited Malays as workers, paying them in a local currency that could only be redeemed at the island store. This exploitative arrangement saw the Clunies Ross family remain as potentates on their 'coral kingdom' until the British Indian Ocean empire eventually disintegrated after World War II.

Small and distant though they are, these islands have connections with broader historical events. Charles Darwin visited for twelve days in 1836 during his fabled voyage on the *Beagle*. These were the only coral atolls that he experienced and on which he based his subsequent theory of atoll formation. Darwin postulated that coral reefs continued growing long after the seamounts that had originally supported them sank away.

The islands have also played a strategic role in some significant events. In 1914, HMAS *Sydney* (I) disabled and captured the German cruiser SMS *Emden* on one of the islands. The survivors of the *Emden* were given medical attention and became prisoners of war. Before the engagement, a party of fifty or so German sailors destroyed the telegraph and cable communications facilities ashore on Direction Island. They escaped and managed to steal a schooner, sailing it to Turkey, an impressive feat of navigation, particularly in wartime.

In World War II, the islands were part of a global signals intelligence network, known as 'Y Service', operated by the British military forces. This once again made the islands a potential enemy target. British troops were garrisoned there, including the Ceylon Defence Force. But there was conflict between the Ceylonese and their British commanders, eventually leading to a mutiny in 1942. Three of the mutineers were executed.

Although the Japanese continually flew over the islands and once bombarded them from a submarine, they made no attempt to land. Towards the end of the war, the islands became a base for British and Dutch fighters and bombers supporting the Allied retaking of Singapore and Malaya.

In 1955, the islands were separated from the colony of Singapore, to which they had been joined after the war, and became Australian territory. The Clunies Ross family continued to control the islands and their people in a manner unacceptable to the Australian government and the family was bought out in the 1970s but allowed to stay in their home. In the 1980s, they were told to leave and, after a High Court case found in their favour, they finally had to leave when the Australian government banned all official business with the island, bankrupting the family who then moved to the mainland.

Today, the Cocos Keelings are a unique collection of islets peopled by around 600 people of mostly mixed European–Malay background, many following Sunni Islam. After their long and troubled history, they are now, along with Christmas Island, part of the Australian Indian Ocean Territories, administered through Western Australia. Their position near sea lanes means that the islands may again have some future strategic role in the Indian Ocean.

The people of the Cocos Islands have been petitioning the Australian government for recognition as Indigenous

Australians. In the meantime, one of the main industries is tourism—'Welcome to Paradise', promises the Cocos (Keeling) Islands Tourism website. It certainly looks like Paradise now.

Sea Country

The Murujuga Aboriginal Corporation is made up of five language groups living in the Dampier region of Australia's north-western coast. This area is also home to the rich rock carvings of the Burrup Peninsula, thought to be more than 40,000 years old. Murujuga stories tell of a time when the seas rose and drowned their settlements and everything within them. The people were forced to move further inland to continue their way of life.

For a long time, these stories were thought by many to be myths, with no relation to actual historical events. But in 2019 a team of scientists working with the traditional owners searched the Murujuga (which means 'hip bone sticking out') area of the Dampier Peninsula and proved that the oral traditions were accurate.

Around 10,000 years ago, melting ice raised sea levels around the world. In this part of it, land that had been dry for up to 160 kilometres from what was then the coast disappeared beneath the rising waters. When archaeologists dived at two sites in the area, they discovered hundreds of stone tools that confirmed the existence of busy communities where the waves had rolled for the last ten centuries. This is the first discovery of sunken First Nations settlements in Australia, but scientists believe there must be many more. When the glaciers melted, perhaps 2 million square kilometres of the continent disappeared. It is likely that many other settlements went the same way and are awaiting discovery and further research that will tell us more about the long pre-history of Australia.

Stories of great floods also appear in the traditions of First Nations communities around the country. Over twenty legends have been identified that relate to the formation of what some call 'sea country', meaning the continuation of their current territory past the high tide mark and out into the far ocean along Australia's long, sloping continental shelf.

Other Kimberley region people, often referred to as the Bardi Jawi grouping, also have stories about the rising seas. In their traditions, Brue Reef, an isolated feature about 90 kilometres north of Cape Leveque, was once occupied by an individual named Jul and his cannibalistic relatives. It was called Juljinabur. When a family from another island came drifting towards Juljinabur, Jul, fearing they would be eaten by his relatives, hid them until he was able to help them escape in a double-hulled canoe. When Jul's relatives discovered this there was a big fight that brought about the sinking of the island, leaving only the reef that is there today.

Elsewhere, the Bidjandjura people of the Great Victoria Desert relate the story of two brothers travelling south from desert country. The elder brother, Malgaru, had firesticks and a water bag. The younger, Jaul, had neither. As they journeyed, Jaul became thin and thirsty because Malgaru would not share the water from his kangaroo skin bag. They came to Biranbura, a dry area to the west of Fowlers Bay, South Australia. Malgaru hid his water bag in the rocks. A quarrel with his brother followed and Malgaru went hunting. As soon as he was out of sight, the parched Jaul rushed to the rocks to satisfy his thirst. In his haste, he punctured the tight skin of the waterbag with his club. Water poured out. Malgaru came running back and tried to stop the rushing water, but he could not. The water flowed across the land, drowning Malgaru and Jaul and forming what is now the sea.

As First Nations custodians and researchers continue to explore the physical and creative aspects of these traditions, it seems likely that more sea country will be revealed and documented, adding to our understanding of even more amazing places.

Not So Sunny

Queensland's Whitsunday Islands and Passage were named after the English Whitsun custom marking the feast of Pentecost by Lieutenant James Cook in 1770. They are now a favourite sailing, diving and general tourism destination. But the many beauties of the area have a less sunny history.

The pleasant-sounding Queensland area known as Cape Bowling Green is a long headland and sandspit near Ayr. Jutting well out into the ocean, the low-lying feature is hard to see from the ocean and caused the sinking of several ships in the colonial period.

A wooden lighthouse was built on the headland in 1874 to aid the increasing sea traffic along the coast. This had to be moved after several years due to erosion. Shifted again for the same reason in 1908, the isolated light has been steadily improved and upgraded as one of a chain of such beacons along that section of the Queensland coast. The light may or may not have been sighted by the steamship *Yongala* in March 1911 as she battled cyclonic winds and seas.

The steel freight- and passenger-carrying SS *Yongala* cruised between the Western Australian goldfields and eastern ports from 1903. A substantial vessel over 100 metres long and weighing over 3500 tons, the ship was named after the South Australian town of Yongala, meaning 'good water' in the Ngadjuri language. *Yongala* was well built and well fitted out, but she lacked one feature that sealed her fate.

Steaming from Mackay for Townsville in March 2011, *Yongala* was last sighted by the Dent Island lighthouse keeper as she entered the Whitsunday Passage. A cyclone warning had been issued shortly after the steamer departed Mackay, causing other ships in the area to seek shelter. But *Yongala* had no wireless and was unaware of the danger into which she was heading. The alarm was raised in Townsville two days after the ship failed to arrive on schedule. Identifiable remnants of her cargo were found along the beach at Cape Bowling Green, confirming the worst fears. The state mounted a large search effort that found wreckage strewn along the coast but the only body found was that of a racehorse. *Yongala* had disappeared on 23 March with no trace of her 122 passengers and crew. The Marine Board of Queensland inquiry was thorough but was forced to conclude that 'the fate of the Yongala passes beyond human ken into the realms of conjecture, to add one more to the mysteries of the sea'.

That was how things stood until the 1940s, when Australian Navy ships located an unknown wreck about 20 kilometres east of Cape Bowling Green. In 1958 a diver brought up a safe from the wreck and a few years later it was shown to be from the *Yongala*. Today, the wreck is a popular diving attraction, along with a few of the other ill-fated vessels lying in the Whitsundays. One of these is the schooner *Louisa Marie*.

In August 1878, the schooner was beached on Whitsunday Island for cleaning. The four men aboard established friendly relations with the local Ngaro people but after a few days a group of First Nations peoples came over from the island group then known as Molle Island, apparently bringing upsetting news. Not knowing what this might have been and becoming fearful for their own safety, the sailors hauled the schooner back into the water.

Next day, two went ashore for fresh water, leaving Captain McIvor and the Scottish cook, John Morrison, aboard. After they'd left, a group of Ngaro people attacked the ship, apparently led by the Molle Island visitors. McIvor was thrown overboard and speared through the cheek from one of the canoes circling the schooner. Fortunately for the captain, his attacker took no further interest and left him struggling in the water as he drew the spear out of his cheek.

Some while later, the other two sailors returned with the fresh water and picked up the exhausted McIvor. They saw their attackers take the sails of the *Louisa Marie* into their canoes and then set fire to the schooner. There was no sign of Morrison.

The three survivors made off and were later picked up by another boat, returning to the spot to find only the topmast and mainmast heads protruding from the water. A party went ashore and there was a confrontation on the beach. Shots were fired but, according to the newspaper account of events, no one was injured. The survivors and their rescuers then sailed to Bowen.

John Morrison was declared dead and that seems to have been the end of this enigmatic confrontation. Whether the crew of the *Louisa Marie* provoked the attack, or whether it was related to local issues is not known. The incident remains one of colonial Australia's many unexplained acts of violence.

Red Palms in the Desert

In 1894, Lutheran missionary and scholar Carl Strehlow collected a story from the Arrernte people of Central Australia. The tradition told of gods bringing palm seeds from the distant north to Palm Valley (Alyape), 120 or so kilometres south-west of Alice Springs. This was their explanation for the remarkable native palms that line the banks of the Finke River, including the rare red cabbage palm (*Livistona mariae*).

More than 120 years later, scientists confirmed that the ancestral seeds of the red cabbage palms had indeed been carried by human hands from near present-day Darwin far south to the Palm Valley possibly 30,000 years before. The lead ecologist, Professor David Bowman, was interviewed about this discovery and said 'We're talking about a verbal tradition which had been transmitted through generations possibly for over 7000, possibly 30,000 years'.

Now part of the 46,000-hectare Finke Gorge National Park, Palm Valley is a popular destination for four-wheel drivers. As well as the palms and the mystique of the place, the Finke River is thought to be one of the world's oldest rivers.

The valley is also the focus of a puzzle that partly predates European settlement. In 1834, an anonymous article began appearing in British and other newspapers. The article told of a secret expedition originating in Singapore several years earlier, then sailing to northern Australia, followed by a gruelling overland journey south to the centre of the continent. Here, in an oasis-like area, a member of the expedition, 'Lieutenant Nixon', encountered the descendants of a large group of Dutch shipwrecked about 170 years earlier. Somehow, the survivors had managed to trek across the desert to find the oasis where they had settled and eked out an existence ever since. The only possible location for such an isolated colony is Palm Valley.

This story has been doubted and defended more or less since it first appeared. Doubters point out the many discrepancies of climate, location and identity in the account, including the non-existence of a Lieutenant Nixon and many other discrepancies. The most damning argument against the truth of the story is that there is no physical evidence for hundreds of Europeans living at Palm Valley for possibly several centuries. Nor do the traditional owners of the area seem to know about such a colony but rather have their own Palm Valley traditions.

The area inspired Arrernte artist Albert (Elea) Namatjira, born in nearby Hermannsburg, to paint many of his famous landscapes. Namatjira's mother was born near the valley, giving him a direct family connection with the place and its traditional significance. His paintings use European techniques to portray the country and its features not only as landscapes but also to embrace their sacred significance. The landform itself and the rocks and trees within it are often shown with water at the visual centre of the painting, directly linking the main elements of Country and its traditional meanings.

Namatjira's artistic skills were celebrated and he was granted a conditional citizenship in 1957. This seemingly bizarre honour allowed him more liberty than other First Nations peoples, including permission to buy alcohol for his own use. His situation led to friction in the local community and Namatjira was sentenced to six months' labour, reduced to three months after public outcry and an appeal, for supplying alcohol to Aboriginal people. He was allowed to serve his time at his home on the Papunya Native Reserve but died two months later, reportedly broken by the burdens of his achievements, cultural obligations and inability to use the wealth from his painting to buy his own land even though he was an Australian citizen.

Albert Namatjira is today recognised as one of Australia's great painters and as an activist for the rights of his people. Some of his over 2000 works hang in galleries around the country and he has been honoured in song, film and several times on postage stamps. His life and work have inspired successive generations of Western Arrernte artists, many of whom continue to paint at Alyape, where the traditions of First Nations and settlers meet.

The Pelican Spree

The Big Scrub was a heavily forested region on the New South Wales North Coast bounded by Byron Bay to the east and Lismore to the west. Extending for around 75,000 hectares, it was the country of the traditional owners now known as the Bundjalung Aboriginal Nation. Timber cutting began in the 1840s, followed by land clearing for agriculture in the 1880s. It is estimated that less than 1 per cent of the original forest remained by the close of the nineteenth century.

Life and labour in the Big Scrub were tough and so were many of the characters who lived there, as the yarn of the Pelican Spree amply testifies. It was contributed to a Sydney newspaper in 1899, recounted brilliantly by 'Jimmie Pannikin':

When Gang No. 7½ of cane-cutters cut-out last season, it was found that they had made the record cheque; and to show their joy and pride, they decided to go on the razzle right away in Fourpubbs, instead of merely indulging in a preliminary foretaste on the river, and then saving the rest of their 'beans' for a spree in Sydney.

There was a great commotion in Fourpubbs when it was voiced abroad that Gang No. 7½ was going 'to do in' most of its money at Mick Fadden's hotel, popularly known as the Cane-cutters' Curse Hotel.

Two of the gang, 'Italian' Charlie and Bobby the Rat got the needle into each other before the cut-out; and they loudly threatened to do for each other.

When the gang reached Fourpubbs, Italian Charlie declared his intention of having a pelican spree, whereupon Bobby the Rat announced his determination to have two pelican sprees one after the other.

Here is the original recipe for a pelican spree. First engage a disused barn, or old shanty. Then procure the following ingredients:—One dozen Richmond River rum (home-brewed, if it is to be got at all), three dozen red herrings, six dozen onions, six pound of good old galloping cheese. This stock is to be consumed in three days. If, at the end of that time, the breath is of a bluish-red appearance, and strong enough to sustain the weight of one's swag, one may reasonably conclude that the festival has not been a failure.

Italian Charley selected a shanty just below Mick Donovan's pub. Bobby the Rat pitched his tent in a clump of lantana further down the river bank. When Italian Charlie had completed his pelican spree, he went on a mad drinking bout for three days. By that time Bobby the Rat had successfully concluded his second pelican spree.

Then a truly brilliant idea struck some of the semi-sober cane-cutters. It wasn't the only thing that struck some of them. They lugged the limp forms of Italian Charlie and Bobby the Rat into an old disused stable at the rear of the C.C. Hotel. Two professional beer-chewers were also rolled in—after a solemn verbal agreement. Amateur artists daubed blood (bullocks' blood from Plumley's slaughterhouse) profusely, yet artistically, over the faces and hands and clothes of the four inebriates. Gore was also lavished on the walls, the mangers, the straw bedding. A cane-knife covered with blood and hair was concealed in a corner. A few heavy nulla nullas were blood-toned; and sundry extra touches gave the whole place a ghastly look.

The deadly enemies lay side by side for some hours. Then, to finish the night's carouse, they were rudely roused by the conspirators at the enervating hour of 'two in the morning'.

The conspirators talked of quarrels in the cane-fields, threats, revenge, murder—pointed to the bloodstains and looked scared. Some of them were on the verge of hysterics with drink and want of sleep. Lights were produced, and they showed two of the bloodiest corpses ever seen in the Big Scrub.

Italian Charlie and Bobby the Rat began to comprehend dimly. They felt an awful paralysing fear. Everything was dead against them. Blood on themselves—blood everywhere. It was just as one cane-cutter had sadly pointed out. The two enemies had quarrelled desperately.

The two dead men had interfered for peace sake. The madness of drink, and the madness of hate had led to the awful madness of murder; So the men talked and whispered till the grey dawn. The sport was prime.

Bobby the Rat looked frightened to death. Italian Charlie worked his eyes and twitched his hands and fingers horribly. Just as some of the cane-cutters were about to explain the gruesome joke, Italian Charlie swooped down suddenly, grabbed the bloody cane-knife, and faced the shrinking, shivering Bobby the Rat.

'You dogga! You make me fighta. You maka me killa blooda man. You killa 'nother man. Me an' you be hanga for dis. Me killa you!'

He swung the deadly knife round fiercely. It is a dreadful weapon, fit to slice a man's body when wielded by powerful accustomed hands. The cane-cutters tumbled over each other in their anxiety to get out of the way.

Italian Charlie danced in front of Bobby the Rat, wildly brandishing his cane-knife all the while. He stood near the door, and so effectually blocked exit.

'You tief ! You robba! I chop you to little pieca, my oatha, so, so!' with a swing of the knife round about Bobby the Rat's head.

'We'll all be blanky well killed if somone doesn't down that madman!' said a cockie, who was one of the party. He picked up one of the nulla nullas, and getting behind the cane-cutter let fly with all his might at Italian Charlie, just as latter was making a desperate chop at Bobby the Rat, who stood as one petrified.

The nulla nulla caught Italian Charlie under the chin.

'Oh, Christa!' he yelled, and cut Bobby the Rat's head fair in two.

The blood spurted out and over Charlie's face. He wiped his face with his left hand, gazed in terror at the blood for a moment; then he threw down the cane-knife, rushed madly out of the stable into a ghastly grey light, shrieking and raving like a wild beast. He raced down the road to Twowharves before anyone thought to follow him.

Three days later his body was found in the river between two of the Colonial Sugar Company's cane-punts, at the mouth of Emigrant Creek.

Whoever Jimmie Pannikin was, he knew how to spin a yarn. If such places as Fourpubbs and Twowharves existed, they might have been small settlements near Coraki. Did the Pelican Spree ever happen? Who knows now? But, true or not, it's a great story of the Big Scrub and its memorable characters.

High Country

Was there ever a 'Man from Snowy River'? Arguments about the reality or otherwise of Banjo Paterson's famous creation began soon after the poem was first published in 1890. They still rage today, along with other controversies about heritage and environment in the fabled high country of Victoria and New South Wales, a region with a rich history.

Aboriginal peoples visited the alpine regions to meet, trade, settle disputes and conduct ceremonies, especially the annual Bogong moth festival. They had been doing this for at least

21,000 years when European settlement of the region began in the 1820s. The land-use practices and values of the traditional owners clashed with those of the settlers. Conflict over access to the natural resources of water and food, together with introduced diseases, led to a rapid decline in the First Nations population, many of whom nevertheless contributed to the development of the regional timber, construction and pastoral industries, and continue to do so. The Kosciuszko Aboriginal Working Group stated their traditional and continuing connections in 2006:

> The Mountains are very old and an ongoing life force that strengthens the ancestral link of our people. We have a living, spiritual connection with the mountains. We retain family stories and memories of the mountains, which makes them spiritually and culturally significant to us. Our traditional knowledge and cultural practices still exist and need to be maintained . . .

The descendants of the settlers who pioneered the high country are also passionate about their cultural heritage and traditional practices, especially those related to the grazing of cattle on the alpine pastures and the closely related issue of the wild horses known as brumbies.

For many years, high country pastoralists have been in conflict with environmental groups concerned about damage to the environment caused by cattle and, increasingly, by brumbies. The rapid increase in brumby numbers has led to culling programs, fiercely resisted by many high country people. The leases allowing cattle to graze alpine pastures were ended in the 1960s, leaving many pastoralists bitter, not only about the blow to their livelihoods but also to their cherished way of life. The brumbies are usually seen as the last vestige of that lifestyle and the threats to destroy them are strongly resisted. Defenders of the brumby point out that other developments, such as the mooted Snowy 2.0 hydroelectric scheme and the alpine tourism and skiing industries also cause damage to the fragile environment and so feel uniquely oppressed by environmentalists and government authorities.

Situations like this are not unknown elsewhere. The American historian Karl Jacoby coined the term 'moral ecology' to describe the ethos of local resistance movements that have evolved in parts of the USA when alliances of environmentalists and governments have sought to impose their values on traditional customs and lifestyles.

A significant report on the high country conflict was pending release in 2021, with all sides hoping for a mutually agreeable resolution of some kind. Meanwhile, the brumbies continue to run free, as does their powerful national image, fostered by books such as Elyne Mitchell's *The Silver Brumby* and films like *The Man from Snowy River*, as well as the original poem.

Arguments over who the man might have been are almost as fraught and long-lasting as the conflict over the high country itself.

The main contender is a man named John 'Jack' Riley. High country folk love a good yarn almost as much as they love their horses. And there's no shortage of tales about Riley and the suicidally steep ride he is said to have made. The most common version is that a station-bred horse had gone wild and 'was running on the Leatherbarrel Mountain, on the road to Kosciuszko from Groggin'. This 'outlaw', as such horses are known, had become something of a legend, defying all attempts to catch him. Riley was one of a group who determined to capture the horse and made elaborate trapping preparations. But the wily beast eluded them, galloping down a steep slope that not even mountain cattlemen would dare. Except Jack Riley.

Jack rode his gallant mount straight down the hill and through the scrub in a mad dash that ended with the outlaw being forced into the pen his hunters had set up for the capture. Riley became a local legend and years later, when Paterson was visiting the Snowy, as he often did, he stayed one night with Riley in his hut. There he was regaled with the story by the man himself. The poet turned the tale into Australia's most famous poem, the galloping rhythm of the bush ballad form perfectly suiting the hell-for-leather yarn of Riley's wild ride.

But there are a few problems with this version of events. It seems that Riley may not even have been in the high country when Paterson visited and wrote the poem. Other contenders have been put forward, including an Aboriginal tracker known only as 'Toby'. He appears as the hero of a remarkably similar yarn published three years before 'The Man from Snowy River'. Did Paterson take his inspiration from this story? No one knows for sure.

The legend of the wayward 'colt from old Regret' and 'the stripling on a small and weedy beast' who 'sent the flintstones flying' is still a bush reciter's favourite, and 'The Man from Snowy River' is destined to be with us for a long time yet—whoever he was.

And down by Kosciusko, where the pine-clad ridges raise
Their torn and rugged battlements on high,
Where the air is clear as crystal, and the white stars
    fairly blaze
At midnight in the cold and frosty sky,
And where around the Overflow the reed-beds sweep
    and sway
To the breezes, and the rolling plains are wide,
The man from Snowy River is a household word today,
And the stockmen tell the story of his ride.

Paroo Legends

The Paroo is the only free-flowing river remaining in the Murray–Darling basin. But it has to rain a lot in its northern catchment area to turn its scattered waterholes into a running stream that sometimes makes it across the border to Wilcannia in New South Wales. Here, it joins the Darling River. The Paroo and surrounding region are important wetlands, with mud springs, rich flora and fauna resources and some remnant opal mining from the long-gone roaring days.

Along the Paroo's 600-kilometre course are some legendary towns, mostly founded in the wake of explorers passing through Bidjara, Budjiti, Gwamu/Kooma, Kunja, Mardigan and Murrawarri country from the 1840s. Hungerford and Eulo are two Queensland settlements with colourful histories.

Hungerford was renowned in bush lore as an especially forbidding place. Henry Lawson's short story summed it up nicely in the days when people travelled only on foot, by horse or perhaps by uncomfortable cart, drays or coaches:

The country looks just as bad for a hundred miles round Hungerford, and beyond that it gets worse: a blasted, barren wilderness that doesn't even howl. If it howled it would be a relief. I believe that Bourke [sic] and Wills found Hungerford, and it's a pity they did.

Lawson was similarly uncomplimentary about the Paroo River area in another of his characteristically gloomy poems:

With blighted eyes and blistered feet,
With stomachs out of order,
Half mad with flies and dust and heat
We'd crossed the Queensland Border.
I longed to hear a stream go by
And see the circles quiver;
I longed to lay me down and die
That night on Paroo River.

As far as we know, Lawson never wrote about another Paroo town, the small hamlet of Eulo. But a few lesser-known rhymesters did. At least, they wrote about Eulo's only claim to fame: Isabel Richardson, better known as Isabel Gray. She came to Australia, probably as a governess, around 1868 and quickly married the first of what would be three husbands. The first died young, and Isabel then married Richard Robinson. Eventually, the couple ended up in Eulo where they took over the Royal Mail Hotel and most of the other few stores in town.

Founded in the 1870s, Eulo was a place that travellers from all directions passed through on their way to somewhere else. Business was good, especially in the accommodation, hospitality and related spheres. As one of the few women in this part of the world, Isabel came to be known as 'the Eulo Queen'. She is said to have entertained lavishly in her bedroom, charging gentlemen outrageous prices for grog—and for her personal services if they were so inclined. She became very wealthy.

The Queen ruled over her dusty domain, known to all and sundry. Her flamboyant style included a girdle fashioned from nautilus shell and opal, her favourite stone, and a no-nonsense ejection technique to deal with troublemakers addled by her sly grog.

Richard Robinson died in 1902 and a year later the Queen married for the third time.

Well into her fifties, Isabel claimed to be thirty-five. Whether her 29-year-old husband, Tasmanian Herbert Gray, believed that we don't know. But he was no paragon of virtue himself as he seems to have already been married to someone else. Still, they made a go of it for a good while, until Isabel took herself off to England for an expensive trip in 1913. Not long after her return, she prosecuted Gray for assault. She won the case but generously paid his fine.

But the times had turned against Eulo and its queen. Economic depression in the 1890s had put a hole in Isabel's bank account and a continuing decline in traffic passing through the town saw her gradually lose much of what remained of her wealth. By 1926 she was living on her dead husband's military pension. She died three years later in a mental hospital at Toowoomba, her wealth by then just £30.

The Eulo Queen was well remembered in the recollections of the generation who knew of her as they aged into the 1930s:

Thirty years back the name and fame of Mrs Robinson, 'The Eulo Queen,' was known throughout the length and breadth of Western New South Wales and Queensland. As a hotel-keeper at Eulo she made much money, and would have been financially Independent to-day had she not been over ambitious . . .

Several poets, including Edward Sorenson, romanticised her life. 'Shebeen' is an Irish word for an illicit pub:

None knew the west till they knew the queen,
The Westerners used to say—
Her castle-keep was a bush shebeen,
And her name was Isobel Gray.

She queened it over the roving throng,
Who stayed for a royal night;
And rattled the roof with a royster song
In the glow of the bar-room light.

Wild spirits in from the farthest West,
And drovers from many a mile,
Knew the Eulo Arms as a travellers' rest,
And a home for, a little while.

Tho' she'd run the rule o'er the rouseabout,
Who flashed as the cheque-proud do,
She was ever a friend of the down-and-out,
A mother and sweetheart; too.

Her name was echoed in hut and shed,
'Twas scrawled by many a pen;

Her charms were sung and her wiles were spread,
On the trails of the cattlemen.

For in her reign, to the outmost post,
The Westerners used to say,
The Eulo Arms to a roving host
Were the arms of Isobel Gray.

The Eulo Queen Hotel and Caravan Park today celebrates the story of Isabel Grey, providing accommodation for tourists seeking a taste of outback southern Queensland history. Visitors can also learn about megafauna, the giant dinosaurs that once roamed the continent, including an oversized wombat, or diprotodon. Sadly, the town no longer runs the World Lizard Racing Championships, another of the many quirky competitions in which Australians seem to take particular delight, including Queensland's Tully Golden Gumboot and the Dunny Races at Cunderdin's Ettamogah Pub, as well as the Darwin Beer Can Regatta, to name but a few.

A Home in the Blizzard

The story of Douglas Mawson's sole survival from an epic Antarctic trek is well known. On a sledging expedition to Oates Land, over 500 kilometres to the east, Mawson's companions, Belgrave Ninnis and Xavier Mertz, died. Mawson was lucky to make it back to the jumble of wooden huts at Cape Denison that made up the base of his Australasian Antarctic Expedition. As he staggered down the last snow slope towards the huts, he saw the smoke of the departing *Aurora*. He had just missed the ship that was to take him and his fellow expeditioners home after a season of polar exploration.

Fortunately for Mawson, a number of his men stayed behind to form a rescue party. They were almost as pleased to see Mawson as he was to see them, despite his dreadfully emaciated condition. But the elation soon gave way to the hard and very cold reality. Their cramped collection of huts was to be their home in the blizzard for yet another winter in Antarctica. Not all Mawson's men would weather it well.

Sidney Jeffryes was born in Toowoomba, Queensland, in 1884. He trained as a telegraph operator, becoming skilled in tapping out Morse code along the wires strung precariously around the country and connecting Australia with the world. But telegraphy was an old technology. The newly developed wireless telegraphy, using radio waves to transmit messages rather than land-bound wires and undersea cables, was the next big thing. Jeffryes trained on wireless and worked as an operator on several ships before unexpectedly landing a late posting to collect Mawson's expedition.

Early wireless was unreliable, especially in Antarctic conditions. For Mawson to remain in contact with Australia he needed to establish an intermediate base on Macquarie Island, halfway between Hobart and Cape Denison. This halved the distance wireless signals needed to travel, allowing messages to pass between Hobart and Cape Denison via the station on Macquarie Island. That was the plan.

It turned out that the wireless equipment at Cape Denison was not up to the task. Jeffryes was to bring updated equipment with him to improve the communication from Cape Denison. He arrived there in February 1913, just as Mawson returned from his incredible survival ordeal, and was able to quickly get the wireless working, allowing the expedition to report what had happened to Mawson's companions and his own lucky escape from death.

Jeffryes was good at his job and a conscientious, even enthusiastic, wireless operator and collector of scientific and technical data. He established the first ongoing two-way wireless communication between Antarctica and Australia. But the enforced captivity of the men in the huts began to take its toll. In May, Mawson found Jeffryes asleep at his post and missing possibly vital communications with Macquarie Island. The expedition leader wrote in his notes:

> Jeffryes stops up all day—goes for tiring walks, etc, and then is not fit to keep an alert watch during the 8 to 12 hours. This is bad management ... Jeffryes is certainly not the man for [scientific study of radio waves] ... he appears to have no conception of scientific analysis.

The wireless operator was a latecomer to the tight-knit group of expeditioners and may have felt that he was, to some degree, excluded from their camaraderie. By July, he began showing signs of mental unbalance, distrust and aggression towards his companions. As Jeffryes was the only expeditioner able to use Morse code, his declining mental condition was a serious threat. Mawson had another expeditioner, Frank Bickerton, learn Morse. This was a wise decision.

Over the next few weeks, Jeffryes was sometimes better, sometimes worse. He told Mawson that he was 'resigning', leading to a group discussion in which it was decided that he would continue to operate the wireless in cooperation with Bickerton. This arrangement seemed to work satisfactorily until September, when Jeffryes tried to send a message to Australia via Macquarie Island that five of the expeditioners were insane and conspiring to murder him and Mawson. The message was not received, but Bickerton and Mawson now took over most of the wireless work. Early the next month Mawson finally relieved Jeffryes of his duties.

In December, the expeditioners gratefully left their ice-bound lodgings and returned to Australia. Jeffryes, by then a virtual outcast among the small group, was kept away from the welcoming festivities in Adelaide during February 1914. But he seemed to have recovered his mental health. He was paid off and it was assumed that he would return to his family in Toowoomba. He did not.

The following month Jeffryes was found starving in the bush near Stawell, Victoria. He was suffering from exposure after trying to live off the land. Apprehended and taken to court, he pleaded to be allowed to go back to the bush to die. Instead, he was sent to various asylums. After attacking an asylum staff member, he was committed to the notorious 'J Ward' for the criminally insane in Ararat Hospital for the Insane. His family was reportedly unhappy with Mawson's apparent lack of interest in the health and wellbeing of his troublesome expeditioner. Sidney Jeffryes was never released and died in 1942, another casualty of history.

It was not until 2010 that Jeffryes was rehabilitated from the obscurity into which he had been cast. The Australian Antarctic Division named a glacier after him, acknowledging his contribution to the study of early wireless in polar conditions.

In 2013 Joe Bugden composed a chamber opera based on the sad story and in 2018 the Mawson's Huts Foundation placed a commemorative plaque on Jeffryes' grave.

Mawson's huts in Antarctica have been preserved and are covered by various forms of heritage recognition and protection. Over the Christmas–New Year period of 2021–2022 six expeditioners voyaged to Cape Denison to work on the preservation of the ice-bound cabins and to search for artefacts. The site is a difficult place to access at the best of times, so there are few tourists, but it can occasionally be visited through an annual adventure cruise. Alternatively, the Mawson's Huts Foundation operates a much warmer replica on the Hobart waterfront.

Slim Dusty with his Ford Customline and the 'pub with no beer' model, in 1960.

6
IMAGINED PLACES

Where the Pelican Builds Its Nest

There was an old bush belief that nobody had ever seen where pelicans build their nests. It was assumed that the birds nested in the best land, far away from settled areas, 'out where the pelican builds its nest', and this became a common reference to the unexplored parts of the country, particularly in far New South Wales and Queensland.

In 1881, Mary Hannay Foott published her poem 'Where the Pelican Builds':

> The horses were ready, the rails were down,
> But the riders lingered still,—
> One had a parting word to say,
> And one had his pipe to fill.

Then they mounted, one with a granted prayer,
And one with a grief unguessed.
'We are going' they said, as they rode away—
'Where the pelican builds her nest!'

They had told us of pastures wide and green,
To be sought past the sunset's glow;
Of rifts in the ranges by opal lit,
And gold 'neath the river's flow.
And thirst and hunger were banished words
When they spoke of that unknown West;
No drought they dreaded, no flood they feared,
Where the pelican builds her nest!

The creek at the ford was but fetlock deep
When we watched them crossing there;
The rains have replenished it thrice since then
And thrice has the rock lain bare.
But the waters of Hope have flowed and fled,
And never from blue hill's breast
Come back—by the sun and the sands devoured—
Where the pelican builds her nest!

The poem was very popular at the time and in the years following. It still appears in anthologies though the pioneering tragedy on which it is based is long forgotten.

Cornelius and Albert Prout were the sons of a naval officer. Like many young adventurers of the 1860s and 1870s, they decided to try their luck on the land in western Queensland. With some help from the settlers who were already around Windorah, they quickly established a number of properties, always moving further out west. Still young and restless, they became entranced with El Dorado–like yarns of bountiful country in what is now the Northern Territory. They also listened to First Nations stories about a great river beyond the western horizon.

In December 1877 they departed on their great adventure from Springfield Station near Windorah with another man named Baker, twelve horses and plenty of supplies and equipment for a long trek. As they left, station owner James Scanlan warned them of the dangers they were sure to encounter in the harsh, arid western lands. 'We are going to do it or die,' they reportedly told him.

Months passed. Nothing was heard of the expedition. Eventually a search party was sent out, led by surveyor W.H.J. Carr-Boyd. They had no success until local people told them of 'something strange that had occurred in the distance'. Carr-Boyd found the Prouts' camp and:

> the remains of Cornelius, also a skeleton of one horse with its bridle on, tethered to a tree. A pint pot was found on which was scratched: 'Two days without water, C. Prout.' The diary of Cornelius also was found at the camp, but Carr-Boyd said it was lost on the way in . . . His watch also was found, a photograph of his mother, and a few letters.

Some of the horses were found in mid-1878 by a hard-riding bushman named Scarr, who identified them from the brands. He also found other remains of the missing party, including:

> old horse-dung, a lot of pieces of blue blanket, pieces of felt hat and calico, a pair of moleskin trousers nearly whole and not much worn, but cut up both legs, and what appear to be

old blood-marks, and a nearly new common twill shirt (not Scotch twill) which appears to have been dropped hastily as if a man was in the act of wringing it after washing.

Scarr brought these remnants in. He was convinced from his discussions with local Aboriginal people that the explorers had been murdered and eaten, though little evidence of this seems to have been produced other than his deeply prejudiced opinion: 'I have left all the other things in a bundle on my marked tree, so that if anyone goes there they will know how to treat the blacks on that creek.'

The bodies of Albert Prout and Baker were never found.

The Outside Track

'The Outside Track' was a term for the life path travelled by those who worked and survived at the edge of society, wandering from place to place, working whenever they needed to or where they could find a job. In his poem 'The Outside Track', Henry Lawson recalls the beery parting of a mate named Len from a group of his friends.

> There were ten of us there on the moonlit quay,
> And one on the for'ard hatch;
> No straighter mate to his mates than he
> Had ever said: 'Len's a match!'
> 'Twill be long, old man, ere our glasses clink,
> 'Twill be long ere we grip your hand!'—
> And we dragged him ashore for a final drink
> Till the whole wide world seemed grand.

Imagined Places

For they marry and go as the world rolls back,
They marry and vanish and die;
But their spirit shall live on the Outside Track
As long as the years go by.

The port-lights glowed in the morning mist
That rolled from the waters green;
And over the railing we grasped his fist
As the dark tide came between.
We cheered the captain and cheered the crew,
And our mate, times out of mind;
We cheered the land he was going to
And the land he had left behind.

We roared Lang Syne as a last farewell,
But my heart seemed out of joint;
I well remember the hush that fell
When the steamer had passed the point
We drifted home through the public bars,
We were ten times less by one
Who sailed out under the morning stars,
And under the rising sun.

And one by one, and two by two,
They have sailed from the wharf since then;
I have said good-bye to the last I knew,
The last of the careless men.
And I can't but think that the times we had
Were the best times after all,
As I turn aside with a lonely glass
And drink to the bar-room wall.

But I'll try my luck for a cheque Out Back,
Then a last good-bye to the bush;
For my heart's away on the Outside Track,
On the track of the steerage push.

Characteristically, Lawson creates an atmosphere of sentimentality, alcohol and despair that marked the lives and deaths of these nomads. Some married and settled down but others were fated to remain wanderers 'As long as the years go by'. While many of these men were battlers, humping their swags around the bush, others were a class of men well known in colonial society. This group included many younger sons of upper- and middle-class British families disinherited by the system of primogeniture, or inheritance by the oldest son only.

It is this nomadic and masculine lifestyle that Lawson and poets like Kipling hinted at in their elegies on 'the younger son' and 'the Gentleman Rover abroad' and in this popular poem, 'The Lost Legion':

There's a Legion that never was listed,
That carries no colours or crest,
But, split in a thousand detachments,
Is breaking the road for the rest.
Our fathers they left us their blessing—
They taught us, and groomed us, and crammed;
But we've shaken the Clubs and the Messes
To go and find out and be damned
    (Dear boys!),
To go and get shot and be damned . . .

Travellers on the Outside Track could also include those known as 'remittance men', individuals who had been sent to the colonies with an allowance from their families on condition that they did not return home. Often, these were the family 'black sheep', some of whom continued their wastrel or otherwise unacceptable ways in Australia, New Zealand, Southern Africa, Canada and along the steamer routes of the British Empire. They were usually well educated and had often served in the army, making them well able to look after themselves drifting along the steamer and rail routes of the empire, taking whatever work was available—if they could not avoid it—and living lives often devoid of lasting relationships. Australian poet Judith Wright captured the sad futility of this life in one of her early poems 'Remittance Man', as did the Canadian poet Robert William Service in his 'The Rhyme of the Remittance Man'.

Colonial Australia thrived on these wanderers of the empire. They joined exploring expeditions, drove cattle, tramped the track with swags, worked in colonial administration and sometimes taught school. Their backgrounds and skills also served many of them well as soldiers in the colonial wars in which Australia took part, or in other conflicts as soldiers of fortune. Some found love and settled down to domestic life and regular work, playing their part in peopling the country. Many were still young enough to go to World War I. By the time that was over, so was the Outside Track, at least for those generations celebrated and commemorated by Lawson and Kipling. British society was transformed by the loss of so many young and middle-aged men in the war. The footloose younger sons and remittance men faded away, assisted by changes to British inheritance laws that allowed younger sons to inherit their share of the family and business assets.

Where was 'the Outside Track'? It was nowhere, and everywhere. It was not a physical reality but a way of life, a series of loose connections among several generations of young to middle-aged men whose life chances were determined by their birth. Some were crushed by it—alcoholism, crime and suicide were not uncommon among them. But many rose above their circumstances and the stereotype that developed about them. Whether they were black sheep, successful prospectors or rural entrepreneurs, the men who circled Australia and the empire along the Outside Track contributed a great deal to the development of Australia and, for better or worse, to the British empire in general.

Matilda Country

The story of the town and country surrounding Winton in Queensland's channel country could stand for just about every regional centre in Australia. As well as its history, the place has connections with not one but two significant events that came to play a large part in Australia's imagination of itself.

After the ill-fated explorer Ludwig Leichhardt passed through the area in the 1840s, followed by William Landsborough during the 1860s, the first Europeans briefly settled before being driven away by drought. It was not until the 1870s that the Pelican Waterhole, as the local water source was known to Europeans, began evolving into Winton.

Development quickly followed as the population grew from perhaps 150 to 1000 or so twenty years later. Cobb & Co.

coaches served the town from around 1880 and the two railway lines eventually arrived. Winton had two banks, churches, a court, a newspaper, a school, four pubs and most of the services necessary to sustain regional livelihoods in the late nineteenth century. However, the tragic accompaniment of this pioneering activity and enterprise was the violent dispossession of the traditional owners from the late 1870s and into the early twentieth century.

Droughts frequently troubled the region, as they do today, and grassfires were a persistent problem on the large pastoral properties in the surrounding country. Several of these would play a role in the creation of Australia's best-known song.

In the summer of 1895, the poet Andrew Barton 'Banjo' Paterson arrived in Winton to continue his ultimately ill-fated eight-year courtship of Miss Sarah Riley, the second daughter of a well-to-do Geelong family. On this trip he met Christina Macpherson, an old school friend of Sarah's, and also a guest at her brother Bob Macpherson's Dagworth Station, a two-day buggy ride from Winton.

Shortly before this, the shearers on Dagworth refused to work under the dictates of the 1894 agreement offered by pastoralists. Bob Macpherson resolved to shear with non-union workers. The strikers burned down the Dagworth woolshed in early September 1894. Inside, 140 lambs awaiting shearing were burned to death while over forty shots were exchanged between defenders and attackers.

The next day, shearer Samuel 'Frenchy' Hoffmeister's heavily armed body was found at Four-Mile Billabong outside Kynuna. Bob Macpherson, together with three trooper police, rode to the billabong to inspect the body. The subsequent inquest returned a finding of suicide, a verdict that hardly anyone, then or since, has believed.

As well as these recent events, the visiting Paterson would almost certainly have heard about the death of another swagman at another local billabong a few years earlier. This swaggie had drowned, by accident it seems, in the Combo Waterhole attempting to escape police after being detected stealing and eating one of Bob Macpherson's sheep.

These incidents, together with the phrase 'Waltzing Matilda', heard possibly for the first time at Winton, provided Paterson with the inspiration for the poem. Christina Macpherson played what she remembered of a brass band marching tune, 'Craigielea', on her autoharp, a form of zither in vogue at the time. These words and music became the first 'Waltzing Matilda'. A version of the song was collected at the North Gregory Hotel in Winton by visiting English musician Thomas Wood in the early 1930s. He published his arrangement a few years later in his travelogue, *Cobbers,* and this version went on to become the one most people know today, propelled to fame by the 1938 recording of Australian bass-baritone Peter Dawson.

Between its original composition and Dawson's kookaburra-enhanced rendition, 'Waltzing Matilda' underwent several other transformations. So, although it was not quite an 'overnight success', the slight ditty about a swaggie, a sheep and the forces of the law and property is now often said to be one of the world's most recorded songs, as well as Australia's unofficial national anthem and internationally recognised musical emblem.

'Waltzing Matilda' is not Winton's only claim to iconic fame. The fledgling aeronautical company Queensland and Northern Territory Aerial Services Ltd was registered there in 1920. Subsidised by the local council, the company built a landing field the following year. After a few more years, they moved operations to Longreach where, under the name Qantas, they began to grow into Australia's national air carrier. But Winton can justifiably claim to be the birthplace of Qantas.

Today, Winton and its surrounding area celebrates its past with a strong emphasis on the birth of the national song and the national airline. It has also developed a Dinosaur Trail based on the excavation of dinosaur bones since the early 2000s. Like many rural and regional towns, it aims to attract tourism to bolster a local economy flagging from the decline in agriculture, resources and the struggle to maintain population. The COVID-19 pandemic has not helped the town or the region.

But Winton and its people have seen good and bad times through the inevitable ups and downs of 150 or so years. Resilience, fortitude and innovation are built into the pioneer heritage of the bush and the outback. As with most other parts of Australia, many terrible mistakes have been made in relation to First Nations peoples and the environment. The challenge now is to go forward to build a viable future for all those who live in 'Matilda Country'.

The Prince of Ballyhoo

Many are familiar with the Sunraysia brand of dried fruits. Some may also have heard of Sunraysia itself, a vaguely defined area straddling the Victorian and New South Wales borders. Like a number of unofficial regions, Sunraysia exists mainly in the collective imagination of those who live and work there. It only came into being through the aspirational enterprise of one man, with the assistance of a number of people who entered a brand-name competition in 1919.

The entrepreneur who created Sunraysia was once described as the 'prince of ballyhoo', a reference to the persuasive power of his tongue. Born into a family of Mildura irrigationists and market gardeners in 1884, Clement John 'Jack' De Garis led a thrusting life of business, marketing and large-scale ambition. He also had the unusual distinction of killing himself not once, but twice.

'C.J.', as De Garis was also known, began in the family business early and by the age of seventeen was running the Mildura branch. He went into debt to expand operations and to establish the ambitious Pyap Village Estate in South Australia where grapevines and orchards were grown with Murray River water. In 1919, C.J.'s marketing skills were employed by the Australian Dried Fruits Association to stimulate consumption of produce from the Mildura area around the country. Heavily influenced by American marketing techniques, he published recipe books and other promotional materials, including an early promotional film.

He also held a competition for a brand name that would focus the consumer's mind on Mildura dried fruits. The winning entry was 'Sun-raysed' (later tweaked to Sunraysia) and it was not long before C.J. had commissioned a 'Sun-Raysed Waltz' and other promotional gimmicks featuring that name. He also managed to link the brand with the Spanish flu epidemic raging at that time:

I fear no more the dreaded 'flu,
For Sunraysed fruits will pull me through.

As part of his drive to establish a real place to go with the brand label, C.J. started a newspaper, the *Sunraysia Daily*, the first official use of the name for an imaginary place that was effectively conjured into being through the magic of marketing.

Always restless, De Garis sold his Pyap venture and moved to Western Australia where he established another visionary agricultural settlement on an extensive property at Kendenup. This began well, with over 300 settlers moving onto the land to raise vegetables and fruit. Unfortunately, the entrepreneur had borrowed too heavily and the venture soon foundered under large debts. He went to America where he claimed he was promised sufficient funds to bail out the settlement but this money never eventuated. A royal commission cleared him of a charge of fraud, but his other businesses ran into financial trouble. He turned to get-rich-quick schemes in real estate and oil-drilling but was overwhelmed by failure and debt. In January 1925 he wrote nearly seventy farewell letters. One read, in part:

> The strain has been too long and too strong, and I have cracked up under it . . . Think as pleasantly as you can of me, who came nearer to being a big success than people think; and who consequently became the greatest failure. Regards and regrets.
> De Garis.

Then he disappeared.

Few believed he had taken his life and a search was quickly mounted. A very much alive De Garis was found by detectives on a boat bound for New Zealand. Legend has it that his silver tongue convinced one of the arresting officers to buy a block of land.

Escaping a charge of passing a dud cheque and any consequences there might have been for faking his death, C.J. set about restoring his tattered fortunes. Less than a year later he woke up 'believing I had the greatest day's work of my life to accomplish and the certainty of all the debts paid'. But whatever promises had been made, real or illusory, they came to nothing. Later that day he gassed himself to death.

Clement John De Garis was a man of many talents, perhaps too many for his own good. As well as his business and marketing skills, he was a noted aviator, a playwright and an author. He wrote short stories and published shortly before his real death a novel/memoir of his life under the pseudonym 'K.J. Rogers'. It was titled *Victories of Failure: A Business Romance*.

Perhaps the 'prince of ballyhoo's' most enduring legacy was the creation of Sunraysia. Today the area is a thriving straggle of centres on both sides of the border, with Mildura as the main town. Citrus, stone fruit and almonds are grown and there is some winemaking. Tourism is important to the region and the *Sunraysia Daily* is still published more than a century after C.J. De Garis brought it into being.

Cuppacumalonga Hill

The creator of 'The Sentimental Bloke', 'Ginger Mick' and other much-loved characters of the past also wrote verse for children. Here, he conjures up a vision of a pleasant, homely place that can be reached after travelling through an idyllic bush landscape in the company of a cattle drover:

Imagined Places

'Rover, rover, cattle-drover, where go you to-day?'
I go to Cuppacumalonga, fifty miles away;
Over plains where Summer rains have sung a song of glee,
Over hills where laughing rills go seeking for the sea,
I go to Cuppacumalonga, to my brother Bill.
Then come along, ah, come along!
Ah, come to Cuppacumalonga!
Come to Cuppacumalonga Hill!

'Rover, rover, cattle-drover, how do you get there?'
For twenty miles I amble on upon my pony mare,
To walk awhile and talk awhile to country men I know,
Then up to ride a mile beside a team that travels slow,
And last to Cuppacumalonga, riding with a will.
Then come along, ah, come along!
Ah, come to Cuppacumalonga!
Come to Cuppacumalonga Hill!

'Rover, rover, cattle-drover, what do you do then?'
I camp beneath a kurrajong with three good cattle-men;
Then off away at break of day, with strong hands on the reins,
To laugh and sing while mustering the cattle on the plains—
For up to Cuppacumalonga life is jolly still.
Then come along, ah, come along!
Ah, come to Cuppacumalonga!
Come to Cuppacumalonga Hill!

'Rover, rover, cattle-drover, how may I go too?'
I'll saddle up my creamy colt and he shall carry you—
My creamy colt who will not bolt, who does not shy nor kick—
We'll pack the load and take the road and travel very quick.

And if the day brings work or play we'll meet it with a will.
So Hi for Cuppacumalonga!
Come along, ah, come along!
Ah, come to Cuppacumalonga Hill!

Sadly, this wonderful place never existed, but its mellifluous name has lived in the minds of generations of children. The publication in which it appeared in 1921, *A Book for Kids*, is still in print today.

The Pub with No Beer

Dan Sheahan sat glumly in a fly-haunted corner of Ingham's Day Dawn Hotel. Oddly for a pub of the period, he was drinking a glass of wine. He was also scribbling something on a crumpled piece of paper. It was 1943 and the pub had been the scene of a serious drinking session by American soldiers the night before. Today, thirsty sugar farmer Dan couldn't get a beer. The soldiers had drunk the place dry. Dan was consoling himself with some murky red syrup and a few heartfelt verses he called 'A Pub without Beer'.

That's how the usual story goes, anyhow, and it could even be true. Whether it is or not, this seems to have been the genesis of what became an iconic Australian song. Dan got his lament published in Bill Bowyang's popular column of bush lore and bulldust, called 'On the Track'. In those days, amateur scribblers filled columns of country newspapers with ballads about droving, shearing and carrying a swag. Dan's poem added a new dimension to these trials and tribulations of bush life in an evocative sketch of the scene, 'lonely away from your kindred and all'.

The poem went on to describe the bored barmaid studying her painted nails, the cranky cook and the boss smoking in silence and 'joking no more'. Dan mentioned wartime rationing and recalled the navvies and cane-cutters who once caroused in the now mostly empty pub. He finished with a celebration of 'the brew of brown barley, what charm is thine' and compared pubs to 'high h[e]aven down here'.

Since that dismal moment when Dan Sheahan penned these verses, the song now known as 'The Pub with No Beer' has had a fabled history.

Country music performer Gordon Parsons was an occasional member of Slim Dusty's early roadshows during the mid-1950s. One whisky-fuelled evening in western New South Wales, he mentioned to his drinking partner, country singer Chad Morgan—known on stage as 'The Sheik of Scrubby Creek'—a poem about beer he'd picked up in his travels. Gordon had no idea where the poem came from. It had been floating around in bush camps and pubs for a few years like many other such recitations syndicated through country newspaper chains and taken up by bush versifiers. Out of this event, Parsons somehow emerged with an early version of the song destined to be famous, using the tune of American composer Stephen Foster's 'Beautiful Dreamer' and with revised lyrics similar to those eventually recorded by Slim Dusty in 1957.

In those days, country music was very popular in the bush but had virtually no following in the cities where recording companies and radio stations were located. The opportunities for having a country record played on the radio were limited to very late at night, very early in the morning, or not at all but somehow 'The Pub with No Beer' broke through the prejudices against 'hick music' and received increasing airplay in Brisbane, then Sydney.

Busy touring country towns and shows, Slim Dusty did not hear for a few months that his song was a hit. It kept being one for years. Not only in Australia but in Britain, Ireland, Canada, Europe and the USA. It was recorded by many international artists and propelled Slim Dusty to stardom.

Meanwhile, the pub with no beer itself became two pubs without beer. When Gordon Parsons penned his own version of Dan Sheahan's original lyric, he was thinking of a pub at Taylors Arm, New South Wales, close to his childhood home. This eventually led to both pubs claiming the valuable title. The Day Dawn pub in Ingham was demolished and rebuilt as Lee's Hotel and still claims to be the premier location of the legend. It went up for sale in 2021. The asking price of this slice of Australiana? Just $3.485 million. Not bad for a pub without beer.

The Land where the Crow Flies Backwards

In the 1950s, anthropologist Jeremy Becket recorded a Gurnu country singer named Dougie Young. Douglas Gary Young was born in Queensland in 1933 and left school early to work as a stockman. A riding accident in 1957 ended his career and he took to writing and singing songs about Aboriginal life and experience in and around Wilcannia, where he lived at the time. One of his best-known songs is 'The Land where the Crow Flies Backwards', an autobiographical expression of black pride.

Dougie lived a rough life of hard times and hard drinking and died in 1991. But he and his songs are legendary in the bush, especially (though not only) among First Nations peoples. His ability to use everyday life and the things people said in his songs make them unique time capsules of an Australia now mostly lost. Who now knows where the crows fly backwards and why?

In February 1905, a drover calling himself 'H7H' was staying in a Queensland town. He was following the cattle for a livelihood and wrote to a newspaper that he was 'gradually getting towards the setting sun and am writing you from Windorah, the land where the crow flies backwards, and they lift the sun in the morning with a crowbar'.

Whoever H7H might have been, he was a great observer of outback life and legend and a fine yarn-spinner to boot. His description of Windorah could stand for just about any outback town around the turn of the twentieth century:

> Windorah is a place that 'has been,' and God only knows if it will ever be again. To look at the town reminds you of one of those ancient cities one often reads about, lost for years in the sand-drift and then dug out by some searcher after ancient relics. The town is situated between a stony plain and a sandridge. Half the houses are in a state of decay, for the most part given over to the housing of fowls, goats, pigs, and other domestic animals. Like most bush towns, grog had a good deal to do with the prosperity or otherwise of Windorah, and nearly every second house appears to have been given over at one time or other to the sale of liquor.

The observant drover was travelling to Boulia, then up the Georgina River bound for Urandangie and Camooweal. There he would join a mob of cattle to be driven across the Northern Territory to the Ord River in north-western Australia. He was then planning to return to southern Queensland with another 4000 head. In his newsy letter he speaks of 100-kilometre rides, dry waterholes and:

> Coming up from Toompine to Maroo things are not too good so far as the travelling stock route is concerned ... and between the T.W. tank on Ardoch resumption and the broken dam on the Thylungera boundary—nearly forty miles [60 km]—there is no water for travelling stock.

When rain does fall, it quickly creates 'bankers', with the floodwaters brimming over the banks of previously dust dry watercourses. An excuse for a party!

> Mr. Campell was busy shearing at Maroo—putting some 1800 through—but was quite satisfied to knock off for a day or two when he got a fall of about 3 in. [8 cm] and all his creeks a banker. In fact, we had a dance at Maroo that night to celebrate the God-send.

After camping for three days and waiting for the waters to fall, the drover needs to move on:

> I decided to make a splash, and, with a good deal of trouble, succeeded in getting the horses, &c. over the Dead Man's Channel without mishap. At the main channel, however, things were different, and I was occupied the whole of this morning putting the camp outfit over and in swimming the horses over behind the boat.

Across the country, the network of overlanding cattle drovers is busy fording flooded creeks and pushing big mobs improbably long distances:

> I hear of drovers en route to Retreat for wethers, but I can hear nothing as to numbers, &c., supposed to be going south. Some forty bulls are now on the way out from Brinninyabba ... Drover Mason has left for Walhalla, in the Northern Territory, to lift 1500 mixed cattle for Springfield. Drover Rabig and Drover Doyle follow, and take 2000 between them for Springfield.

The rise and fall of cattle numbers and, with them, fortunes, is part and parcel of this way of life, a constant struggle against drought, distance, flood and the 'pleuro':

> Thylungera was busy brumby-running when I passed. It has about thirty-five to date. I hear there is a probability of more cattle coming to Thylungera. The herd now numbers from 1700 to 2000. In days gone by 35,000 was the tally. The water dries very fast in Kyabra Creek on Thylungera. In a hole where we watered 1700 cattle in December last, you could hardly get a drink for 500 now and then you would require to cut the mob up into small lots.

This was the land where crows fly backwards during the mostly dry times to keep the dust from their eyes.

The backward-flying crows might have some relationship to another fantastic feathered creature of bush lore and legend, the 'Oozlum bird'. Immortalised by poet W.T. Goodge, the Oozlum's defining characteristic is the ability, if that is the right word, to fly around in ever-decreasing circles until it disappears up its own fundamental orifice. Wits have long compared this peculiar behaviour with that of politicians for some reason. But while politicians might do this in reality, the Oozlum exists only in the great Australian imaginary of the bush and the outback.

The Roaring Days

Henry Lawson's famous poem 'The Roaring Days' is about the goldrush era of the mid-nineteenth century, remembered substantially from his own childhood experiences on the goldfields at Gulgong, New South Wales.

> The night too quickly passes
> And we are growing old,
> So let us fill our glasses
> And toast the Days of Gold;
> When finds of wondrous treasure
> Set all the South ablaze,
> And you and I were faithful mates
> All through the roaring days!
>
> Then stately ships came sailing
> From every harbour's mouth,
> And sought the land of promise
> That beaconed in the South;
> Then southward streamed their streamers
> And swelled their canvas full
> To speed the wildest dreamers
> E'er borne in vessel's hull.

Imagined Places

Their shining Eldorado,
Beneath the southern skies,
Was day and night for ever
Before their eager eyes.
The brooding bush, awakened,
Was stirred in wild unrest,
And all the year a human stream
Went pouring to the West.

The rough bush roads re-echoed
The bar-room's noisy din,
When troops of stalwart horsemen
Dismounted at the inn.
And oft the hearty greetings
And hearty clasp of hands
Would tell of sudden meetings
Of friends from other lands;
When, puzzled long, the new-chum
Would recognise at last,
Behind a bronzed and bearded skin,
A comrade of the past.

And when the cheery camp-fire
Explored the bush with gleams,
The camping-grounds were crowded
With caravans of teams;
Then home the jests were driven,
And good old songs were sung,
And choruses were given
The strength of heart and lung.

Great Australian Places

Oh, they were lion-hearted
Who gave our country birth!
Oh, they were of the stoutest sons
From all the lands on earth!

Oft when the camps were dreaming,
And fires began to pale,
Through rugged ranges gleaming
Would come the Royal Mail.
Behind six foaming horses,
And lit by flashing lamps,
Old 'Cobb and Co.'s', in royal state,
Went dashing past the camps.

Oh, who would paint a goldfield,
And limn the picture right,
As we have often seen it
In early morning's light;
The yellow mounds of mullock
With spots of red and white,
The scattered quartz that glistened
Like diamonds in light;
The azure line of ridges,
The bush of darkest green,
The little homes of calico
That dotted all the scene.

I hear the fall of timber
From distant flats and fells,
The pealing of the anvils

As clear as little bells,
The rattle of the cradle,
The clack of windlass-boles,
The flutter of the crimson flags
Above the golden holes.

Ah, then our hearts were bolder,
And if Dame Fortune frowned
Our swags we'd lightly shoulder
And tramp to other ground.
But golden days are vanished,
And altered is the scene;
The diggings are deserted,
The camping-grounds are green;
The flaunting flag of progress
Is in the West unfurled,
The mighty bush with iron rails
Is tethered to the world.

The term 'Roaring Days' was also used more broadly to refer to the era of pastoral expansion from around the 1830s. A distinctive colonial lifestyle, values, attitudes and language developed around male bush workers. A range of character types evolved, including the shearer, the overlander and the bullocky, as well as the digger on the goldfields. These were celebrated in song, verse and art and often seen as typical of an emerging Australian character, distinctive from that of the mostly British 'new chums' and immigrants from other countries.

Lawson, along with many other writers, Banjo Paterson and Will Ogilvie among them, composed reams of verse about the wild decades of the wool industry, overlanding mobs of cattle, digging for gold and bushranging. However, when Lawson wrote 'The Roaring Days', that era—if it ever existed outside the rose-tinted spectacles of nostalgia for youthful times—was coming to an end. The colonies generally became more industrialised as railways were built and more people lived in the cities than in the bush. That location—basically New South Wales, Victoria and Queensland—that time and the men, mainly, who typified it were nostalgically recreated in the creative imagination of the nation as 'the Roaring Days'.

In that world, epic yarns and glorious lies were swapped around boozy campfires, vast mobs of cattle were overlanded, a season's shearing cheque was 'knocked down' in sly grog shanties and legendary horsemen performed improbable feats. Romantic and appealing though the image was, the 'Roaring Days' of colonial history were a place in the collective mind of a mostly urbanised nation, more than they were a reality.

'Where they rise the sun with a golden bar'

> Out on the fringe of the Never Never,
> Out where the heat waves dance for ever,
> Out where the pigs for daylight root,
> And the pigeons fly with felted boots,
> Where they rise the sun with a golden bar,
> On the bunyip station of the great 'Speewah.'

An old shearer sent this recollection of his younger days to a local newspaper in the 1930s. He was one of many who spun yarns of a fabulously large station running an unimaginably large number of sheep shorn by armies of the fastest shearers ever known. The tales began to trickle into country newspapers in the 1890s, but lies like this had been told and retold long before then, probably since the 1870s, or earlier, going by the reminiscences of old shearers.

There were few outrageous exaggerations that were not made about the Speewah and its chief character, the oversized superhero shearer who could shear three sheep with just two blows of his shears and needed eight 'loppies', or rouseabouts, to carry the fleeces away. One shearer recalled his younger days in the columns of a 1920s newspaper:

> I have often heard of a big gun shearer who was in the zenith of his fame the year blucher boots were thirty bob a pair. Under the nom de plume of Rooked [sic] Mick, and using blades 8 feet [2.5 m] long, a back chain for a driver, and a 400 gallon [1800 L] tank for a water pot; he rang all the sheds from the Darling, to the Diamantina. His greatest feat, and one I think that will live for ever, was shearing three hoggetts in two blows . . .

Another correspondent to the same newspaper, Luke, corrected the misspelling of Mick's name and gave his own version of the legend:

> Now in my time 'Crooked Mick' never ventured as close to civilisation as the Darling or the Diamantina, and the Lord knows they were well outback. He continued his operations

to the Speewah, where the sheds were so big that the boss of the board had to go round on a bicycle and where a man, if he got fired, went out one door to turn up next day at another door and be re-engaged, as he was unknown. And out in the Speewah they cooked the plum duffs in 40,000 yard tanks and to save the roasted bullocks whole, which were cut up by means of circular saws. Oh, yes ! They did things on the grand scale out on the Speewah!

Crooked Mick's prowess with the blades was almost matched by his cooking skills. As well as his giant plum duffs, his pastries were said to be so light that they simply floated away across the vast Speewah station, which, as a shearer by the name of Stuart recalled with an extra flourish or two:

> was a mythical place, somewhere away out in the Territory, like the Hesperides of old. There shearing was plentiful and there was work for all. The sheds were immense—the boss of the board had to ride round on a bi-cycle. If a man was unlucky enough to get 'speared' he just walked out one door and half-a day later walked in another and was put on again. Every thing was on a gigantic scale. Bullocks were washed whole and cut up by means of circular saws. As for puddings— well they used to dump them in the dam and boil them there, hoisting them in and out by means of steam cranes. These, too, were cut up in similar fashion to the bullocks.

By the time shearer and writer Julian (John) Stuart tacked a few of the many bits and pieces of this yarn together, Crooked Mick had become a 'superman':

> ... with feet so big that he had to go outside to turn round. It took a large-sized bullock's hide to make him a pair of moccasins. He was a heavy smoker.—It took—one 'loppy' (rouseabout) all his time cutting tobacco and filling his pipe. He worked at such a clip that his shears ran hot, and sometimes he had half a dozen pairs in the water-pot. To cool. He had his fads, and would not shear in sheds that faced north. When at his top it took three pressers to handle the wool from his blades, and they had to work overtime to keep the bins clear. He ate two sheep each meal— that is; if they were small merinos—but only one and a half when the ration sheep were Leicester crossbred wethers.

When Mick was 'between sheds', Stuart reported, he worked as a fencer, swinging an axe in each hand. When he dug the holes for the posts, Mick used a shovel in one hand and a crowbar in the other, at the same time, of course. And:

> Once, when taming a Dawson River brumby (which had killed or crippled every man whomever tackled him) he nearly died of starvation. The outlaw had kept on bucking continuously, and on the third day the rider yelled for food. His mates cooked a lot of preserved potatoes, which they threw at him when they could get near enough. He caught some open mouthed, but a good deal of the food was wasted, as the horse bucked sideways and in circles. Lumps of the spuds lodged in Mick's beard, which reached to his waist, and on his moustache, which was so long that he used to tie it at the back of his head ...

Not all Speewah tales featured Mick. Snake stories are among the bush liar's favourite fantastications:

> I've heard a lot about snakes being very thick in different parts of Australia, but I think the Speewah is the leading snake district of the lot. All the bunks in the stockmen's huts are hung on four fencing wire, and slush lamps are kept burning all night, the little snakes are generally used for boot laces, and the big ones for belts. Outsizes in snakes are generally made into horse rugs, and the extra outsizes are used to cover the motor cars and lorries. Ladies use the very long ones for clothes lines.

The snakes came in all colours, including pink, gold and rainbow, usually 'in the beer season', including one 'with a yellow back, green belly and blue eyes, but to tell the truth I had been having a month's beer and other drinks at the pub, so I won't guarantee that the species exists, but I think it does'.

The perpetrator of this whopper concluded by claiming to have heard that the Speewah boundary riders repaired their broken fences with a particularly wiry species of snake, 'but I can hardly believe it. There are some awful liars knocking about the country, and I have no time for them.'

Little was heard of Mick and the Speewah during the 1940s and it was not until writers like Alan Marshall in the 1950s and Bill Wannan in the 1960s picked up on bush lore that they came back into print. But by the 1990s the reviewer of an anthology of Australian humour containing a few Speewah yarns declared that including these tales was a 'resurrection'. However in the twenty-first century Crooked Mick and the Speewah have gone the way of the Oozlum bird, as Australia has become a much more cosmopolitan and sophisticated society.

Of course, we can still tell a lie or three.

The Everywhere Man

It was a cold May night in the town of Richmond, New South Wales, in 1946. The Regent Theatre was only half full for a 'welcome home' function for a group of servicemen and women recently returned from World War II military service. But still, a fine time was had by all. After a grand opening of 'They are Jolly Good Fellows', the mayor offered a cordial welcome home to the soldiers. 'It seems like old times again,' he enthused, although:

> Their joy at having these Servicemen and women home again was, however, tempered with sympathy for those families whose loved ones would not return, the Mayor added. 'We are overjoyed to have you all with us once more. I think the word "home" is one of the greatest in our language, and it is very pleasing indeed for me, on behalf of the citizens of Richmond, to extend you a very sincere welcome home.'

The speeches were followed by a concert from 'a group of ex-Servicemen, members of the R.S.L. who regularly broadcast from a Sydney station'. There were vocalists, impersonators, a contortionist, a piano accordionist, a saxophonist and a performer who, 'with his guitar, was responsible for most of the laughs with his vocal gymnastics, his number, "In Der Fuehrer's Face", being a gem of its kind, which had the audience in hysterics.' From a 1943 short film by the Walt Disney studio, the song lampoons Adolf Hitler and Nazism in general with verses like:

> When der Fuehrer says we is de master race
> We heil (pffft) heil (pffft) right in der Fuehrer's face
> Not to love der Fuehrer is a great disgrace
> So we heil (pffft) heil (pffft) right in der Fuehrer's face . . .

The 'pffft' is pronounced as a juicy raspberry.

The entertaining performer producing the raspberries used the stage name 'Geoff Mack'. His real name was Albert Geoffrey McElhinney and he had cut his performing teeth in Borneo where he was posted as a Royal Australian Air Force aircraft mechanic. His musical skills were soon discovered and put to good use entertaining the troops. After the war, Mack pursued a career in show business, specialising in country-flavoured novelty songs, often of his own composition.

In 1959 he penned a new one around the idea of unusual Australian place names. It began with a spoken introduction by a bloke hitching a lift to Oodnadatta on a semitrailer. The truckie asked his passenger if he'd ever seen a dustier road. The passenger said he had, "Cause I've been everywhere, man'. A popular Australian singer picked up the song, recorded it and released it in 1962. His name was 'Lucky Starr' and 'I've Been Everywhere' became a massive hit, establishing him in an enduring show business career.

Imagined Places

Featuring a dazzling array of tongue-twisting Australian placenames, 'I've Been Everywhere' is one of Australia's most famous songs here or abroad. It cleverly rhymes more than 100 placenames, including Mooloolaba, Muckadilla, Mullumbimby, Goondiwindi (pronounced gun-da-windi) and even Grong Grong, a small town in the Riverina whose name is thought to mean 'bad camping place'.

Good, bad, or indifferent, there weren't too many places the hitchhiking yarn spinner hadn't visited. As the exasperated truckie conceded at the end of the song, his well-travelled passenger had indeed been everywhere, except for one place, and he didn't need help to reach it.

While people today are probably still familiar with a song that was popular more than half a century ago, few know of the many different versions that have blown around Australia and the world. The song became a hit in America, with lyrics rewritten for American towns and has been covered by many well-known artists, including Johnny Cash and, in Australia, Ted Egan. Around 130 cover versions are thought to have been recorded in the United Kingdom, New Zealand, Ireland and elsewhere.

In Nashville, Tennessee, Geoff Mack was inducted into the Songwriters Hall of Fame as early as 1963, though it took another fifteen years for recognition in his home country, with a place in the Hands of Fame at Tamworth, Australia's country music capital. He also received other awards including an Order of Australia.

Born in 1922, Albert Geoffrey McElhinney died in 2017. It took him 95 years to reach the divine place the 'everywhere man' of his most famous song had not yet been.

Capricornia

The stresses and strains of the COVID-19 pandemic propelled Australia's borders into sharp focus. In the only continent to have a single government, most citizens and visitors took interstate travel for granted. When states began to close their borders to protect residents from disease it came as a shock to many, as well as to the Commonwealth government. Everyone, it seems, had forgotten that prior to 1901 Australia was a collection of squabbling colonies unable to agree even on the gauge of intercolonial railway lines. Since 2020 it is apparent that little has changed, as the sharp exchanges between state and federal politicians demonstrated, together with the different approach of each state and territory to public health.

Australia's history since 1788 has been characterised by a continual drawing and redrawing of boundaries. Although the current arrangement of states and territories that make up the Commonwealth is what most living Australians are familiar with, there have always been those who are unhappy with the system and advocate for separation or secession. The best-known of these movements is probably in Western Australia. The colony was reluctant to join the federation of 1901. On several occasions since, Western Australians frustrated with the relationship with the Commonwealth and other states, have promoted secession, once voting for it in 1933.

One secession attempt in the west even succeeded, sort of. The quirky exit of the Hutt River Province from Western Australia as an independent sovereign state, or 'principality' has long amused citizens and tourists alike. The 'micronation' issued its own postage stamps and passports and lasted from 1970 to 2020. It can still be visited on the internet.

Some Torres Strait Islanders have also pursued a separatist path at times, aiming to be independent of Queensland. Also up north, North Queensland has long considered itself and its interests to be better served by a break from the rest of the state, the main recent proponents being members of the Katter's Australian Party. Versions of this proposal frequently use 'Capricornia'—the name of an existing region and federal electoral district—as their preferred name. Advocates want a new state extending north from the Tropic of Capricorn to the Gulf of Carpentaria and west to the border with the Northern Territory.

The first proponent of the idea was a fiery Scots Presbyterian minister, John Dunmore Lang. He arrived in Australia in 1823 and was soon advocating for the colonies to separate from Great Britain. By the 1850s he was publishing his ideas about a separate North Queensland, arguing that the area was so large that it could not be effectively governed or policed from the distant administrative capital of Brisbane. He feared the region would become a 'common receptacle for lawless characters of all descriptions, and no regular government would be practicable within it' until it had declared an autonomous 'Australian Union'. Lang wanted this state to operate under a federal government independent of Britain.

Although Lang's specific proposals did not gain much support, Queensland experienced a range of separatist movements, agitations including the Northern Separation League in the 1860s. The issue was more effectively revived in 1870, though without result due largely to considerable local resistance and a petition to Britain for separation in 1871 was unsuccessful. By the 1890s the campaign was dead, lost in the economic depression of the time, and was not revived until 1910 and then again in the 1920s.

It was in the 1950s that the idea of a separate North Queensland next attracted attention. Fuelled by economic development in central and northern Queensland and lingering fears of Japanese invasion that had started during World War II, the Liberal and then Country parties pushed for separation of north Queensland. Today, colourful politicians and others continue to argue that north Queenslanders are severely disadvantaged by distance. Opponents of a new state sometimes point to the region's history of indentured black labour, particularly in the sugar industry. The implication is that without forced labour, development of the region would have been economically unviable.

One mostly forgotten work of imagination confronted these issues head on. In 1938 Xavier Herbert published his first novel, the sprawling *Capricornia*, set in a more or less imaginary country approximating the Northern Territory and the tropical north in general. Herbert engages fully with the prejudice and the enduring problems and debates over developing Australia's far north, beginning with 'Although that northern part of the Continent of Australia which is called Capricornia was pioneered long after the southern parts, its unofficial early history was even more bloody than that of the others . . . ' The novel continues through its intergenerational cast of 'combos', 'yellerfellas' and 'Javanese princesses' to paint an unsparing picture of toxic racism in language that many contemporary readers would find confronting and probably offensive.

The book won several literary awards and contributed to the development of Baz Luhrmann's film, *Australia* (2008). Writer Randolph Stow hailed it as 'THE Australian classic', yet few read it or are even aware of *Capricornia* today. But the idea of a separate state of some kind in the tropical north, under whatever name, is unlikely to go away. Nor is it likely to disappear from the wider Australian conversation about boundaries and borders.

The Borders

Hardly anyone thinks about borders. The official boundaries between the states and territories are just lines on the map for most of us. But then COVID-19 arrived.

The complete freedom of passage from one part of the country to any other largely disappeared. We reverted to a situation not unlike that before Federation united the fractious colonies that had evolved since 1788. Australians now found themselves stuck on one side or the other of various state and territory borders. Locals who usually walked or drove from New South Wales to Victoria at Albury–Wodonga for work, to visit family or for recreation were no longer able to do so. And vice versa. The same situation played out on most of Australia's internal borders.

Similar restrictions were applied at the New South Wales–Queensland border, and Western Australia simply stopped just about everyone from entering the state or leaving it. This happened even where there was little community incidence of the disease, as in the Northern Territory and, at times,

Tasmania. Visitors to Norfolk Island were threatened with a lockdown and enforced isolation of unknown duration when the pandemic first struck in March 2020.

As well as the clipping of our free-and-easy wings, there were other consequences. Many businesses on either side of borders lost customers because people no longer travelled as they had done or were undergoing one or another of the various forms of isolation that governments periodically, and increasingly erratically, imposed. Together with the disappearance of international tourists and students, hospitality, restaurants and the many enterprises associated with these industries had to cut their activity, often lost staff and sometimes closed their doors forever.

Suddenly, the official boundaries between states and territories became a matter of intense interest and significance. This was an issue few had thought about since the influenza pandemic of 1919 . During the COVID-19 pandemic, states and territories again discovered they had considerable clout, independent of the Commonwealth. Premiers had to be consulted by the prime minister in a National Cabinet. Legal challenges against states were made by business interests, particularly against Western Australia, and questions about who had the power to do what within states became an issue at the federal government level. Related questions around state authority also sparked some of the largest street demonstrations seen in Australia since the days of the Vietnam War.

Deciding where borders should be, agreeing to them and changing them has been a lengthy and often divisive thread of Australian history. In complete ignorance of traditional First Nations territories, Europeans at first just called the whole continent 'New Holland' or 'New South Wales'. But it wasn't long before various groups began agitating for a place of their own with the appropriate boundaries to separate themselves from the rest of the colony. Van Diemen's Land, now Tasmania, became a colony in 1825; the Swan River, later Western Australia, in 1829; South Australia from 1836; Victoria in 1851 and Queensland in 1859. The Northern Territory and Australian Capital Territory followed at different times, together with various islands, including south-east New Guinea. Even New Zealand was a colony of New South Wales until 1841. So, although we have mostly thought of the country as an undivided whole—'a single jewel', as historian Alan Atkinson put it—it is riven by many internal and external borders and related tensions.

One of the issues in the Federation debate of the nineteenth century was the passage of goods across the borders. Before Federation, the colonies controlled, and charged for, goods passing through their borders. Most feared that a commonwealth would deprive them of this income, which it did. Others argued for the better efficiencies of having a single system in which there was unencumbered movement of goods through the whole country. Federation provided this, despite the ongoing problem of different-gauge railway lines.

But during the COVID-19 panic, we reverted to something like the pre-Federation system, with all forms of transport being restricted. The consequences of this were especially severe in the west, where many goods are transported by train, road or air across the Nullarbor Plain. The borders were closed early in the pandemic and remained that way until early 2022. Allied with restrictions and related difficulties elsewhere in the country, this had a major impact on the building industry and deliveries of mail and goods, leading to prolonged shortages, particularly over the summer of 2021–22.

In many parts of the world, borders are highly volatile zones, their existence the product of history and warfare. They may be contested and patrolled by military and are often difficult to cross. Australia has avoided such situations and there is no likelihood of border wars. But the return of these convenient dividers as significant constitutional and practical barriers highlights the conditional nature of places we have taken for granted.

While they exist on paper and are, as we now know, able to be closely controlled, Australia's internal borders are a part of the imagination of Australia. It began in the distant past when the continent was an unknown southland and continued in the hearts and minds of the politicians and people who debated and, ultimately, voted to create the constitutional pattern of the country we live in today.

Barbara Ellis in front of the Big Banana at Coffs Harbour, in the late 1960s.

7
OUR PLACE

Big Australia

A big country needs big things. Australia has lots. It's difficult to travel through regional or even remote areas without coming across a BIG something. Sometimes they are in prominent places, such as beside a main road or at the centre of a town or tourist area. Some are more or less hidden away in seemingly odd locations. Whatever they represent and wherever they are, Australia's Big Things are almost everywhere.

Many of these more than 150 signature structures represent aspects of Australian identity, including plants, animals, activities and people. The Australian Capital Territory boasts not one but two Big Galahs kissing each other in Watson and a Big Bogong Moths sculpture in Acton.

Great Australian Places

New South Wales has the Big Banana at Coffs Harbour, several Big Chooks (Mount Vernon and Moonbi), a Big Blue Heeler at Muswellbrook and—wait for it—the Big Cheese at Bodalla. There are other 'Big' icons in the state as well, including a Big Prawn at West Ballina, a Big Murray Cod at Tocumwal and, celebrating the giant 'Hexham Greys' of folklore, Hexham has its own Big Mosquito, known affectionately as 'Ozzie the Mozzie'. There's a Big Merino at Goulburn, a Big Kookaburra at Kurri Kurri, a Big Funnel Web Spider at Jamberoo and some Big Ugg Boots in the Hunter Valley.

And, of course, someone just had to do it. In the early 2000s, locals were concerned at a state government decision not to reuse wastewater in the Kiama area of New South Wales. In protest, they commissioned a 1 metre x 5 metre foam poo. The object has been displayed at various locations in the years since.

Up in the Top End, the traditional owners of the area are celebrated in the 17-metre Anmatjere Man sculpture at Anmatjere near the Aileron Roadhouse. There is a Big Boxing Crocodile at Humpty Doo, built in 1988 to celebrate the winning of the America's Cup yacht race five years earlier. There are quite a few references to alcohol in big Territory structures, including the Big Beer Can at Ghan, the Big Stubbie at Larrimah and the Big Wine Bottle at Daly Waters.

To be fair, quite a few places sport signs related to grog. But surprisingly the state famous for its wine, South Australia, has only one: the Big Church Block Bottle, and that was taken away from its site at the Wirra Wirra Winery in 2016. But the Croweaters have plenty of others, such as the Big Ant at Poochera, the Big Bobtail Lizard at Port Lincoln, a Big Wombat at Bookabie, a Big Yabby at Clayton and a Big Cockroach at Lower Light, among many more.

Inevitably, Tasmania has a Big Tasmanian Devil, as well as a Big Platypus and a Big Apple. Some affect an especially quirky charm, like Deloraine's Big Coffee Pot, built by fitting a handle and spout to either side of a grain silo. Tassie has also created a sculpture in the University of Tasmania, where there is a Big Slide Rule in the School of Mathematics and Physics.

Perhaps academics have a stronger sense of humour than we might think. Over in Western Australia the Edith Cowan University campus at Joondalup flaunts an image over four times larger than its rival in a Spanish university. This is said to be the world's largest permanent periodic table of the elements. It's educational, of course, but they've even installed a periodic picnic table nearby (get it?) for visitors who want to view their international triumph at its most impressive. The west also boasts its own Big Apple, Orange, Banana, Lobster, Marron, Prawn, Crocodile and Whale. If you should ever find yourself on a sightseeing trip at the industrial area between South Hedland and Port Hedland, you'll even come across a Big Wheelbarrow.

Smaller than many other states, the 'Cabbage Patch', Victoria, is no laggard when it comes to bigness. They have the usual array of oversized native species, including Abalone at Laverton North, Koala at Dadswells Bridge and a Lizard at Marysville. The Mallee is especially well represented with the Big Mallee Bull at Birchip, a Mallee Fowl at Patchewollock and a Mallee Root at Ouyen. Victorian structures sometimes project whimsical wit, such as the Big Dead Fish atop the Fishy Pub at Fish Creek and the outsize model of an old-fashioned clip purse for spare change outside the former GPO in the Bourke Street

Mall, known as 'The Public Purse'. Not satisfied with one big bushranger at Glenrowan, there is also a Big Ned Kelly at Warrenheip.

Last, but definitely not least, is Queensland, with possibly the biggest batch of big things in the country. There are Big Apples, Bananas, Pineapples, Barramundi, Brolgas, Cassowaries and Crocodiles galore, not to mention the Big Cane Toad. Captain Cook gets a look-in at Cairns. Tolga has a Big Peanut and Yatala a Big Pie, while Bundaberg had to have a Big Rum Bottle. There's a tribute to the Aussie lawn with a Big Mower at Beerwah and, oddly, another Big Ned Kelly at Maryborough. Perhaps Ned stayed at the motel graced with his image?

And they still can't get enough big stuff in Bananaland. In 2021 at Calen, north of Mackay, a couple of blokes knocked up the Big Thongs outside the hotel using conveyor belt rubber from the local mine. 'They're built to last, like a good old pair of Aussie thongs', said one of the co-creators.

It's easy to laugh at these icons of local, regional and national identity. Many are purely commercial or self-conscious exercises in public art. But others, especially the local makeshift structures, project that dry sense of humour for which Aussies are renowned. In colloquial terms, they often 'stir the possum' or 'take the piss' and are usually meant as tongue-in-cheek takes on those things that we associate with the country and its people.

One of the earliest big things reflects these motivations. Queensland's 7.9-metre-tall Big Golden Gumboot at Tully was erected in 2003 as a nod to the area's highest rainfall in 1950. The frog clinging to the side whimsically reinforces the structure's environmental genesis. The town was in need of an economic boost from tourism as the sugar cane industry faded. Local opinion is reportedly divided about the value of the Gumboot, but the townsfolk paid for the cost of construction and have always footed the not-insubstantial cost of maintaining the concrete welly. It symbolises their community and its sense of belonging to a very soggy place.

The Old Tin Shed

They called him 'Huge Deal McIntosh', though his proper name was Hugh D. McIntosh, colourful entrepreneur and builder of the now-lost Stadium in Sydney, New South Wales. A huge expanse of wooden bleachers covered, more or less, by a vast corrugated iron roof, the Stadium was host to generations of boxers, wrestlers and entertainers over its sixty-odd-year history.

In 1908, McIntosh leased the site of the Chinese market gardens in Rushcutters Bay, promoting the place as an outdoor sporting venue. At that time, boxing was a popular international sport, as well as the focus of heavy gambling. McIntosh aimed to put Australia on the international prize-fighting circuit with Bill 'Boshter' Squires pitted against Canadian heavyweight Tommy Burns at the first Stadium event, an open-air bout attended by thousands.

A few months later the stadium hosted a historic bout that attracted a crowd of between 20,000 and 40,000. Fight fans filled the space to see Burns lose the World Heavyweight Boxing Championship to Jack Johnson. The African American Johnson was a big and powerful man after whom large artillery shells were named in World War I. These sensational events made

McIntosh a lot of money and a few years later he had an octagonal structure built, a great barn, able to hold up to 12,000 people. It became part of the fabric of the city's sporting and entertainment culture for generations of Australians.

Its creator was born to Scots Irish parents in Sydney in 1876. His early life was impoverished and chequered but he emerged as a promoter of bicycle racing in the 1890s, then moved on to the opportunities he correctly saw in the boxing game. He also invested in many other businesses including hotels, vaudeville theatres, newspapers and the early Australian film industry. One of his promotional ideas was to film the Burns v Johnson fight and take it to America, where he planned to pursue even bigger business ventures. He would spend many years living the high life in America and Britain as well as in Australia. Here, he was involved in politics, eventually managing to have himself elected a member of the New South Wales Legislative Council.

Despite his expensive lifestyle and controversial public profile, McIntosh was continually in financial trouble and was finally bankrupted in 1932. Ever the optimist and with his trademark unflagging energy, McIntosh opened the Black and White Milk Bar in London, as usual, capitalising on current fads. It was a great success but failed a few years later when he tried to expand. He died broke in London in 1942.

A much more famous Stadium personality was the extraordinary Australian boxer Les Darcy. Born near Maitland, New South Wales, in 1895, the muscular Darcy had most of his fights at the Stadium and became a superstar of the era. Like McIntosh, he aspired to an American career but, like thousands of other men of his age, he was expected to enlist in World War I. He did not, drawing intense criticism and accusations of cowardice. He responded by saying that he wished to go to America to secure his family's finances, after which he would travel to Britain and join the services there. But, in a spectacularly bad piece of timing, he secretly and illegally sailed for America the day before the first conscription referendum. If this had been a 'yes' vote, Darcy would have been forced to enlist. It was not, but controversy followed him across the Pacific.

McIntosh is rumoured to have used his American contacts to ensure Darcy could not get a fight when he arrived there. After some humiliating vaudeville show fights and some cancelled professional bouts, Darcy took American citizenship and volunteered for the army.

Then he was contracted to fight in Memphis, Tennessee, his call-up being deferred to allow the bout. He began training but fell ill soon after. His condition worsened and his fiancée, Winnie O'Sullivan, rushed from Sydney to his bedside, arriving just before he died.

The great Les Darcy—non-drinker, non-smoker, devout Catholic and supporter of his family—had been floored by blood poisoning, the result of a poorly treated dental injury sustained in one of his last Australian fights. Darcy's body was farewelled by large crowds in San Francisco and again back in Sydney and in his hometown. The legend grew that the Americans were so fearful of his prowess in the ring that they engineered his death. A similar belief exists about the demise of the famous racehorse Phar Lap. Both beliefs are myths.

Wars, scandals and troubles did not stop the Stadium entertaining its audiences. Boxing and wrestling were matched by roller derbies in the 1950s and 1960s, and from 1954 international entertainers were brought to the barn by the flamboyant

American impresario, Lee Gordon. He presented Ella Fitzgerald, Johnny Ray, Frank Sinatra and Louis Armstrong, among others. Sydney promoter Harry M. Miller booked Judy Garland and other stars, and when rock-and-roll got underway, Bill Haley and the Comets appeared at the Stadium, as did local acts like Johnny O'Keefe, and Col Joye and the Joy Boys. In 1964 the Beatles played several concerts at the ageing venue, known by then in the showbiz world as 'The Tin Shed'.

It couldn't last, of course. In 1970 the Eastern Suburbs Railway ended the Stadium's unusually long run. Those who experienced the draughty, noisy and barebones building usually remember it with affection. As its historian wrote, it was also a kind of microcosm of Sydney's raffish society, where 'politicians and wealthy men in tailored suits rubbed shoulders with broken-nosed battlers and ticket scalpers'.

What Did the King Say to the Duke?

It was a sunny and momentous day. The ninth of May 1927. After many years, a parliament house had finally been built in Canberra. The nation's assembly now had a purpose-built place to meet, debate and legislate.

The building and surrounding area were decorated with flags and 'At the entrance stretched an awning of purple-and-gold. Stands accommodated 500 official guests, and in the lawn stands there were 600 present by special invitation. Half-way down the lawn and on each side there were spectators numbering 10,000.'

The Duke of York, destined to be King George VI, was there to perform the honours, together with the Duchess of York.

Prime Minister Stanley Bruce, cabinet ministers, backbenchers, military men and senior public servants were in attendance, along with the press and interested members of the public. Everyone was invited. Well, not quite everyone.

No invitations had been sent to the original inhabitants of the land on which Parliament House and the growing capital city of Canberra were built. But their envoys came anyway.

Jimmy Clements, known as 'King Billy', was a 'clever man' of the Wiradjuri people. He and a companion, John 'Marvellous' Noble were both old enough to have witnessed early settlement. Now they had humped their swags the three-day walk from Brungle, near Tumut, to Canberra. They planned to take part in the grand opening ceremony and to lay out their sovereign claim to Canberra and the country all around.

The two Wiradjuri men, dressed in swagman mode and without shoes, were encouraged by the police to leave. But the crowd in attendance disapproved, someone calling out that 'the Aborigine had a better right than any man present to be there'.

The opening ritual went ahead as planned. The duke was reportedly impressed when Marvellous offered him 'an approved military salute', acknowledging it with 'a special wave'. Jimmy managed to secure a meeting with the duke, though what exactly was said was not recorded. One of Jimmy's descendants, Dean Freeman, thinks it likely that the Wiradjuri Elder explained their culture and their special connection with the land. In particular, Jimmy wanted it to be known that Wiradjuri people were still occupying their country. What the future King of England—and Australia—might have made of this we can only guess.

Jimmy Clements died a few months later, remembered as a man with artistic talent and a 'splendid physique and personality'. It was the common practice at the time for Aboriginal people to be buried outside the consecrated ground of church cemeteries. When Marvellous Noble died in 1930 he was buried in this way. But King Billy received an interment within the consecrated ground at Queanbeyan Riverside Cemetery, together with the full final rites of the Anglican church. It is thought that he might have been baptised at some point in his life, though nobody can be sure.

As well as his respectful burial, many thought King Billy should be commemorated with a statue. He wasn't. Nor was Marvellous Noble. But there are now renewed calls for a memorial commemorating the events and confirming the continuing right of First Nations peoples to the land and their right to be seen and heard.

A number of photographs taken on the grand day. One of them captured King Billy, recumbent on his bare earth in front of Parliament House. He is not far from where the Aboriginal Tent Embassy has staked a claim to First Nations sovereignty since 1972. That may be the most fitting memorial to Jimmy 'King Billy' Clements and John 'Marvellous' Noble.

The Bridge

Sometimes known as 'The Coathanger', more usually just as 'the Bridge', Sydney's most famous icon was the largest steel-arch span in the world when it was opened in 1932. The first sod was turned in 1923 and construction of the arch began from the north and south sides of the harbour in 1928. Would the two halves meet exactly in the middle? People made bets one way or the other. Some lost their money when the arching steel joints, fastened by hand-driven hot rivets, merged perfectly.

The ghost of a diver who drowned while working on the construction of the edifice is said to haunt the bridge. He was one of the sixteen workers who died on that job. For many of the thousands of rivetters, steel workers, labourers and tradesmen who worked on the bridge, it was their only chance to earn an income, the construction phase from 1923 to 1932 falling partly during the Great Depression. At one point, it was dubbed 'the iron lung', a reference to its lifesaving characteristics.

The bridge was instantly famous around the country and internationally, seen and promoted as a symbol of Australia's modernity and success. It also served to encourage immigration, enhanced by its location on the harbour. It was a rite of passage for immigrants arriving by sea to be on deck to witness the underside of the giant girders as their ship came in to dock.

Labor Premier Jack Lang insisted on opening the wonderful structure on behalf of the people of New South Wales, rather than allowing the state's governor, representative of the crown, to do the job. In the event, neither did. The right-wing Captain de Groot galloped up and slashed the ribbon with his sword. The people were not much troubled and an estimated 300,000 surged across the span, taking possession of their road, rail and foot bridge. They would be paying for it for decades to come. The structure was reputed to have cost over £6 million, a debt not paid off until the late 1980s, with the help of tolls and the state lotteries.

One of the walkers that day was a nine-year-old boy named Lennie Gwyther. He was there, together with his pony Ginger Mick, named after the C.J. Dennis character of World War I. Lennie and his patient companion rode from the family farm at Leongatha, Victoria, all the way to Sydney just to be there for the grand opening. Lennie also wanted to go to the Royal Easter Show and see the ships on the harbour. But on this day, he achieved his main ambition when he and his pony walked the length of the bridge, together with an estimated 300,000 people, and with up to one million others also taking part in the broader event.

The bridge would not be opened again for such a mass possessioning until its fiftieth anniversary, when more than half a million people walked across from either side, reclaiming the pedestrian possibilities of the structure for a few enthusiastic hours. In 2000 the Peoples' Walk for Reconciliation saw another large contingent of walkers, as well as reminding the world of the iconic nature of the bridge during the Olympic Games. The Millennium celebrations saw the bridge lit up with a spectacular fireworks display. In contrast, the bridge's seventy-fifth anniversary was so regulated by a government fearful of the upcoming polls, in which public transport was to be a major issue, that it passed almost without notice.

Despite the controversies and traffic congestion, Sydneysiders love their bridge, though not everyone has been impressed. Visiting around 1950, American writer James Michener later wrote 'Sydney Bridge [sic] is big, utilitarian and the symbol of Australia, like the Statue of Liberty or the Eiffel Tower. But it is very ugly. No Australian will admit this.'

'She's a Beauty!'

Never mind that Karl Benz had already invented the first car to be realistically powered by an internal combustion engine, Herbert Thomson and Edward Holmes of Armadale reckoned they had a better idea. Why not put a steam engine onto the horse-drawn carriage usually described as a 'phaeton? They did. It was called the Thomson Motor Phaeton and chuffed onto what then passed for roads in 1899 following several years of development. It was said that 'Australia caught its breath in amazement' as the buggy completed an 'epoch-making' trip from Bathurst to Melbourne at an average speed of eight and a half miles (14 kilometres) an hour.

Other Australians attempted to build steam- and petrol-driven cars, though most of our early automobiles were imported, until Harley Tarrant began to make them in the 1890s. After first experimenting with a kerosene-powered vehicle he developed a locally built and assembled two-seater with a petrol engine. It sold well. But by 1907, the Ford Model T was a better and cheaper choice for motorists than his own make. Astutely, Tarrant ceased to produce his own cars and purchased a Ford franchise for Victoria.

A saddlery business called J.A. Holden & Co. had been founded in Adelaide in the 1850s but subsequent generations of the family moved into the automobile business and, through mergers and expansions, prospered until the Great Depression of the 1930s. The American General Motors company bought the struggling manufacturer in 1931 and it became General Motors-Holden. The Australian government was keen to encourage local automobile manufacturing and associated industrial facilities in the lead-up to World War II and the quest for an Australian-designed and built automobile was eventually won by GM-H. In 1948 GM-H produced the endearingly dumpy vehicle that came to be known as the 'FX'. It was unveiled by Prime Minister Ben Chifley, who famously declared 'She's a beauty!'

As the company grew, it opened factories in many places, including Fishermans Bend in Melbourne, Pagewood, New South Wales, and even, briefly, in New Zealand. By 1963 their plant was up and running in Elizabeth, South Australia. Her Majesty Queen Elizabeth II came to see and be seen the following year and the Holden in all its various models continued on its way as the quintessential Aussie car. Models like the Kingswood, Monaro and, ultimately, the Commodore, achieved cult-like status among automobile aficionados and resonated with a public marketed into pride in 'our' car.

But it all started slowing down from 2013. The company received grants of $270 million from the state and Commonwealth governments just the previous year but failed to attract funding from a new Coalition government in Canberra. Holden management announced that production would cease in 2017. Reaction was swift and savage. People, especially those who worked for Holden or were dependent on their business, wanted to know what had gone wrong. Many reasons were given over the next few years, as attempts to save the operation lurched from one plan to another. Insufficient sales. Excessive labour costs. Difficulty of competing with global brands. Some smelled one or more rats, pointing the finger at management and governments.

Recriminations and industrial action dogged the gradual closing down of Holden and the loss of jobs that went with it. The Elizabeth plant in South Australia came to symbolise the struggle of workers and many others against the inevitability of closure and the loss of work, skills and national manufacturing capability. On 20 October 2017, the last shift at the plant in Elizabeth joined the thousands of GMH employees who had already had their final pay packets. The last car to come off the assembly line was a red Commodore sedan.

The Holden lion logo and other signage was removed from the Elizabeth plant in 2018. A new owner has since redeveloped the site as the Lionsgate Business Park, a hub for industrial manufacturing and construction. The new identity promises to bring jobs back to a region devastated by the end of Australia's love affair with its favourite car. The Holden brand was finally 'retired' in 2021. General Motors rationalised its American and global operations, withdrawing fully from Australia and New Zealand. Prime Minister Scott Morrison accused the company of taking billions in taxpayer subsidies over the years and then simply allowing the brand to 'wither away'.

Despite its place in our affections, historians point out that the Holden was never really an 'Australian' car, owned as it was by an American company and, at various times, largely assembled rather than made here. But Australians took Holden cars to their hearts and wallets, as they transported people to and from and through the ever-expanding post-World War II suburbs. The Holden Kingswood, Monaro, Commodore and other classic models are still fondly remembered by many.

For those still pining for old Holdens, take a trip to Condobolin, New South Wales. There you will find a paddock full of artistically repurposed Holden utes, the inspiration of Graham and Jana Pickles. Old utes were located, cleaned and given over to local and visiting artists to be colourfully repainted and sometimes reshaped and imaginatively mounted. There is a vertically displayed ute featuring Dame Edna Everage on the dunny, the work of artist Karen Tooth. A 1962 EJ ute sits atop an array of spear plants, created by muso Stephen Coburn. Coburn collaborated with another muso, Jim Moginie, on the conversion of a 1957 FE into 'UteZilla', a giant kangaroo complete with a joey that looks like the children's TV cartoon character Bluey. These and the other inventive recreations are popular with tourists and won top gong at the national Australian Street Art Awards in 2020.

They can take our factory away, but they'll never take our Holdens.

The Bushranger of Research

This backhanded compliment was applied to the Australian scientist chiefly credited with the development of penicillin, opening the way for many other lifesaving drugs.

The evolution of penicillin was a series of scientific accidents. A French physician named Ernest Duchesne made the initial discovery in the 1890s but his work was forgotten. In 1928 Scottish scientist Alexander Fleming allegedly sneezed on some bacterial culture plates he was working with. He then went on holiday, leaving the plates in his laboratory. When he returned, he found a mould had grown that turned out to be penicillin. However he made his wonderful discovery, Fleming was unable to manufacture it in useable quantities and abandoned this research. It would take more than a decade of hard work and another stroke of luck to eventually produce the world's first wonder drug.

Born in South Australia in 1898, Howard Florey won a prestigious Rhodes Scholarship to Oxford University when he was in his early twenties. He followed a research career in science and became Chair of Pathology in the Sir William Dunn Institute of Biochemistry at Oxford in 1934. It was from this eminent position that Florey was able to develop a different approach to research. Instead of operating with teams of similarly trained and qualified scientists, he built a multidisciplinary group who brought different expertise and so different ideas to any given research problem. Chief among these was the German-trained Ernst Chain. In the course of his work, Chain came across both Duchesne's and Fleming's earlier work. Florey and Chain, with assistance from other team members, went on to produce penicillin in the laboratory, tested it on animals and finally, in 1941, on humans. After initial setbacks, the drug delivered impressive outcomes, duly reported by Florey in the leading medical journal *The Lancet*.

The problem then was how to produce enough penicillin for a world at war, as well as to combat the number of deadly infections that even the smallest cut or graze might produce. Facilities were not available in war-torn Britain, but Florey had good contacts in America, where he went with the new wonder drug. Its enormous value was quickly recognised and the resources and facilities needed to produce the drug in large quantities were provided. Further human trials were successful and penicillin went into everyday use in hospitals and military situations, saving millions of lives. Florey was knighted in 1944 and the following year, with Fleming and Ernst Chain, shared the Nobel Prize in Physiology or Medicine.

These three men were very different characters. Fleming was easygoing and always happy to speak with the press of the day, while Florey was immersed in his work and notoriously difficult to work with or for. The professor with the solid Australian accent he never lost was known as the 'bushranger of research at Oxford for his drive and persistence in obtaining research funding'. He and Chain both had short tempers and clashed over many issues, including Florey's refusal of Chain's strong pleas to patent penicillin rather than gifting it to humanity. Florey was not the kind of man to be dazzled by his own brilliance and once said frankly, 'We had a bit of luck with penicillin—a great deal of luck'.

Honours and accolades were showered on Florey, including his election as the first Australian President of the Royal Society. He remained closely tied to his homeland, contributing to the development of the Australian National University. He and others from his team, including Chain, continued their researches and contributed to the further development of lifesaving drugs made possible by their work on penicillin. Florey is acknowledged as one of Australia's and the world's greatest scientists, his image appearing on stamps and banknotes.

The laboratory at Oxford where he and his colleagues carried out their groundbreaking research is recognised on the List of Overseas Places of Historic Significance to Australia: 'His laboratory at Oxford University is of outstanding significance to Australia as the place where this revolutionary research, which has helped alleviate suffering around the globe, took place.'

The Show

They say that more people take part in them than go fishing each year. 'The Show!', as annual agricultural shows are usually known, has been with us in one form or another for a very long time.

From early in modern Australia's story the agricultural show has been the focus of annual celebration and plain old-fashioned fun. Based on eighteenth-century rural events and hiring fairs in Britain, the agricultural societies that ran the shows were among the first organised institutions in most colonies. Then known as 'Exhibitions', the earliest was in New South Wales in 1823. Given the farming basis of the Australian settler economy, the founding of such organisations is not surprising, allowing as they did the exchange of techniques, implements and goods. The societies that ran them became very influential in the business and political spheres of colonial life, as their members were often large landholders with considerable resources of their own and a strong interest in seeing the economy prosper.

Although they began as farming trade fairs, it was not long before other events crept in. At first these were mostly rural in character, including competitions such as woodchopping, campdrafting, tent-pegging, shearing demonstrations and ploughing, as well as stunning displays of regional produce. Later, rodeos were imported from the USA and 'the Show', wherever held, became a great popular carnival as well as a serious rural business venue. The grand parade of the competing animals has always been the highlight for serious show-goers.

But most visitors to city shows are there for the fun and excitement of the uniquely Australian showbags, the rides and the razzle-dazzle. Sideshow Alley began as a raggle-taggle scattering of joints and old-time fair games like hoopla and the coconut shy. It gradually evolved as 'showies', the travelling entertainers who run the attractions, became more organised from the early twentieth century. Sideshow Alley was more or less officially recognised as an important element of the shows in the 1920s, although the laughing clowns, hoopla stalls and 'freak shows' had been a defining feature of the fun from the nineteenth century onwards.

The annals of the shows are rich with legendary characters, none more colourful, perhaps, than Jimmy Sharman. In 1911, the scrapping fighter Jimmy Sharman started what was to become the most famous of all the travelling boxing tents. He had plenty of competition as he travelled around country towns and city shows with his signature call 'Who'll take a glove?' Many did and provided their paying friends, family and punters with the shock or delight of seeing them beaten by the professionals of the boxing troupe. Mostly the defeats were relatively gentle and black eyes and bloodied noses were a badge of honour: at least you'd had a go. Jimmy Sharman was a hands-on entrepreneur who also fought in his own shows, reputedly losing only one of many bouts before he became too old to wisely take on the local hopefuls.

As with many live animal shows and 'freaks' ('special people' in non-judgemental showie parlance), the boxing tents came to be seen as an unacceptable form of entertainment. From around the 1950s, Sideshow Alley began moving towards 'rides'. At first dodgem cars, roller-coasters, Ferris wheels and similar mechanical attractions provided a more physical experience for show-goers. Then larger and more elaborate rides began to appear, especially from the United States fair and carnival industry. Today, glaring, blaring machines designed to thrill patrons with stomach-wrenching movements, upwards, downwards, sideways or in circles dominate Sideshow Alley. Some of the older, more sedate stands live on in the form of laughing clowns and joints of one kind or another featuring prizes, mainly for children. Some form of haunted house or ghost train remains a standard, though the considerable verbal artistry of the spiel and the psychology of spruiking has disappeared.

'The front of the show gets the dough' was an old-time showmen's saying that emphasised the importance of the spruiker, the person who attracted the crowd with a 'spiel', a carefully chosen and delivered monologue designed to entice paying customers inside the tent. The aim of this art form was to connect with the third of the crowd arrayed below the 'line-up board' who were undecided about whether to part with their hard-earned. About 30 to 40 per cent of the crowd were probably going to buy a ticket, while the rest had no intention of entering, no matter what wonders the spruiker promised. It all depended on selling a few key words, as showman Jack Allan recalled in his spiel for his troupe of Chinese acrobats:

> And now presenting a galaxy of oriental extravaganza long to be remembered. It's the best show I have ever seen in my life so I know it will be the best show you would ever have seen, because I've seen more than you, and if I'd seen a better one than this I would have it here for your edification.

Good spruikers were recognised experts who could, and did, earn a solid living at shows around the world, making the difference between breaking even—or worse—and making a profit.

Today, there are over 700 agricultural shows in Australia, though their number has been declining. Around 400 families follow the seasons around the show circuit. Showies generally live in well-appointed caravans and their children, on the east coast at least, attend the National School for Travelling Show Children that helps with the difficulties of getting an education while on the move for much of the year.

The Country Hall

The Derby Town Hall in Tasmania's north-east is a picturesque but otherwise unremarkable example of thousands of small halls in Australian communities. These humble structures, usually thrown up by local volunteer labour and skill, provided a place for community activities of all kinds, from the dances of the past through to political meetings and everything in between.

It was tin that brought the first European settlers to Derby in 1874. Lots of it. A mine was established there by the Krushka brothers, who left their legacy in the town that quickly grew. Their mine was known as Brothers Mine, later renamed Briseis after the 1876 Melbourne Cup winner, and the original town was called Brothers Home until it was later changed, possibly to honour the three-time British Prime Minister Edward Smith-Stanley, the fourteenth Earl of Derby, although he had died in 1869.

As with other minerals, the possibility of striking it rich attracted many to the settlement, which grew quickly and haphazardly to over 3000 people by the end of the nineteenth century, many of them Chinese. Mining operations were producing large amounts of tin and the area was said to be one of the richest of its kind in the southern hemisphere.

The humble metal we know as 'tin' (stannum) has a glorious history. Mixed with copper it forms the tough alloy bronze, as early smiths discovered, leading to the technological revolution of the Bronze Age around 3000 BC. Tin was later essential for making pewter, a poor person's version of silver widely used for eating and drinking implements from medieval times. By the eighteenth century, tin was on the way out as cheap and serviceable ceramics became widely available for household use. But from the beginning of the nineteenth century, it had a large and ongoing revival. The 'tin can' had arrived. These were made with iron or steel, but a coating of tin was used to stop them rusting. Until the advent of aluminium and plastic in the twentieth century, the humble 'tin' held, transported and preserved foodstuffs of all kinds around the world, leading to a huge demand for the metal that put Derby on the map and kept it there until 1929.

That year, torrential rains caused the dam that served the mine to burst. Fourteen people were drowned as floodwaters swept through the town and surrounding area. Mr Kerrison of Derby told how he saw several of his workers swept away in 'a huge wave of muddy water'. He first became aware of the disaster when his wife noticed that the hill was slipping away:

> I was standing at the back door, and when I saw the water I called out, 'Run for your life, the dam has gone', said Mr Kerrison.

We ran up the hill about 20 yards. As I turned. I saw the water rush in a huge muddy foaming wave towards the stables. It took the stables in its course, with several of the men and eight draught horses. The water came within a few feet of our verandah, and our house is about 70 or 80 ft. [20–25 m] above the level of the river.

I thought I had nerve, but I never want to see such an awful sight again. I saw the water rush across the flats to where the men were working in the lower face.

It was impossible to warn the men, as it all happened so quickly.

There was some finger-pointing at the inquest, with some concern about the construction quality of the dam. But after hearing from a number of expert witnesses, the jury found that the deaths were caused:

> through drowning in a rush of water down the Cascade River and over the Briseis mine workings following the bursting of the Briseis Company's dam; and that the bursting of the dam was the result of an abnormal and unprecedented volume of water, which might have been caused by a cloudburst, or by an extraordinary rainfall in the catchment. No blame was attachable to anyone.

The mine was closed, reopening after five years at a lower level of production and eventually closing for good after World War II. As the population inevitably faded away, the town's buildings fell into disrepair. But the Derby Hall survived, providing a meeting place and a social space for dances, debutante balls, fetes and much more. Its pressed tin walls gave it pleasing acoustics, still valued by musicians today.

After visiting the Derby Town Hall in 1988, folksinger Phyl Lobl wrote a song celebrating the history and spirit of the Derby Hall and, by extension, every other country hall in Australia:

> On a dampened Derby morning when the clouds string out like washing
> And you see the mine bones pushing through the patches in the fog.
> Past the dinosaured remains you can hear the old-time tunes,
> Floating far beyond the mullock and the ragged heaps of slag,
> 'Varsoviana' and 'Mazurka' bouncing off the tin lined walls.
> Paint in faint and fading pictures memories of the Derby Hall.
>
> From the concerts came the sounds of 'La Paloma' played on gum leaf,
> The songs of Gladys Moncrieff, cover versions by the score.
> Lilting Irish tenor voices that had just begun to harden,
> While sopranos murdered fairies at the bottom of the garden,
> 'Road To Mandalay' and 'Aves' bouncing off the tin lined walls.
> Paint in faint and fading pictures memories of the Derby Hall.
>
> When the boys went to the fighting serving under foreign skies,
> There were memorable evenings of farewells with sad goodbyes.
> And when the boys came back again the welcomes were the same,

Though there weren't so many of them, just that list of golden names,
But the 'Last Post' and 'Reveille' bouncing off the tin lined walls.
Paint in faint and fading pictures memories of the Derby Hall.

What a proud and wondrous moment when the 'queen-of-queens' was crowned,
How they'd laboured over dresses matching trinkets they had found.
There was taffeta with laces, marcasite with pearls,
Such a powdering of faces for the prettiest of girls,
'Fox Trot', 'Gypsy Tap' and Tango bouncing off the tin lined walls.
Paint in faint and fading pictures memories of the Derby Hall.

There were fetes with stalls and toffees and fancy-dress parading
With costumes a kaleidoscope of shifting shapes and shading.
But now there is the TV and in these later days,
The hall is used for indoor cricket, sport and exercise,
Shuttlecock and plastic ping pong bouncing off the tin lined walls.
Paint out faint and fading pictures memories of the Derby Hall.
Paint out faint and fading pictures memories of the Derby Hall.

The Milk Bar

They're usually called 'delis' in Western Australia, 'corner shops' in New South Wales and 'milk bars' in Victoria. The terms for the local shop that sold bread, milk, soft drinks, the papers, lollies and, originally at least, sodas and milkshakes, tend to be pretty interchangeable from state to state. These basic, usually family-run businesses are nearly all gone now, victims of the grocery and fast-food chains.

Milk bars proper are something of an Australian hybrid. British oyster parlours and American soda or ice-cream stores are partial predecessors. But the first local enterprise of this sort is usually said to have been a shop at number 24 in Sydney's Martin Place established by Mick Adams in 1932. He was inspired by the American diner where sodas could be purchased and served along a bar. Mick substituted milkshakes for sodas and called his shop a 'milk bar'. Opening day was a big affair, with the 'Black and White 4d Fruit Milk Bar' being launched by the lord mayor and the first day's takings donated to a local children's charity. After the ceremony, it was promised that 'the "dairy maids", prominent Sydney girls with Miss Madge Elliott as their director will take charge behind the bar'. Photographs of the establishment feature a row of young women in white uniforms ready to serve up the milkshakes. The idea of drinking milk at a bar was an exotic one at a time when the most usual beverage consumed at a bar was beer. Despite that, or because of it, the business was a roaring success.

Mick's pioneering milk bar was a very plush Art Deco affair, with mirrors, chandeliers, and a black-and-white tiled bar and floor, graced with pastoral scenes painted on the wall. Other businesses of this type quickly sprang up around the country. It is estimated that in the 1930s there were around 4000 milk bars in cities, suburbs and country towns. Many of these places evolved into what were effectively restaurants available to workers unable or unwilling to eat out at more expensive establishments. There was more than a hint of class attitude and values involved.

As time went on, the much humbler local convenience outlets offering basic items of everyday needs, children's confectionery and the like began to install the minimal equipment needed to whip up milkshakes, malted milk and related drinks. Unlike the tiled palaces of the cities and larger country towns, these places were often just a room built at the front of a house in which the family running the business lived.

Many of these more basic shops were also run by immigrant families. Mick Adams (formerly Joachim Tavlarides) was from Greece, and Italians often took up the milk bar trade as did Vietnamese immigrants later. Having a milk bar allowed an immigrant family to live in the attached house and everyone could pitch in with the many tasks involved in stocking and operating a corner shop, with the numerous lines of small items they often sold along with bread, milk and lollies. Some foods outside the usual steaks, chips, eggs and three veg options generally favoured by Australian diners were introduced through the milk bars. These included homemade pastries such as baklava, ice-cream and sometimes even fresh fruit and vegetables.

In the 1950s and 1960s, some milk bars became youth hangouts with pinball machines and jukeboxes, usually with an emphasis on American pop music and fashions. This was pretty much the high point of the local corner shops, whatever name they were known by. Since then they have been fading away, mourned by people nostalgic for their young days and the better times that supposedly existed in the past. They have become the focus of commemorative photographic books, documented by social media pages, and even been heritage-listed by local councils. Many have become private residences and some transformed to neighbourhood cafes, bakeries and restaurants.

In 2021, one of the last Greek milk bars, the Olympia in Sydney's Stanmore, finally closed down. It had fallen into disrepair and been closed by the council several years before. After more than sixty years tending the shop, the aged owner retired to a nursing home. The plight of the old place inspired a Facebook support group with over 4000 members, and the building has been placed on the New South Wales Heritage Register.

Sun, Sand and Surf

He was known to all as 'Matey', a bitzer dog who became a legend in the early years of Surfers Paradise, nowadays Queensland's answer to Miami. Where Matey came from, nobody knew. He just turned up one day and began making himself an indispensable element of the 1940s and 1950s tourist experience. He moved into the Surfers Paradise Hotel and never left until he died in the late 1950s. His fame arose from guiding lost and possibly inebriated visitors back from their revels to the comfort of their rented beds.

Alan 'Polly' Mitchell knew the dog well: 'Matey was a local identity and loved by all', he recalled in a 2013 interview. Polly had seen Surfers grow from a sleepy beachside getaway to the international resort location it is today and became the champion of the bronze statue of Matey erected through public subscription in the late 1950s. He successfully campaigned for glass eyes to be added to the statue and for it to be included in the heritage register of the Gold Coast. A keen historian as well as colourful larrikin of the old school, Polly died in 2017, but thanks to his efforts you can now see a shiny-eyed Matey at Cavill Park, Surfers Paradise.

While they may not have any canine statues, most beachside communities have similar yarns about their local characters, animal and human, and about their tragedies, as well as a fund of lore and legend. For those who live on the coast, and for the many who visit, the beach is the focus of a way of life and leisure, as well as one of the great Australian dreams of equality and our right to celebrate the outdoors in general and sun, surf and sand in particular.

We have come to take our abundance of staggeringly beautiful beaches for granted. With hardly any exception, all Australian beaches are open to all of us, all the time. In other parts of the world beaches may be privatised, permanently polluted or militarised. The beach and all it stands for has become a central part of modern Australian lifestyle, pleasure, and recreation. But it wasn't always so.

Sea bathing did not become a widespread leisure activity until the late nineteenth century. Early Victorian-era taboos on the public display of flesh meant that respectable folk did not enter the water at all. If they did, they needed to be well covered up. Attitudes gradually changed and it became fashionable to swim, though still displaying as little skin as possible. It was not until the early twentieth century that the prohibitions on bathing began to be lifted as people demanded more freedom on the sand and in the sea, embracing the healthy image of the 'sun-bronzed Aussie'.

These freedoms were sometimes hard won. There was resistance to attempts by local councils to determine what people could wear, or not, at the beach. In 1907 a proposal by Waverley

Shire Council, New South Wales, that men should wear tunics similar to those worn by women bathers provoked mass protests at the popular Sydney beaches of Bondi, Coogee and Manly. In later years, further battles were fought over the respectability of swimwear, particularly men's trunks. After World War II, the wearing of bikinis, then considered too revealing, was fiercely contested for some years and can still be an issue in some situations. A young woman was reportedly banned from her suburban Sydney unit for wearing a bikini at the pool in 2020. As many pointed out, this seemed rather absurd when topless bathing is not unknown and the G-string has become popular.

The absurdity of this outdated moral policing was highlighted by the growth of the surfing movement, where males with long, preferably blond, locks became the standard look. Surfboard riding in Australia is usually dated from the visit of board master Duke Kahanamoku in 1914–15 and his well-publicised demonstrations of Hawaiian longboard riding. Although there had probably been some forms of wave riding and body surfing enjoyed in Australia since the mid-nineteenth century, and possibly earlier, it was the Duke's impressive mastery of the waves that provided the impetus for the surfing movement we now have, with its distinctive clothing, music, language and art.

As the beach grew in popularity, so more swimmers got into trouble. The surf lifesaving movement got underway in the early twentieth century, both as a response to the attempted over-regulation of local government and as a volunteer beach monitoring, rescue and training movement. Originally a mainly Anglo-Celtic male activity, the movement has strong roots in beachside communities and came to be widely considered a symbol of the Australian way by the 1930s. A mass rescue of over 200 distressed bathers at Bondi beach in 1938 confirmed the heroic national status of the lifesaver.

Interrupted by World War II, the movement regrew, peaking in the 1950s then declining as a new generation of surfers rebelled against what they saw as the rules and strictures imposed by lifesavers. Beaches might be patrolled by local council 'inspectors' who had licence to demand bathers cover up and, at one point, even police the length of men's hair. Such seemingly quirky attitudes of the past are now long forgotten and surf lifesaving continues today, although it is said to be in decline in some areas as people are either less inclined to volunteer or simply do not have the time.

Australia's treasure chest of coastal glories ranges from isolated and near-pristine stretches of sand and surf, through the popular bathing beaches of the suburbs and towns that ring our shorelines to the glitter of Surfers Paradise. They all resonate with the laidback lifestyle of surfing, tanning—and simply enjoying life. Between land and sea, the beach is a little of both, a zone where distinctions of wealth or position do not apply in the sun-bronzed egalitarianism of 'swimmers', 'cossies' and 'budgie smugglers'.

The Centre of Australia

Where is the centre of the place Australians call home?

The exact centre of the continent can be found on a road without a name at a place called Ghan with the coordinates −25.6091, 134.3619. It is marked with a scaled-down version of the flagpole above Parliament House in Canberra. On the marker is a plaque commemorating the official opening of what is known as the Lambert Centre of Australia in 1994.

Who was Lambert and why is calculating the centre of Australia such a big deal? The answer turns out to be a confusing saga.

The first thing to get your head around is that there is no single centre of Australia. That's right. There are a number of possible centres, their exact position depending on the method used to calculate the point. Our 'wide brown land' is so irregular in shape and so large that the curvature of the earth is a complicating factor in doing the sums.

The early explorers of inland Australia were keen to be the first to stand at the centre. Charles Sturt's third expedition of 1844–45 in search of an inland sea was also inspired by his wish to find the middle of the continent:

> Let any man lay the map of Australia before him, and regard the blank upon its surface, and then let me ask him if it would not be an honourable achievement to be the first to place foot at its centre. Men of undoubted perseverance and energy in vain had tried to work their way to that distant and shrouded spot.

He found neither a sea nor the centre, though one of his companions on this expedition, John McDouall Stuart, did reach what he thought was the centre sixteen years later. On Sunday 22 April 1860, Stuart wrote in his journal that he was at 'Small Gum Creek, under Mount Stuart, Centre of Australia—today I find from my observations of the sun, 111° 00′ 30″, that I am now camped in the centre of Australia. I have marked a tree and planted the British flag there.' That's it then, right? No.

Subsequent calculations have suggested a number of different centres. In the 1930s, explorer and geologist Dr C.T. Madigan travelled through central Australia and used the common-sense technique of working out the centre of gravity using a piece of metal in the shape of Australia and a plumb line. His calculations put the centre around 11 kilometres away from the Lambert location.

Pretty good, but a more sophisticated version of this method digitises thousands of points on the coastline and uses some tricky maths to assign each one a weight. Where these notional weights balance out would be the centre, at 23° 07' South, 132° 08" East.

In 1988 the Royal Geographical Society of Australasia worked out another version of the centre for the Australian Bicentennial. They used a method similar to the coastal weightings approach and came up with a centre at 25° 36' 36.4" South, 134° 21' 17.3" East. This is where the Lambert Centre marker is located, named in honour of one-time director of the Division of National Mapping, Dr Bruce P. Lambert.

Other methods have also been tried. One involves moving a series of concentric circles over a map of Australia until one of them touches the coastline at three points. After more maths and scaling from the map used, the centre can be calculated at 23° 02' South, 132° 10' East.

If you're more of a straight-line person, the geodetic median point method might appeal more than the circular approach. A square is drawn around a map of the continent, touching it at each corner. Two lines are drawn between the four corners.

Mind-numbing mathematics are again involved but, basically, where the lines intersect is the centre of Australia, or one of them, at least. This one turns out to be 23° 33′ 09.89″ South, 133° 23′ 46.00″ East.

Intriguingly, whichever method is used and despite the physical irregularities and complexities of our country, the coordinates for the centre of Australia are all fairly close together, around Alice Springs and the nearby MacDonnell Ranges.

Unless you are, or have access to, a mathematician, cartographer or surveyor, best not to try any of this at home. Instead, check out the Geoscience Australia website, where they've also done all the clever calculations to work out the centres of each state and territory.

Wherever those centres might be and whatever their scientific importance, for most of us the centre of the country is simply the heart of the place where we all live.

ACKNOWLEDGEMENTS

As always, many people have helped with the research, writing and publication of this book. My grateful thanks to Maureen Seal, Kylie Seal-Pollard, Olya Willis, Rob Willis, Phyl Lobl, Bruce Watson, Elizabeth Weiss and the talented editorial staff at Allen & Unwin.

Thanks also to readers of my previous books who have contributed ideas, thoughts and story clues. We often assume that the stories we know must be familiar to everyone else. But in researching and writing these Great Australian Stories over the years, I have learned that this is often not the case. Stories might only be known to particular groups of people, or to those who live in the same area, work in the same industry, or share some common interest or activity. Writing about these many fascinating tales has been a good way for me to learn so much more about Australia and its people and also to share their great yarns around.

IMAGE CREDITS

Chapter 1
'School celebration of centenary of Fort Dundas establishment, NT Centenary 1824–1924, Leichhardt's Expedition', 1924. Jessie Litchfield/Christa Roderick Collection, Territory Stories, Image ID PH0110/0081 (https://hdl.handle.net/10070/874801).

Chapter 2
'Landing the sub-marine telegraph cable, coming from Java to Port Darwin', 1871. Samuel White Sweet/Peter Spillett Collection, Territory Stories, Image ID PH0238/0407 (https://hdl.handle.net/10070/730691).

Chapter 3
'John Bailey collection of photographs showing Bob Buck leading the expedition to recover Lasseter's body in Central Australia', 1930. John (Jack) Bailey/State Library of NSW, Image ID MK2DZ7aEjqZBm.

Chapter 4
'Mr. Albert Botteri, Lydia Botteri and Mrs. Rose Botteri, with unidentified woman on the left, standing under sign which reads Bonegilla', 1955. State Library of Victoria, Image ID H2002.24/1.

Chapter 5
'Group of hikers in bushland around campfire, smoking, having a drink, packs on the ground beside them, one sitting on a rock', c. 1937. State Library of Victoria, Image ID 1799173.

Chapter 6
'Slim Dusty with his Ford Customline and the "pub with no beer" (model)', February 1960. Norm Danvers/Australian Photographic Agency, State Library of New South Wales, Image ID IE1108591.

Chapter 7
'Barbara Ellis in front of the Big Banana', c. late 1960s, courtesy of the Big Banana Fun Park Coffs Harbour.

NOTES

Chapter 1: Pioneering Places

Turn Again

page 8 'good to be done there': From the diary of Captain John Saris, 18 November 1605, quoted in T.D. Mutch, 'The First Discovery of Australia with An Account of the Voyage of the "Duyfken" and the Career of Captain Willem Jansz', *Journal of the Royal Australian Historical Society*, vol. XXVIII, part V, Sydney, 1942.

page 8 'significant historical sites in Australia': Geoff Wharton, 'The Pennefather River: Place of Australian national heritage', in *Gulf of Carpentaria Scientific Study Report*, Royal Geographical Society of Queensland, 2005, p. 35. See also James Henderson, *Sent Forth a Dove: Discovery of the Duyfken*, UWA Press, Nedlands, 1998.

page 8 'a big mob of logs': Another version says the Aboriginal people took it for a large pelican: Henderson 1998, p. 158.

page 8 'their sailors as "devils"': Henderson, pp. 143ff; Peter Sutton, 'Stories about Feeling: Dutch–Australian Contact in Cape York Peninsula, 1606–1756', in Peter Veth, Peter Sutton and Margo Neale (eds), *Strangers on the Shore: Early coastal contacts in Australia*, National Museum of Australia Press, 2008, pp. 35ff.

page 9 'their ship and sailed away': L.A. Hercus and Peter Sutton (eds), *This Is What Happened: Historical narratives by Aboriginals*, Australian Institute of Aboriginal Studies, Canberra, c. 1986. See also Barbara Miller, *The European Quest to Find Terra Australis Incognita: Quiros, Torres and Janszoon*, Barbara Miller Books, Sydney, 2014, pp. 169–184 for further discussion of Wik-Munkhan oral traditions.

Notes

Possession Island

page 10 'of the *Endeavour* barged in': Dr Shayne T. Williams, 'An Indigenous Australian Perspective on Cook's Arrival', *The Voyages of Captain James Cook*, British Library, https://www.bl.uk/the-voyages-of-captain-james-cook/articles/an-indigenous-australian-perspective-on-cooks-arrival, accessed February 2022.

page 11 'another spear or other weapon': 'Shield', British Museum Accession no. Oc1978,Q.839, described at *British Museum*, https://www.britishmuseum.org/collection/object/E_Oc1978-Q-839, accessed February 2021.

The Futile Fort

page 12 'feed her children, then disappeared': Maryanne Mungatopi, 'Palaneri—the Creation Period', *Tiwi Land Council*, https://tiwilandcouncil.com/index.cfm?fuseaction=page&p=248&l=2&id=60&smid=120, accessed February 2022.

page 14 'intended for food and labour': John Morris, 'The Tiwi and the British: An ill-fated outpost', Special section: 'Genocide'? Australian Aboriginal History in International Perspective, *Aboriginal History*, ANU Press, Canberra, vol. 25, 2001, pp. 243–261, http://press-files.anu.edu.au/downloads/press/p72971/pdf/ch1612.pdf, accessed February 2022.

page 14 'the country's north took place': Derek Pugh, *Fort Dundas: The British in North Australia 1824–29*, eBook, Alchemy Pty Ltd, 2017.

page 14 'was at a reduced rate': Conor Byrne and Nibir Khan (with Adam Steer and Liz Trevaskis), 'Light finally shed on unknown WWII frontline war stories from the Tiwi Islands', *ABC News*, 17 February 2022, https://www.abc.net.au/news/2022-02-17/tiwi-islands-unknown-frontline-war-stories/100817320, accessed February 2022.

The Bloody Bridge

page 16 'times have been much mythologised': T. Causer, '"The Worst Types of Sub-Human Beings"? The Myth and Reality of the Convicts of the Norfolk Island Penal Settlement, 1825–1855', in Professional Historians Association (NSW) (eds.), *Islands of History: Proceedings of the 25th Anniversary Conference*, Anchor Books, Sydney, 2011; 'History of Norfolk Island', *Wikipedia*, https://en.wikipedia.org/wiki/History_of_Norfolk_Island, accessed February 2022.

Notes

Long Harry's Legacy

page 19 '"chronic bronchitis" in September 1885': David Green, 'Garrett, Henry Beresford', *Dictionary of New Zealand Biography*, first published in 1990, republished in *Te Ara—the Encyclopedia of New Zealand*, https://teara.govt.nz/en/biographies/1g5/garrett-henry-beresford, accessed 25 February 2021. Henry Garrett, *Recollections of Convict Life in Norfolk Island and Victoria: With prison portraits, being sketches of criminals and prison governors, including the early life, career and death of John Price and of the bushrangers, Billy Morgan, Burgess, &c. / by Henry Garrett, alias Rouse, the bushranger*, Dunedin Public Library, Dunedin, 1973 (first published serially in the *Otago Witness*, 13 March to 14 May 1886); James Wilson, 'Garrat [sic] the Bushranger', *Otago Witness*, 28 June 1911, p. 92.

page 19 'shine out of his carcass': Tony Wright, 'The mysterious bushranger who terrorised Victoria and New Zealand', *The Age*, 14 June 2019, https://www.theage.com.au/national/victoria/the-mysterious-bushranger-who-terrorised-victoria-and-new-zealand-20190612-p51x1h.html, accessed February 2022.

Mrs Penfold's

page 21 'George's Church in nearby Woodforde': Julie McIntyre, 'Penfold, Mary (1816–1895)', *People Australia*, National Centre of Biography, Australian National University, https://peopleaustralia.anu.edu.au/biography/penfold-mary-29651/text36618, accessed September 2021.

page 23 'That is pure and true': Bertram Stevens, *An Anthology of Australian Verse*, Angus & Robertson, Sydney, 1906, pp. 134–5.

Old Ireland at Baker's Flat

page 25 'of most nineteenth-century settlers': Kelsey M. Lowe, Susan Arthure, Lynley A. Wallis and Joshua Feinberg, 'Geophysical and Archaeological Investigations of Baker's Flat, a Nineteenth Century Historic Irish Site in South Australia', *Archaeological and Anthropological Sciences*, vol. 12, no. 1, January 2020, DOI: 10.1007/s12520-019-01003-2, accessed February 2022; Arthure, S. 'Kapunda's Irish Connections' in S. Arthure, F. Breen, S. James and D. Lonergan (eds),

Notes

Irish South Australia: New histories and insight, Wakefield Press, Adelaide, 2019, pp. 58–73.

The Land We Live Inn

page 27   'in the yard to bleach': 'Eighty years ago', *Albury Banner and Wodonga Express* (NSW), 19 August 1938, p. 28.

page 28   'the Land We Live Inn': *Wellington Times* (NSW), 11 June 1936, p. 9; *The Sydney Morning Herald* (NSW), 21 January 1858, p. 4.

page 28   'as her obituary put it': *Barrier Miner* (Broken Hill, NSW), 28 July 1927, p. 3.

page 29   'each fined for disorderly conduct': Will Carter, *Wellington Times* (NSW), 29 June 1939, p. 8.

page 29   'is now a private residence': Mick Roberts, 'The Land We Live Inn: Drunken gold-digger had his locks lopped while asleep in Sofala pub', *Time Gents: Australian Pub Project*, 17 November 2014, https://timegents.com/2014/11/17/the-land-we-live-inn-sofala-nsw/, accessed November 2021. This site has more yarns of the pub, and many others.

Glorious News for the Diggers!

page 33   'the croaking of the bullfrogs': 'Saturday evening at the Lachlan', *The Star* (Ballarat), 23 August 1862, p. 2, https://trove.nla.gov.au/newspaper/article/66326599, accessed February 2022.

The Singing Wire

page 36   'Kaititja (Kaytetye) people were killed': The Centre for 21st Century Humanities, *Colonial Frontier Massacres in Australia, 1788–1930*, University of Newcastle, https://c21ch.newcastle.edu.au/colonialmassacres/detail.php?r=700, accessed February 2022.

Sea Lines

page 37   'such cable in the world': J. Given, 'The Most Connected Place on the Planet'. Originally published in *Communication, Politics and Culture*, vol. 43, no. 1, 2010, pp. 120–42.

page 38   'world for the first time': Bill Burns, *History of the Atlantic Cable & Undersea Communications,* http://atlantic-cable.com/Cables/1871Java-PortDarwin/index.htm; accessed February 2022. *The Sydney Morning Herald*, 5 February 1872, p. 2.

Notes

page 39   'Java, providing a backup facility': Broome to Java Submarine Telegraph Cable Nomination for Historic Engineering Marker Plaques and Ceremony Report, May 2008, https://portal.engineersaustralia.org.au/system/files/engineering-heritage-australia/nomination-title/Broome_Java_Nomination_Ceremony_Report.pdf, accessed February 2022.

The Wire Frontier

page 40   'newspaper heading in July 1868': *The Queenslander*, 18 July 1868, p. 11.

page 40   'The controversy continued': *The Queenslander*, 29 January 1881, p. 146, and 5 February 1881, p. 178.

page 41   'eastern Australia during the 1880s': *South Australian Register*, 23 June 1885, p. 5.

page 41   'to its existing 580-kilometre length': 'Niche Continuing to Undertake Work on the NSW Wild Dog Fence Extension Project', Niche Environment and Heritage, https://niche-eh.com/2020/08/24/wilddogfence/, accessed February 2022.

page 42   'with those of the land': A.G. Fisher, C.H. Mills, M. Lyons, W.K. Cornwell and M. Letnic, 'Remote Sensing of Trophic Cascades: Multi-temporal Landsat imagery reveals vegetation change driven by the removal of an apex predator', *Landscape Ecology*, vol. 36, 2021, pp. 1341–58, https://doi.org/10.1007/s10980-021-01206-w, accessed February 2022.

page 42   'her by then ex-husband, compensated': Belinda Middleweek, *Feral Media? The Chamberlain Case forty years on*, Australian Scholarly Publishing, North Melbourne, 2021.

The Sheds

page 44   'is probably unsurpassed in Australia': Micaela Hambrett, 'Old Errowanbang Woolshed has endured 135 years of history on the land, but its future is in doubt', *ABC News*, 20 March 2021, https://www.abc.net.au/news/2021-03-20/old-errowanbang-woolshed-who-should-pay-to-preserve/13235388, accessed February 2022.

page 44   'the same dilemma as Errowanbang': Patrick Martin, 'Is saving the Cordillo Downs woolshed the most difficult renovation job in Australia?', *ABC News*, 7 May 2019, https://www.abc.net.au/

Notes

news/2019-05-07/cordillo-downs-station-woolshed-restoration-in-public-hands/11082728, accessed February 2022.

page 45 'knuckle down at Goorianawa': *The Windsor and Richmond Gazette*, 13 April 1928, p. 2.

page 46 'the other in reasonable time': 'Tuppence' in *The Bulletin*, 23 January 1929, p. 25.

A Golden Pipeline

page 48 'caused by worry and overwork': *The West Australian*, 14 March 1902, p. 3.

page 49 'out at $8 million': Isabel Moussalli, 'Iconic Goldfields Pipeline tipped to be replaced, ending a century of history', *ABC News*, 24 January 2020, https://www.abc.net.au/news/2020-01-24/goldfields-pipeline-built-by-cy-oconnor-set-to-be-replaced/11895482, accessed August 2021.

Chapter 2 Dangerous Places

The Eye of the Needle

page 52 'and were delivered to Sydney': 'Narrative of the shipwreck of Captain Hamilton and the crew of the Sydney Cove', *Asiatic Mirror*, Calcutta, 1797–98, in *Historical Records of New South Wales*, vol. III, 1796–1799, Appendix A, pp. 757–69.

page 53 'off and carried to safety': *Launceston Examiner*, 17 September 1845, p. 5 (from the *Port Phillip Herald*, 13 September 1845).

page 54 'found the "much scarred" boy': *The Argus*, 3 June 1878, p. 5.

B LXV

page 56 'or some combination of those': Boorloo Shire, 'Burke and Wills—The Dig Tree', *Explore Bulloo*, https://www.explorebulloo.com.au/downloads/file/11/dig-tree-information-sheet-pdf, accessed February 2022.

page 57 'hypothermia, their fates were sealed': Dave Phoenix, 'Did Burke and Wills Die Because They Ate Nardoo?', *Dig: The Burke and Wills Research Gateway*, https://webarchive.nla.gov.au/awa/20220704054300/; http://pandora.nla.gov.au/

Notes

pan/194331/20220704-1543/burkeandwills.slv.vic.gov.au/ask-an-expert/answers.html, accessed March 2022.

page 58 'tree was the famous icon': Maddelin McCosker, 'Researcher casts doubt on legitimacy of Burke and Wills Dig Tree', *ABC News*, 13 October 2017. https://www.abc.net.au/news/2017-10-13/new-doubt-cast-over-burke-and-wills-dig-tree/9043600, accessed February 2022.

page 58 'twenty-hour drive west from Brisbane': Royal Queensland Historical Society, 'The Dig Tree', http://www.thedigtree.com.au, accessed February 2022.

Stringybark Creek

page 60 '3 o'clock the next afternoon': *The Age*, 9 August 1880.

page 61 'with the exception of Lonigan': Also known as the 'Euroa Letter' and held in the Public Records Office of Victoria, https://prov.vic.gov.au/explore-collection/online-galleries-and-exhibitions/ned-kelly, accessed February 2022.

The Street of Evil

page 62 'most filthy language and conduct': *The Argus*, 18 January 1854, p. 5.

page 64 'want to stay here always': Quoted in Annie Hider, 'Growing Up in the City', https://web.archive.org/web/20110811082604/http://museumvictoria.com.au/littlelons/grow.html, accessed July 2021.

page 65 'An' that's Romance': C.J. Dennis, *The Songs of a Sentimental Bloke*, Angus & Robertson, Sydney, 1915.

Windy Gully Candles

page 68 'the mine closed in 1970': New South Wales Government, '1902 Mount Kembla Coal Mine Explosion', *NSW Resources Regulator*, https://www.resourcesregulator.nsw.gov.au/safety-and-health/events/learning-from-disasters/learning-from-disasters-timeline/mount-kembla-1902; accessed February 2022; Jamie Radford, 'What happened tragic day of Mt Kembla Mine disaster', *Illawarra Mercury*, 25 July 2014, http://mineaccidents.com.au/uploads/mt-kembla-disaster.pdf, accessed February 2022; 'Mt Kembla Mine Disaster: The victims', *Kembla Jottings*, https://kemblajottings.wixsite.com/kemblajottings/victim-and-survivor-profiles, accessed November 2021.

Notes

page 69 'lit to honour the dead': *The Australian*, 31 July 2002, p. 6. See also Piggin, S., 'Voices still call from the black pit', *Weekend Australian*, 3–4 August, 2002, p. 26; Stuart Piggin and Henry Lee, *The Mt. Kembla Disaster*, Oxford University Press, Melbourne, in association with Sydney University Press, 1992.

The Fatal Railway Station

page 73 'Brookfield's fate than I am': *The Barrier Miner*, 23 March 1921, p. 1.

page 73 'presumably for dissection and inspection': Daniel Keane, 'Australia's first political assassination is just as mysterious today as it was a century ago', *ABC News,* 20 March 2021, https://www.abc.net.au/news/2021-03-20/centenary-of-australian-political-assassination-at-riverton/13250748, accessed February 2022; Nerida Campbell, 'The Wobblies', Sydney Living Museums, https://sydneylivingmuseums.com.au/ww1/wobblies, accessed February 2022.

Razorhurst

page 76 'marks against the Bavin Government': *Truth* (Sydney), 13 January 1929, p. 1.

page 77 'as Kate famously put it': *Sydney Morning Herald*, 1 October 1954, p. 8.

Escaping the Island

page 80 'mainland from St Helena—CATCH HIM': 'How gunman Charles Leslie escaped from St. Helena Gaol', *Truth* (Brisbane), 7 December 1924, p. 1.

page 80 'Ryan, Deacon, Deakin and Hayes': Clem Llewellyn Lack, 'Pirates, Blackbirders, and Other Shady Characters', *Journal of the Royal Historical Society of Queensland*, vol. 6, no. 2, 1960 (1959–60), pp. 360–88.

Greased Lightning Let Loose

page 81 'Sydney beachside suburb of Maroubra': 'Sydney (NSW)', *Speedway and Road Race History*, http://www.speedwayandroadracehistory.com/sydney---olympia-motor-speedway-maroubra-speedway.html, accessed October 2021.

page 82 'was her brave mechanic, "Bob"': I.M. Brodie, 'A queen of speed', *The Australian Women's Mirror*, 21 April 1925, p. 23.

Notes

page 83 'and his clothes were torn': *The Sun* (Sydney), 9 January 1927, p. 2.

The Woman Who Ran The Radio

page 86 'vital part of wartime Australia': 'Ruby Boye-Jones', Queensland Maritime Museum, https://maritimemuseum.com.au/eventsandexhibitions/exhibitions/womenatsea/ruby-boye-jones/, accessed September 2021.

page 86 'Guadalcanal saved the South Pacific': James Burrowes, 'Coastwatching', *The Last Coastwatcher*, https://thelastcoastwatcher.wordpress.com, accessed September 2021.

page 86 'Garden Island Chapel Remembrance Book': Alan Powell, 'Boye-Jones, Ruby Olive (1891–1990)', *Australian Dictionary of Biography*, National Centre of Biography, Australian National University, https://adb.anu.edu.au/biography/boye-jones-ruby-olive-12242/text21963, published first in hardcopy 2007, accessed online 25 September 2021.

page 86 'force the Coast Watchers': 'The Coast Watchers', *Kokoda Track Memorial Walkway*, https://www.kokodawalkway.com.au/the-coast-watchers/, accessed September 2021.

Two Up, One Down

page 88 'been doing the day before': Courtney Howe and Matt Dowling, 'The day Leonard Fuller put Brocklesby on the map after landing two planes at once', *ABC News*, 1 October 2021, https://www.abc.net.au/news/2021-10-01/the-day-a-pilot-landed-two-planes-in-a-paddock-in-regional-nsw/100502830, accessed October 2021.

page 89 'damage he had inflicted': Len's military records are in the National Archives of Australia, at A9300, Fuller L G.

page 89 'found in Blacksmith Park, Brocklesby': *Monument Australia*, https://monumentaustralia.org.au/themes/conflict/ww2/display/111556-50th-anniversary-of-the-avro-anson-aircraft-collision/photo/3, accessed October 2021.

page 89 'landing, reportedly without human intervention': *The Australian Women's Weekly*, 12 October 1940, p. 7.

Saving Silver Town

page 90 'damage to this historic place': Kelly Fuller and Caitlin Dougan, 'Firefighters "went all in to save Yerranderie", a former silver mining gem in the wilderness', *ABC News,* 7 March 2020, https://www.abc.net.au/news/2020-03-07/fight-to-save-the-historic-silver-mining-village-of-yerranderie/12029180, accessed February 2022.

page 91   'as might be imagined . . .': 'A trip to Yerranderie', *Windsor and Richmond Gazette,* 28 August 1909, p. 12.

page 92   'unsuccessfully, for a wage increase': 'Wages dispute', *The Sydney Morning Herald,* 17 July 1901, p. 5.

page 92   'or so miners working there': *The Worker* (Wagga), 18 June 1908, p. 13.

page 92   'Dharug, Dharawal, Wiradjuri and Gundungurra': *Lithgow Mercury,* 28 June 1909, p. 1.

The Field of Thunder

page 93   'four bora, or ceremonial rings': Jonathan Kumintjara Brown, 'Maralinga Aftermath, Crater Where Four Bodies Were Found', 1996, accessible online via *The Australian War Memorial,* AWM2017.255.1, https://www.awm.gov.au/collection/C2478456, accessed February 2022.

page 93   'ever since the tests ended': Ken Eastwood, 'Woomera: Nuclear danger zone', *Australian Geographic,* 10 May 2010, https://www.australiangeographic.com.au/travel/travel-destinations/2010/05/woomera-nuclear-danger-zone/., accessed February 2022.

page 94   'later had a stillborn child': Colin James, 'Aborigines died in test site bunker', *The Advertiser,* 10 July 2001, http://web.archive.org/web/20050619225230/http://www.theadvertiser.news.com.au/common/story_page/0,5936,6407166%5E26839,00.html, accessed September 2021.

page 94   'than in the general population': Megan Palin, 'New generations of Australian families suffering deformities and early deaths because of 'genetic transfer', *News.com.au,* 10 March 2016, https://www.news.com.au/lifestyle/health/health-problems/new-generations-of-australian-families-suffering-deformities-and-early-deaths-because-of-genetic-transfer/news-story/5a74b7eab2f433402aa00bc2fcbcbea4, accessed September 2020.

page 95   'happy and a sad day': Nance Haxton, 'Maralinga returned to traditional owners', *ABC News,* 18 December 2009, https://www.abc.net.au/news/2009-12-18/maralinga-returned-to-traditional-owners/1185536, accessed September 2020.

Notes

page 95 '"Mamu Pulka", or "big evil"': Mike Ladd, 'The lesser known history of the Maralinga nuclear tests—and what it's like to stand at ground zero', *ABC News*, 24 March 2020, https://www.abc.net.au/news/2020-03-24/maralinga-nuclear-tests-ground-zero-lesser-known-history/11882608, accessed September 2021.

Chapter 3: Sacred Places

The Rock

page 98 'We continually recreate the Tjukurpa': Quoted in Diana James, 'Tjurkupa Time', in Ann McGrath and Mary Anne Jebb (eds), *Long History, Deep Time: Deepening Histories of Place*, ANU Press, Canberra, 2015, https://press-files.anu.edu.au/downloads/press/p319821/html/ch02.xhtml, accessed February 2022.

page 98 'venomous snakes known as Liri': *Ayers Rock Resort*, 'Meet the Anangu', https://www.ayersrockresort.com.au/our-story/anangu-culture, accessed July 2021.

page 98 'Uluru, "He shakes off tourists"': Quoted in Diana James, 'Tjurkupa Time', in Ann McGrath and Mary Anne Jebb (eds), *Long History, Deep Time: Deepening Histories of Place*, ANU Press, Canberra, 2015, https://press-files.anu.edu.au/downloads/press/p319821/html/ch02.xhtml, accessed February 2022.

page 99 'climber to reach the summit': *W.C. Gosse's Explorations, 1873*, South Australian House of Assembly, Adelaide, 1874, p. 9.

page 100 'a written treaty, or "Makarrata"': Roslynn Haynes, 'Uluru', in Melissa Harper and Richard White (eds), *Symbols of Australia: Imagining a Nation*, NewSouth, Sydney, 2021.

The Wurrwurrwuy Stones

page 101 'the first who came . . .': Quoted in Sandy Blair and Nickolas Hall, 'Travelling the "Malay Road": Recognising the heritage significance of the Macassan maritime trade route', in Marshall Clark and Sally K. May (eds), *Macassan History and Heritage: Journeys, encounters and influences*, ANU Press, Canberra, 2013; Department of Sustainability, Environment, Water, Population and Communities, 'National Heritage Places: Wurrwurrwuy Stone Arrangements',

Notes

https://www.awe.gov.au/parks-heritage/heritage/places/national/wurrwurrwuy, accessed March 2022.

The Devil's Marbles

page 103 'went their separate ways . . .': quotation from 'Kirda and Kurdungurlu', Northern Territory Parks and Wildlife Service, *Devil's Marbles (Karlu Karlu) Conservation Reserve Joint Management Plan*, February 2009, p. 1, https://dtc.nt.gov.au/__data/assets/pdf_file/0008/249047/Devils_Marbles_JM_Plan. pdf, accessed February 2022.

Hallowed Grounds

page 106 'pieces of the "true cross"': Rafael Epstein, 'The unofficial history of the MCG', *ABC Drive*, 24 September 2019, https://www.abc.net.au/radio/melbourne/programs/drive/unofficial-history-of-the-mcg/11544628, accessed October 2021.

page 107 'from the jaws of defeat': Ray Sparvell, 'Wind in the willows: Cricket legends remember the WACA's greatest hits', *WA Today*, 4 September 2015, https://www.watoday.com.au/national/western-australia/wind-in-the-willows-cricket-legends-remember-the-wacas-greatest-hits-20150903-gjene1.html, accessed November 2021.

The Tree of Knowledge

page 108 'setting up a tent city': 'Shearers' Strike Camp Site, Barcaldine', *Queensland Government Heritage Register*, https://apps.des.qld.gov.au/heritageregister/detail/?id=600019, accessed February 2022.

page 108 'as the "Tree of Knowledge"': Glenn Davies, 'Townsville's "Tree of Knowledge" claims first place', *Independent Australia*, 7 May 2021, https://independentaustralia.net/politics/politics-display/townsvilles-tree-of-knowledge-claims-first-place, 15062.

page 109 'the famous "Freedom on the Wallaby"': *The Worker* (Brisbane), 16 May 1891, p. 8.

Mer

page 113 'the *Native Title Act 1993*': Screen Australia Digital Learning; 'Land Bilong Islanders', *MABO: The Native Title Revolution*, National Film and Sound Archive, https://www.mabonativetitle.com/

mer_35.shtml, accessed February 2021; Noel Loos, 'Mabo, Edward Koiki (Eddie) (1936–1992)', *Indigenous Australia (Australian Dictionary of Biography)*, National Centre of Biography, Australian National University, https://ia.anu.edu.au/biography/mabo-edward-koiki-eddie-16122/text28064, accessed 2 February 2021.

page 113 'kilometres of Torres Strait waters': Duane W. Hamacher, 'The moon plays an important role in Indigenous culture and helped win a battle over sea rights', *The Conversation*, 12 February 2021, https://theconversation.com/the-moon-plays-an-important-role-in-indigenous-culture-and-helped-win-a-battle-over-sea-rights-119081, accessed February 2022.

Sad Waterlilies

page 114 'last respects to the girls': *Queensland Times, Ipswich Herald and General Advertiser*, 23 March 1891, p. 2.

page 115 'of the Babies of Walloon': *The Dawn*, 1 May 1891, p. 18.

page 115 'of Australia's history and folklore': Peter Pierce, *The Country of Lost Children: An Australian anxiety*, Cambridge University Press, Melbourne, 1999.

page 116 'drowned somewhere up in Rockhampton': Andrew Korner, 'Babies' grave adds to saga of Walloon', *The Courier Mail*, 27 November 2012, https://www.couriermail.com.au/news/queensland/ipswich/babies-grave-adds-to-saga-of-walloon/news-story/3fe276695dfd997712b3895654a12eac, accessed October 2021.

page 116 'site by a Catholic priest': Pfoley, 'Blessing for the babies of Walloon', *The Courier Mail*, 25 March 2015, https://www.couriermail.com.au/news/queensland/ipswich/blessing-for-the-babies-of-walloon/news-story/6b1bef06e0a6d7760ba52691d72afa9f, accessed October 2021.

Places in the Heart

page 121 'Jimmy Turner, North Unley': *The Advertiser*, 31 May 1919, p. 8.

Here Is Their Spirit

page 123 '"Here is their spirit"': *The Advertiser* (Adelaide), 31 May 1919, p. 8.

Notes

Misery Hill

page 124 'one from World War II': Commonwealth War Graves Commission, 'Codford St. Mary (St. Mary)', *Commonwealth War Graves*, https://www.cwgc.org/visit-us/find-cemeteries-memorials/cemetery-details/45456/CODFORD%20ST.%20MARY%20(ST.%20MARY)%20NEW%20CHURCHYARD/

page 126 'who have no known grave': Australian War Memorial, 'War Graves' (EO5494), https://www.awm.gov.au/articles/encyclopedia/war_graves, accessed February 2022.

'I am the last of the Tasmanians'

page 128 'her people at Oyster Cove': J. Clark, 'Smith, Fanny Cochrane (1834–1905)', *Australian Dictionary of Biography*, National Centre of Biography, Australian National University, https://adb.anu.edu.au/biography/smith-fanny-cochrane-8466/text14887, published first in hardcopy 1988, accessed online 21 October 2021.

page 128 'first services were in May 1901': Geoff Ritchie, 'Methodist Church, Nicholls Rivulet', *On The Convict Trail*, 30 December 2013, https://ontheconvicttrail.blogspot.com/2013/12/methodist-church-nicholls-rivulet.html, accessed February 2022.

page 129 'Memory of the World Register': The recordings can be heard at the 'Fanny Cochrane Smith's Tasmanian Aboriginal Songs', 1899, *Australian Screen,* National Film and Sound Archive, https://aso.gov.au/titles/music/fanny-cochrane-smith-songs/clip1/, accessed February 2022.

page 129 'the next one was me': Bruce Watson, 'The Man and the Woman and the Edison Phonograph: Race, history and technology through song', https://www.brucewatsonmusic.com/documents/TMATWATEP_article_2016.pdf, accessed February 2022

The Star of Taroom

page 130 'important items have been repatriated': Paul Turnbull, *Science, Museums and Collecting the Indigenous Dead in Colonial Australia*, Palgrave Macmillan, Cham, Switzerland, 2017.

page 132 'and high-profile act of reconciliation': Jon Daly and David Iliffe, 'The stolen star', *ABC News*, 18 August 2021, https://www.abc.net.au/

Notes

news/2021-08-18/stolen-aboriginal-artefact-return-heals-first-nation-iman-taroom/100332960, accessed August 2021.

A Plait of Hair

page 132 'by the Taliban in 2001': World Wildlife Fund Australia, 'Supplementary Submission to Productivity Commission Inquiry into Resources Sector Regulation', undated, https://www.pc.gov.au/__data/assets/pdf_file/0011/256664/subdr093-resources-attachment1.pdf, accessed October 2021.

page 133 'higher volumes of high-grade ore': Calla Wahlquist and Lorena Allam, 'Rio Tinto blew up Juukan Gorge rock shelters "to access higher volumes of high-grade ore"', *The Guardian*, 4 August 2020, https://www.theguardian.com/australia-news/2020/aug/04/rio-tinto-blew-up-juukan-gorge-rock-shelters-to-access-higher-volumes-of-high-grade-ore, accessed October 2021.

page 133 'community within Australia and internationally': The Senate Joint Standing Committee on Northern Australia, *Never Again: Inquiry into the destruction of 46,000-year-old caves at the Juukan Gorge in the Pilbara region of Western Australia,* Interim report, December 2020, https://www.aph.gov.au/Parliamentary_Business/Committees/Joint/Northern_Australia/CavesatJuukanGorge/Interim_Report/section?id=committees%2Freportjnt%2F024579%2F75133, accessed October 2021.

page 134 'Kunti Kurrama and Pinikura people': Anna Henderson, 'Indigenous artefacts pulled out of Juukan Gorge before Rio Tinto blast sitting in shipping containers, inquiry hears', *ABC News*, 28 August 2020, https://www.abc.net.au/news/2020-08-28/indigenous-artefacts-juukan-gorge-caves-storage-concerns/12605566, accessed October 2021.

page 134 'imperatives of governments and corporations': The Senate Joint Standing Committee on Northern Australia, *Never Again: Inquiry into the destruction of 46,000-year-old caves at the Juukan Gorge in the Pilbara region of Western Australia*, Interim report, December 2020.

page 134 'to better protect sacred sites': Kristie Wellauer, Bridget Brennan and Shahni Wellington, 'Juukan Gorge Inquiry says new laws needed to stop destruction of cultural heritage sites', *ABC News*, 18 October 2021, https://www.abc.net.au/news/2021-10-18/juukan-gorge-report-tabled-in-parliament-canberra/100542640, accessed February 2022.

Notes

page 135   'million petroglyphs on the peninsula': James Liveris, 'Fears pollution will destroy world's biggest collection of rock art "within 100 years"', *ABC News*, 29 October 2021, https://www.abc.net.au/news/2021-10-29/fears-murujuga-pilbara-rock-art-at-risk-from-industry-pollution/100572050, accessed October 2021.

Chapter 4: Unsettling Places

Hell's Gate

page 141   'produce the most unfortunate results': *Colonial Times and Tasmanian Advertiser*, 10 March 1826, p. 2.

page 141   'bushrangers, on 4 May 1826': L. L. Robson, 'Brady, Matthew (c. 1799–1826)', *Australian Dictionary of Biography*, National Centre of Biography, Australian National University, https://adb.anu.edu.au/biography/brady-matthew-1822/text2089, published online 1966, accessed online 10 August 2021.

The Massacre Hill

page 142   'the rope round my neck': Carboni Raffaello, *The Eureka Stockade*, printed for the author by J.P. Atkinson, Melbourne, 1855, p. 8. (The author's birth name was Carboni Rafaello).

page 144   'the building of the stockade': *The Argus*, 3 December 1904, p. 17.

Cullin-La-Ringo

page 146   'known as "the history wars"': 'History Wars', *Wikipedia*, https://en.wikipedia.org/wiki/History_wars#Stuart_Macintyre's_The_History_Wars, accessed October 2021.

page 146   'known as Cullin-La-Ringo in 1861': Also 'Cullinlaringo' and variously said to be derived from Gaelic or Spanish.

page 147   'November, killing at least sixty': The Centre for 21st Century Humanities, 'Expedition Range', *Colonial Frontier Massacres in Australia, 1788–1930*, University of Newcastle, https://c21ch.newcastle.edu.au/colonialmassacres/detail.php?r=650, accessed September 2021. Estimates of the number of Aboriginal people killed vary, see 'Historical Society Cullin-la-ringo Massacre recalled', *Morning Bulletin*, 4 September 1954, p. 6.

Notes

page 148   'Wills's participation in reprisal killings': A letter from Wills's mother is said to contain damning information, but this seems to have disappeared.

page 148   'years later, even to strangers': Russell Jackson, 'Research discovery suggests AFL pioneer Tom Wills participated in massacres of Indigenous people', *ABC News*, 18 September 2021, https://www.abc.net.au/news/2021-09-18/suggests-afl-pioneer-tom-wills-participated-indigenous-massacres/100463708, accessed September 2021.

A Troubled Light

page 149   'with badly damaged internal organs': Queensland State Archives, 'Bustard Head Lighthouse', *Stories from the Archives*, 28 April 2021, https://blogs.archives.qld.gov.au/2021/04/28/bustard-head-lighthouse/, accessed August 2021.

page 150   'the station named George Daniels': *Morning Bulletin* (Rockhampton), 6 September 1912, p. 3; 21 September 1912, p. 9.

page 152   'it about two inches long': *Central Queensland Herald*, 12 September 1935, p. 63.

Ironstone Mountain

page 152   'production and vast wealth—for some': Mount Morgan Promotion and Development Inc., 'The Discovery of Mount Morgan', *Mount Morgan, Historic Township*, https://www.mountmorgan.org.au/History/The-Discovery-of-Mount-Morgan, accessed September 2021.

page 152   'per cent over ten years': Peter Frankopan, *The Silk Roads: A New History of the World*, Bloomsbury Publishing, London, 2015.

page 153   'oil reserve in the world': Queensland State Archives, 'How BP Nearly Never Existed', *Stories from the Archives*, 14 February 2020, https://blogs.archives.qld.gov.au/2020/02/14/how-bp-nearly-never-existed-the-william-knox-darcy-story/, accessed September 2021.

page 154   'and the mitigation of suffering': 'Building Australian Medical Research', *Walter and Eliza Hall Institute of Medical Research*, https://discovery.wehi.edu.au/timeline/highlights/walter-and-eliza-hall-trust, accessed September 2021.

page 155   'an ongoing environmental remediation challenge': Queensland Government, 'Mount Morgan Remediation Project', https://www.qld.gov.au/environment/land/management/abandoned-mines/remediation-projects/mount-morgan, accessed September 2021.

Notes

Visions Splendid

page 155 'areas of the British Empire': Kingsley Fairbridge, *The Autobiography of Kingsley Fairbridge*, Oxford University Press, London, 1927. Also, various other editions.

page 156 '"men", mostly of British origin': Rhodes Fairbridge (ed.), *Kingsley Fairbridge Farm School Information Booklet*, The Fairbridge Society Inc, Pinjarra, 1951.

page 157 'have potential beyond farm work': Molong Historical Society, 'Life at Fairbridge', https://www.migrationheritage.nsw.gov.au/exhibition/fairbridge-farm-school/life-at-fairbridge/index.html, accessed February 2022.

page 158 'who lived and worked there': Australian Government, 'Child Welfare Timeline', *Find and Connect*, https://www.findandconnect.gov.au/featured-stories/timeline/, accessed September 2021.

The Country Knows the Rest

page 159 'And the country knows the rest': 'The Country Knows the Rest' by Graham Seal, recorded by Margaret and Bob Fagan on *Landmarks on the Journey*, 2019.

page 161 'For the Company underground. Nor overground': Composed about 1839, from Mark Gregory's research on Frank MacNamara, at *Frank the Poet—Francis MacNamara—1811–1861*, https://frankthepoet.blogspot.com/2011/01/for-company-underground.html, accessed February 2022.

page 161 'a hard mine to work': https://web.archive.org/web/20120615104120/http://hosting.collectionsaustralia.net/newcastle/greta/roth.html.

page 162 'a riot by police officers': From the *Cessnock Eagle and South Maitland Recorder*, 18 February 1930, quoted by Terry Callaghan, 'Resources—Norman Brown and the Rothbury Riot', *Terry Callaghan—History and Genealogy*, http://www.terrycallaghan.com/resources-norman-brown-the-rothbury-riot/#_ftn1, accessed February 2022.

A Troubled Triangle

page 164 'encountered several unhappy child presences': Nic Hume, 'St John's Foundling Orphanage', 2011, https://www.appighosthunts.

Notes

com/uploads/7/7/4/4/7744052/st_johns_foundling_orphanage_by_nic_hume.pdf, accessed February 2022.

page 165 '"the occasional Mr Whippy treat"': Louise Thrower, 'Former residents return to St Joseph's Orphanage', *Goulburn Post*, 11 December 2015, https://www.goulburnpost.com.au/story/3553177/former-residents-return-to-st-josephs-orphanage-photos/, accessed July 2021.

page 166 'was survived by three daughters': 'Tragedy at Kenmore', *Young Witness*, 10 July 1917, p. 1.

page 166 'He was sentenced to death': 'The Kenmore Murder', *Goulburn Evening Penny Post*, 29 April 1920, p. 2.

page 166 '"history", declared the local MP': John Thistleton, 'Anger rises over Kenmore neglect, vandalism', *About Regional*, 6 September 2020, https://aboutregional.com.au/anger-rises-over-kenmore-neglect-vandalism/, accessed July 2021.

Unexplained Ipswich Phenomena

page 167 'was an interplanetary reconnaissance saucer': *The Courier Mail*, 29 July 1948, p. 1.

page 168 'would have had that effect': 'Mystery light over Ipswich; Houses shaken', *Queensland Times* (Ipswich), 28 July 1948, p. 2.

page 168 'its speed at 400–500 m.p.h': 'Flying saucer over Queensland', *Queensland Times* (Ipswich), 7 December 1950, p. 2.

page 168 'in Ipswich, elsewhere in Queensland': Katrina Mawer, *QUT News*, 20 May 2013, https://www.qutnews.com/2013/05/20/ufo-sighting-over-ipswich/; accessed February 2022. See also *Queensland Times* (Ipswich), 7 December 1950, p. 2.

page 168 'might fly through the air': Office of the Director of National Intelligence, *Preliminary Assessment: Unidentified Aerial Phenomena*, 25 June 2021, https://www.dni.gov/files/ODNI/documents/assessments/Prelimary-Assessment-UAP-20210625.pdf, accessed September 2021.

page 170 'space junk above the planet': Hannah Walsh and Tegan Philpott, 'UFOs—undesirable flying objects—in night sky over North Queensland easily identified, says expert', *ABC News*, https://www.abc.net.au/news/2021-11-21/ufo-explained-mackay-spacex-elon-musk-satellites/100634840, accessed November 2021.

Notes

'Populate or Perish!'

page 172 'huts, kitchens and the latrines': National Archives of Australia, 'Immigration and Immigrants—Immigration Reception and Training Centres—Bonegilla—Health Inspector Reports', NAA: A1658, 556/4/10, pp. 220–22.

page 173 'to Bonegilla as a child': Bruce Pennnay, *So Much Sky: Bonegilla Training and Reception Centre 1947–1971*, 2008, https://www.migrationheritage.nsw.gov.au/exhibitions/somuchsky/significance.html, August 2021.

page 173 'lives in a new country': Bonegilla stories at New South Wales Migrant Heritage Centre, 'Belongings', https://www.migrationheritage.nsw.gov.au/belongings/index2764.html?migrantaccommodation=bonegilla, accessed August 2021.

The Spirit Stones

page 174 'were cast by human hands': 'Stones still fall after spirit is caught', *Kojonup Courier*, 14 July 1955, p. 1; Stephen Braude, *Australian Poltergeist: The Stone-Throwing Spook of Humpty Doo and Many Other Cases by Tony Healy and Paul Cropper* (Review) *Journal of Scientific Exploration*, vol. 29, no. 1, Spring 2015; Jennifer Gherardi, *Spirit Stones*, Jag Films for ABC Australia, 2005. The rationale behind this well-researched film includes an extensive list of sources and the film includes interviews with eyewitnesses and participants, see *Spirit Stones*, www.spiritstones.com.au, accessed February 2022; Helen Hack, *The Mystery of the Mayanup Poltergeist*, Hesperian Press, Carlisle, WA, 2000. The author was the wife of the Mayanup farmer's son.

Mysteries within Mysteries

page 178 'on what that might be': Sarah Swain, 'Wakehurst Parkway Sydney: Australia's most haunted road', *Nine.com.au*, 31 October 2018, https://www.9news.com.au/national/haunted-roads-wakehurst-parkway-sydney-northern-beaches-ghost-kelly-halloween/20144f16-45d4-4f68-b5cd-d8866e4f4723, accessed February 2022; A.J. Guesdon, 'Roads to Pittwater: The Wakehurst Parkway along Old Oxford Falls Track', *Pittwater Online News*, Issue 365, June 24–30 2018, http://www.pittwateronlinenews.com/

Notes

Wakehurst-Parkway-Along-Old-Oxford-Falls-Track.php, accessed July 2020. Bianca Biasi has made a film on this subject, *The Parkway Hauntings*.

Toxic Town

page 180   'Asbestos Diseases Society of Australia': Asbestos Disease Society of Australia, https://asbestosdiseases.org.au/the-wittenoom-tragedy/, accessed March 2022.

page 180   'People are still dying': Australian Government Asbestos Safety and Eradication Agency, Asbestos Safety Conference 2019, https://www.asbestossafety.gov.au/sites/default/files/documents/2019-11/DAY%202%20PLENARY.pdf, accessed November 2021.

page 180   'can take decades to appear': The University of Western Australia's Occupational Respiratory Epidemiology Group estimated at least 1200 Wittenoom residents and workers have died from mesothelioma and lung cancer. Isabel Moussalli and Andrew Tyndall, 'Last homes in asbestos-riddled Wittenoom to be demolished, but some want to stay', *ABC News*, 12 November 2021, https://www.abc.net.au/news/2021-11-12/wittenoom-closure/100599722, accessed November 2021.

Chapter 5: Wild Places

Ghost Gum Dreaming

page 184   'the greenhouse gas carbon dioxide': Thea Williams, 'Eucalyptus: Five things you might not know about these flowering giants', CSIROscope, 23 March 2018, https://blog.csiro.au/national-eucalyptus-day-five-things-you-might-not-know-about-these-flowering-giants/, accessed February 2022.

page 184   'bladder and related inflammatory diseases': Most A. Akhtar, Ritesh Raju, Karren D. Beattie, et al., 'Medicinal Plants of the Australian Aboriginal Dharawal People Exhibiting Anti-inflammatory Activity', *Evidence-Based Complementary and Alternative Medicine*, 2016, Article ID 2935403, https://doi.org/10.1155/2016/2935403, accessed February 2022.

Notes

page 184   'chest pain, toothache and diarrhoea': Ian Edwin Cock, 'Medicinal and Aromatic Plants—Australia', *Ethnopharmacology, Encyclopedia of Life Support Systems (EOLSS)*, January 2011, https://www.researchgate.net/publication/264424689_Medicinal_and_aromatic_plants_-_Australia, accessed February 2022.

page 184   'feeling of repose and tranquillity': James Griffin, 'Bosisto, Joseph (1824–1898)', *Australian Dictionary of Biography*, National Centre of Biography, Australian National University, https://adb.anu.edu.au/biography/bosisto-joseph-3027/text4439, 1969, accessed October 2021.

page 185   'constellation and the Milky Way': Michael J. Connolly, 'The Southern Cross: Yaraan-doo—the place of the white gum-tree', 2009, https://www.kullillaart.com.au/dreamtime-stories/The-Southern-Cross-Yaraan-doo-The-place-of-the-white-gum-tree, accessed October 2021.

page 185   'monarchs of the eucalyptus genus': *National Register of Big Trees*, www.nationalregisterofbigtrees.com.au, accessed December 2021.

The Great Divide

page 186   'Victoria in a westerly direction': Commonwealth of Australia, *Year Book Australia*, 1910, https://www.abs.gov.au/AUSSTATS/abs@.nsf/Previousproducts/1301.0Feature%20Article1921910, accessed August 2021.

page 187   'the violence of the concussion': William Charles Wentworth, 'William Charles Wentworth—Journal of an Expedition across the Blue Mountains, 11 May–6 June 1813', State Library of New South Wales, https://acms.sl.nsw.gov.au/_transcript/2012/D04270/a1461.pdf, accessed February 2022.

page 187   'other dreadful convulsion of nature': Gregory Blaxland, *A Journal of a Tour of Discovery across the Blue Mountains in New South Wales*, B J Holdsworth, London, 1823, pp. 26–27.

page 187   'in which at least six': The Centre for 21st Century Humanities, *Colonial Frontier massacres in Australia, 1788–1930*, University of Newcastle, https://c21ch.newcastle.edu.au/colonialmassacres/detail.php?r=569, accessed March 2022.

page 189   'The results were inconclusive': Samantha Turnbull, 'Woodenbong in Yowie Country is a good place to start if you're looking for Australia's Big Foot', *ABC News*, 22 November 2018,

Notes

https://www.abc.net.au/news/2018-11-22/woodenbong-and-history-of-yowie-country-curious-north-coast/10505204, accessed February 2022; Tony Healy and Paul Cropper, *The Yowie: In Search of Australia's Bigfoot*, Strange Nation, Sydney, 2006, and subsequent editions.

page 189   'fleeing quickly from human contact': Rosemary Clark, 'Yowies in the Hills?', *Woodenbong Community Website*, http://woodenbong.org, accessed August 2021.

'A Small, Woody Island'

page 191   '"about one-o-clock in the afternoon"': William Dampier, *A New Voyage around the World*, James Knapton, London, 1697, pp. 472–3.

page 192   'cemetery at Geraldton in 2008': Samille Mitchell, 'Identification of HMAS Sydney's "unknown sailor" would solve a decades-old mystery', *ABC News*, 18 November 2021, https://www.abc.net.au/news/2021-11-18/unknown-sailor-hmas-sydney-identification/100629054, accessed November 2021.

page 192   '*Sydney* also expressed their happiness': Kate Midena, 'Identity of "unknown sailor" revealed as 21-year-old Thomas Welsby Clark', *ABC News*, 19 November 2021, https://www.abc.net.au/news/2021-11-19/unknown-sailor-identified-as-thomas-welsby-clark/100633302, accessed November 2021.

Dark Emu in the Stars

page 194   'perceived in the dark clouds': Yubulyawan Dreaming Project, 'Before Galileo' (ABC *Message Stick* episode), 2009, http://ydproject.com/index.php/lowernav/general/httpydprojectcomindexphplowernavgeneralgalileo2/galileo/, accessed February 2022

page 194   'section of the Milky Way': Robert S. Fuller, Michael G. Anderson et al., 'The Emu Sky Knowledge of the Kamilaroi and Euahlayi Peoples', *Journal of Astronomical History and Heritage*, vol. 17, no. 2, Preprint (2014).

page 194   'between First Nations artists and astrophysicists': Tingay, Steven John, 'Ilgarijiri—Things Belonging to the Sky: Connecting Australian Indigenous Artists and Astrophysicists,' *International Journal of the Arts in Society: Annual Review*, vol. 6, no. 1, 2011, pp. 203–12, doi:10.18848/1833-1866/CGP/v06i01/35965.

Notes

page 194   'story of the Dark Emu': Duane W. Hamacher, 'New coins celebrate Indigenous astronomy, the stars, and the dark spaces between them', *The Conversation*, 14 September 2020, https://theconversation.com/new-coins-celebrate-indigenous-astronomy-the-stars-and-the-dark-spaces-between-them-145923, accessed February 2022.

The Burning Mountain

page 195   'cliff, setting the mountain alight': Ros Stone, 'The Story of Burning Mountain', Murrurundi Community Portal, January 2021, https://murrurundi.nsw.au/attractions/burning-mountain/story-of-burning-mountain/, accessed January 2021.

page 195   'where the woman was fossilised': Anon., *Boundaries of the Hunter Valley Aboriginal People. The Wonnaura Koori's*, https://wonnarua.org.au/wp-content/uploads/2021/06/Boundaries-of-the-hunter-valley-aboriginal-people.pdf, accessed January 2021.

The Coral Kingdom

page 197   'originally supported them sank away': Patrick Armstrong, *Under the Blue Vault of Heaven: A Study of Charles Darwin's Sojourn in the Cocos (Keeling) Islands*, Indian Ocean Centre for Peace Studies, Nedlands, 1991.

page 199   'Cocos (Keeling) Islands Tourism website': Cocos (Keeling) Islands, *Wikipedia*, https://en.wikipedia.org/wiki/Cocos_(Keeling)_Islands#Bibliography, accessed February 2022.

Sea Country

page 199   'there must be many more': Jonathan Benjamin, Michael O'Leary, Jo McDonald et al., 'Aboriginal artefacts on the continental shelf reveal ancient drowned cultural landscapes in northwest Australia'; *PLOS One*, 1 July 2020, https://journals.plos.org/plosone/article?id=10.1371/journal.pone.0233912, accessed February 2022.

page 200   'reef that is there today': Patrick Nunn, *The Edge of Memory: Ancient Stories, Oral Tradition and the Post-Glacial World*, Bloomsbury, London, 2018, p. 96.

page 201   'what is now the sea': Nunn, p. 105, quoted in Ronald M. Berndt and Catherine H. Berndt, *The Speaking Land: Myth and Story in Aboriginal Australia*, Penguin, Ringwood Vic., 1989, p. 401.

Notes

Not So Sunny

page 202 'the mysteries of the sea': Maritime Museum of Townsville, 'Yongala Artefacts', https://www.tmml.org.au/yongala-artefacts/, accessed September 2019.

page 204 'many unexplained acts of violence': 'The burning of the Louisa Maria, schooner, by the Blacks', *Maryborough Chronicle, Wide Bay and Burnett Advertiser*, 29 August 1878, pp. 2–3.

Red Palms in the Desert

page 204 'Valley possibly 30,000 years before': David M.J.S. Bowman, J. Gibson, & T. Kondo, 'Outback Plants: Aboriginal myth meets DNA analysis', *Nature*, vol. 520, 2015, p. 33, accessed February 2022.

page 204 '7000, possibly 30,000 years': 'Research findings back up Aboriginal legend on origin of Central Australian palm trees', *ABC News*, 3 April 2015, https://www.abc.net.au/news/2015-04-03/aboriginal-legend-palm-tree-origin-central-australia-research/6369832, accessed October 2021.

page 205 'out an existence ever since': Anon., 'Discovery of a white colony on the northern shore of New Holland', *The Leeds Mercury*, 25 January 1834. The article was also reprinted in a number of other newspapers around the world. Its most likely author was Thomas J. Maslen, spruiker of the theory that there was a giant inland sea, lake or river in the centre of Australia.

page 206 'he was an Australian citizen': Sylvia Kleinert, 'Namatjira, Albert (Elea) (1902–1959)', *Australian Dictionary of Biography*, National Centre of Biography, Australian National University, https://adb.anu.edu.au/biography/namatjira-albert-elea-11217/text19999, published first in hardcopy 2000, accessed November 2021.

The Pelican Spree

page 210 'the mouth of Emigrant Creek': 'A Pelican Spree', *Sydney Sunday Times*, 17 December 1899, p. 11.

High Country

page 211 'and need to be maintained': Australian Alps National Parks, 'Aboriginal People and the Australian Alps', https://

Notes

theaustralianalpsnationalparks.org/the-alps-partnership/education/aboriginal-people/, accessed February 2022.

page 212 'agreeable resolution of some kind': Jess Davis, 'The battle over brumbies', *ABC News*, 21 August 2021, https://www.abc.net.au/news/2021-08-21/brumbies-battle-in-nsw-high-country-kosciuszko-national-park/100372254, accessed August 2021.

page 213 'yarn of Riley's wild ride': From an article in the *Corryong Courier and Walwa District News*, 20 January 1949, reprinted at http://www.murrayriver.com.au/the-man-from-snowy-river-reality-or-myth/, accessed March 2022.

page 213 'Man from Snowy River': 'Snowy man may have been an Aboriginal', *The Canberra Times*, 3 February 1988, p. 1.

Paroo Legends

page 215 'night on Paroo River': *The Bulletin*, vol. 14, no. 743, 12 May 1894, p. 2, section: The Red Page, https://www.austlit.edu.au/austlit/page/C296399, accessed May 2022.

page 216 'by then just £30': J.C.H. Gill, 'Gray, Isabel (1851–1929)', *Australian Dictionary of Biography*, National Centre of Biography, Australian National University, https://adb.anu.edu.au/biography/gray-isabel-6464/text11069, published first in hardcopy 1983, accessed October 2021.

page 217 'over ambitious': 'The Eulo Queen', *Narromine News and Trangie Advocate*, 11 July 1930, p. 5.

page 218 'the arms of Isobel Gray': *Smith's Weekly* (Sydney), 6 August 1932, p. 12.

A Home in the Blizzard

page 220 'no conception of scientific analysis': Australian Antarctic Division, 'Home of the Blizzard: The Australasian Antarctic Expedition', https://mawsonshuts.antarctica.gov.au/cape-denison/another-winter/radio-waves/. Sir Douglas Mawson, *The Home of the Blizzard: Being the story of the Australasian Antarctic Expedition, 1911–1914*, Heinemann, London, 1915.

page 221 'relieved Jeffryes of his duties': Elizabeth Leane and Kimberley Norris (with Ben Maddison), 'Remembering Sidney Jeffryes and the darker side of our tales of Antarctic heroism', *The Conversation*, 16

Notes

October 2018, https://theconversation.com/remembering-sidney-jeffryes-and-the-darker-side-of-our-tales-of-antarctic-heroism-105034, accessed August 2021.

page 222 'and to search for artefacts': Rebecca Hewett, 'Expeditioners set sail for six-week-long project to preserve historic Mawson's Huts in Antarctica', *ABC News*, 30 November 2021, https://www.abc.net.au/news/2021-11-30/mawsons-hut-expeditioners-head-south-to-preserve-history/100658092, accessed December 2021.

Chapter 6: Imagined Places

Where the Pelican Builds Its Nest

page 226 'Where the pelican builds her nest': First published in *The Bulletin*, 12 March 1881, two weeks later in the *Australasian Sketcher*, and again in Foott's collection, *Where the Pelican Builds and Other Poems*, in 1885.

page 227 'they reportedly told him': E.S. Wilkinson, 'Out where the pelican builds', *The Brisbane Courier*, 17 September 1932, p. 19.

page 228 'the blacks on that creek': 'The perils of Queensland exploration. The fate of the Prout Brothers and Baker', *The Queenslander*, 5 October 1878, p. 18.

The Outside Track

page 230 'track of the steerage push': Henry Lawson, *Verses Popular and Humorous*, Angus & Robertson, Sydney, 1900.

page 230 'and be damned . . .': First published in the *New York Sun*, 13 May 1893.

page 232 'the family and business assets': Helen Leggatt, '"Whither Shall We Send Our Son?": A prosopographical analysis of remittance men in New Zealand', *The Graduate History Review*, vol. 9, no. 1, 2020, pp. 20–48.

Matilda Country

page 232 'or so twenty years later': Centre for the Government of Queensland, 'Winton', *Queensland Places*, https://www.queenslandplaces.com.au/winton, accessed July 2021.

Notes

page 233 'into the early twentieth century': Timothy Bottoms, *Conspiracy of Silence: Queensland's Frontier Killing Times*, Allen & Unwin, Sydney, 2013.

The Prince of Ballyhoo

page 237 'official use of the name': 'About Us', *Sunraysia Daily*, https://www.sunraysiadaily.com.au/about-us, accessed November 2021.

page 237 'an extensive property at Kendenup': John Selwood, Matthew Tonts and Roy Jones, 'Closer Settlement Revisited at Kendenup, Western Australia: A historical geography', *Prairie Perspectives: Geographical Essays*, vol. 14, 2011, pp. 34–44.

page 237 'Regards and regrets. De Garis': 'De Garis mystery: Bound for New Zealand', *Advocate*, 10 January 1925, p. 5.

page 238 'buy a block of land': Janet McCalman, 'De Garis, Clement John (Jack) (1884–1926)', *Australian Dictionary of Biography*, National Centre of Biography, Australian National University, https://adb.anu.edu.au/biography/de-garis-clement-john-jack-5941/text10129, published first in hardcopy 1981, accessed online 9 November 2021.

Cuppacumalonga Hill

page 240 'is still in print today': C.J. Dennis, *A Book for Kids*, Angus & Robertson, Sydney, 1921, pp. 15–17.

The Pub with No Beer

page 241 '"high h[e]aven down here"': Bill Bowyang, 'On the track', *Townsville Daily Bulletin*, 30 December 1943, p. 4.

page 241 'where the poem came from': Slim Dusty and Joy McKean, *Slim: Another Day, Another Town*, Hachette, Sydney, 2014.

page 242 'propelled Slim Dusty to stardom': Paul Byrnes, 'A Pub with No Beer', *Australian Screen,* National Film and Sound Archive, https://aso.gov.au/titles/music/a-pub-with-no-beer/notes/, accessed January 2022.

The Land where the Crow Flies Backwards

page 245 'mob up into small lots': H7H, 'Odd stock and other notes', *The Capricornian*, 25 February 1905, p. 19. Also in the *Morning Bulletin* (Rockhampton) 25 February 1905, p. 6.

Notes

The Roaring Days

page 249 'Is tethered to the world': Henry Lawson, first published in the *Bulletin,* vol. 10, no. 514, 21 December 1889, p. 26. This version from Henry Lawson, *In the Days When the World was Wide and Other Verses*, Angus & Robertson, Sydney, 1900, second edition.

'Where they rise the sun with a golden bar'

page 250 'bunyip station of the great "Speewah."': 'The Great Speewah', *The Shoalhaven News*, 17 November 1937, p. 10.

page 251 'country newspapers in the 1890s': 'Stories told round the camp fire. The champion liar of the Queensland Coast', *The Western Champion and General Advertiser for the Central-Western Districts*, 2 August 1892, p. 3.

page 252 'scale out on the Speewah': 'Shearing Records. A Friendly Argument', *Morning Bulletin* (Rockhampton), 19 July 1924, p. 11. See also *The Bulletin*, 23 January 1929, p. 25.

page 252 'similar fashion to the bullocks': Glenmoriston, 'Tinnenburra. Old-time Tyson station. Some random recollections', *Morning Bulletin* (Rockhampton), 30 January 1923, p. 10.

page 253 'back of his head . . .': *The Australian Worker*, 24 March 1926, p. 18.

page 254 'have no time for them': Bill Bowyang, 'On the track', *Townsville Daily Bulletin*, 25 June 1930, p. 14.

The Everywhere Man

page 256 'had the audience in hysterics': 'Richmond honours returned servicemen', *Windsor and Richmond Gazette*, 29 May 1946, p. 7.

page 256 'pronounced as a juicy raspberry': 'Der Fuhrer's Face' (song), *Disney Fandom*, https://disney.fandom.com/wiki/Der_Fuehrer%27s_Face_(song), accessed October 2021.

page 257 'Geoffrey McElhinney died in 2017': 'Geoff Mack', *Wikipedia*, https://en.wikipedia.org/wiki/Geoff_Mack, accessed October 2021.

Capricornia

page 259 'to be independent of Queensland': Jamie Fellows and Mark David Chong, 'Secessionism in Northern Queensland and the Torres Strait Islands: Reality or fantasy?', *James Cook University*

Notes

Law Review, vol. 21, pp. 89–103, http://138.25.65.110/au/journals/JCULawRw/2014/6.pdf, accessed October 2021.

page 260 'then again in the 1920s': Christine Doran, 'Separation Movements in North Queensland in the Nineteenth Century', 1978, https://espace.library.uq.edu.au/view/UQ:207953, accessed October 2021.

page 260 'the tropical north in general': *Capricornia* was first published in a limited edition by Publicist Publishing Company, Sydney, 1937, then by Angus & Robertson, Sydney, 1938.

page 261 'even aware of *Capricornia* today': L. Conor, and A. McGrath, 'Xavier Herbert: Forgotten or repressed?' *Cultural Studies Review*, vol. 23, no. 2, 2017, pp. 62–9, http://dx.doi.org/10.5130/csr.v23i2.5818, accessed November 2021.

The Borders

page 262 'of intense interest and significance': Simon Leo Brown and Georgia Power, 'Will the states keep their newfound power? The history of Australia's Federation gives some clues', *ABC News*, 27 December 2021, https://www.abc.net.au/news/2021-12-27/will-states-keep-newfound-power-history-of-australia-federation/100697002, accessed December 2021.

page 263 'historian Alan Atkinson put it': Alan Atkinson, 'Map', in Melissa Harper and Richard White (eds), *Symbols of Australia: Imagining a Nation*, NewSouth Publishing, Sydney, 2021, p. 67.

Chapter 7: Our Place

Big Australia

page 268 'locations in the years since': Rachel Mounsey, 'Big Poo floats up the coast to flush council's ocean outfall strategy', *Kiama Independent*, 26 November 2019, https://www.kiamaindependent.com.au/story/6512772/big-poo-floats-up-the-coast-to-flush-councils-ocean-outfall-strategy/, accessed March 2022.

page 270 'motel graced with his image': David Clark, *Big Things: Australia's Amazing Roadside Attractions*, Penguin Books, 2004. Amy Clarke, 'Australia's "Big" problem—what to do with our ageing super-sized statues?' *The Conversation* (Australia), 19 September 2017,

Notes

https://theconversation.com/australias-big-problem-what-to-do-with-our-ageing-super-sized-statues-83424, accessed March 2022.

page 270 'said one of the co-creators': Tobi Loftus, 'Big Thongs unveiled as new tourist attraction at country pub in Calen, north of Mackay', *ABC Tropical North*, 27 January 2021, https://www.abc.net.au/news/2021-01-27/big-thongs-unveiled-at-calen-north-of-mackay/13088940, accessed March 2022.

page 271 'maintaining the concrete welly': 'Jordan Silver, 'From the Big Banana to the Big Oyster, Australia's 'big things' are still striving to put small towns on the map', *ABC News*, 26 December 2021, https://www.abc.net.au/news/2021-12-26/big-banana-big-oyster-australias-big-things-striving-small-towns/100554032, accessed December 2021.

The Old Tin Shed

page 272 'broke in London in 1942': Chris Cunneen, 'McIntosh, Hugh Donald (1876–1942)', *Australian Dictionary of Biography*, National Centre of Biography, Australian National University, https://adb.anu.edu.au/biography/mcintosh-hugh-donald-7373/text12811, published first in hardcopy 1986, accessed September 2021.

page 274 'world as "The Tin Shed"': Sydney Living Museums, 'The Wild Ones: Sydney Stadium 1908–1970', https://sydneylivingmuseums.com.au/stories/wild-ones-sydney-stadium-1908—1970, accessed September 2021.

page 274 'broken-nosed battlers and ticket scalpers': Terry Smith, *The Old Tin Shed: Sydney Stadium 1908–1970*, Eric Spilsted Publishing, Sydney, 1999, p. 9.

What Did the King Say to the Duke?

page 274 'there were spectators numbering 10,000': 'Australia's first Parliament at Canberra opened by the Duke of York', *The Daily News* (Perth), 9 May 1927, p. 4.

page 275 'man present to be there': 'Canberra ceremony', *Melbourne Argus*, 10 May 1927, p. 19.

page 275 'it with "a special wave"': 'Incidents of the Ducal visit to Canberra', *Sydney Mail*, 18 May 1927, p. 15.

page 276 'be commemorated with a statue': 'Old King Billy', *Sydney Morning Herald*, 21 September 1927, p. 10.

Notes

page 276 'to be seen and heard': Dan Bourchier, 'King Billy and Marvellous were not invited to the 1927 opening of Parliament House—but that didn't stop their fight for sovereignty', *ABC News*, 21 September 2020, https://www.abc.net.au/news/2020-09-21/king-billy-and-marvellous-fight-for-sovereignty-at-parliament/12682986, accessed March 2022 .

The Bridge

page 278 'it passed almost without notice': Peter Spearritt, 'Sydney Harbour Bridge', Melissa Harper and Richard White (eds), *Symbols of Australia: Imagining a Nation*, NewSouth Publishing, Sydney, 2021, pp. 253ff.

page 278 'No Australian will admit this': James Michener, *Return to Paradise*, Corgi Books, London, 1951, p. 275.

'She's a Beauty!'

page 280 'finger at management and governments': Royce Kurmelovs, *The Death of Holden: The End of an Australian Dream*, Hachette, Sydney, 2016.

page 281 'the brand to "wither away"': 'A History of Holden in Australia—Timeline', *The Guardian*, 19 February 2020, https://www.theguardian.com/business/2020/feb/19/a-history-of-holden-in-australia-timeline, accessed March 2022.

page 282 'Street Art Awards in 2020': Shannon Corvo, 'Holden utes of outback NSW paint tribute to Australia's lost automotive history', *ABC News*, 1 June 2021, https://www.abc.net.au/news/2021-06-01/iconic-utes-unintentionally-memorialise-holden-greatness/100157188, accessed November 2021.

The Bushranger of Research

page 284 'persistence in obtaining research funding': Museum of Applied Arts and Sciences, 'Penicillin Mould from Howard Florey's Lab', https://collection.maas.museum/object/166791, accessed March 2022.

page 284 'penicillin—a great deal of luck': Robert A. Kyle, David P. Steensma and Marc A. Shampo, 'Howard Walter Florey—Production of Penicillin', *Mayo Clinic Proceedings*, vol. 90, no. 6, 2015, pp. e63–e64, doi.org/10.1016/j.mayocp.2014.12.028, accessed March 2022.

Notes

page 284 'around the globe, took place': Australian Government, 'Howard Florey's Laboratory, Sir William Dunn School of Pathology, United Kingdom', *List of Overseas Places of Historic Significance to Australia*, https://www.environment.gov.au/heritage/places/list-overseas-places-historic-significance-australia/howard-floreys, accessed March 2022.

The Show

page 286 'take on the local hopefuls': Bob Morgan, *The Showies: Revelations of Australia's Outdoor Side-Showmen*, B. Morgan, Mitcham, Qld, 1995.

page 286 '"people" in non-judgemental showie parlance': Morgan, p. 91.

page 286 'Alley began moving towards "rides"': Though Fred Brophy continued the tradition until relatively recently, see Fred Brophy and Sue Williams, *The Last Showman: The Life and Times of an Outback Tent-Boxing Legend*, Penguin Random House, Hawthorn, 2016.

page 287 'it here for your edification': Morgan, p. 108.

The Country Hall

page 290 'it all happened so quickly': 'How Briseis Dam burst', *The Register News-Pictorial* (Adelaide), 9 April 1929, p. 2.

page 290 'blame was attachable to anyone': 'Briseis Dam Disaster', *Advocate* (Burnie), 20 June 1929, p. 5.

page 292 'of the Derby Hall': Copyright Phyl Lobl, used with permission. You can listen at 'Then & NOW—A Bass Strait Crossing', *Phyl Lobl: Cultural Maintenance Worker*, https://phyllobl.net/songs/then-and-now-album/, accessed March 2022.

The Milk Bar

page 293 'take charge behind the bar': *The Labor Daily* (Sydney), 31 October 1932, p. 7.

page 295 'New South Wales Heritage Register': '91 year Mr Fatiou closes his historical café for the last time', *Greek City Times*, 4 April 2021, https://greekcitytimes.com/2021/04/04/fotiou-closes-historical-cafe/, accessed March 2022. Effy Alexakis and Leonard Janiszewski, *Greek Cafes & Milk Bars of Australia*, Halstead Press, Braddon ACT,

Notes

2016. Eamon Donnelly, *The Milk Bars Book: Milkshakes, memories and mixed lollies*, Melbourne, 2018.

Sun, Sand and Surf

page 295   'recalled in a 2013 interview': Damien Larkins, 'Matey: Man's best friend sits watch over surfers', ABC Local, 5 June 2013, https://www.abc.net.au/local/audio/2013/06/05/3774965.htm?site=goldcoast, accessed December 2021.

page 297   'the G-string has become popular': Kerry Parnell, 'Bikini wars: We must stand up for our right to bare bottoms', *The Daily Telegraph*, 10 October 2020, https://www.dailytelegraph.com.au/news/opinion/bikini-wars-we-must-stand-up-for-our-right-to-bare-bottoms/news-story/34c73f9bd8d44b06190fedc2dc649d97, accessed December 2021.

page 298   'strictures imposed by lifesavers': Caroline Ford, 'Lifesaver', in Melissa Harper and Richard White (eds), *Symbols of Australia: Imagining a Nation*, NewSouth Publishing, Sydney, 2021, pp. 270–81.

The Centre of Australia

page 301   'of each state and territory': Geoscience Australia, *Centre of Australia States and* Territories, http://www.ga.gov.au/scientific-topics/national-location-information/dimensions/centre-of-australia-states-territories#1, accessed March 2022.